The Story of Nu

Cecil Headlam

Alpha Editions

This edition published in 2024

ISBN : 9789362923790

Design and Setting By
Alpha Editions
www.alphaedis.com
Email - info@alphaedis.com

As per information held with us this book is in Public Domain.
This book is a reproduction of an important historical work. Alpha Editions uses the best technology to reproduce historical work in the same manner it was first published to preserve its original nature. Any marks or number seen are left intentionally to preserve its true form.

Contents

PREFACE ....- 1 -

CHAPTER I Origin and Growth...- 2 -

CHAPTER II Development of Nuremberg.............................- 22 -

CHAPTER III Nuremberg and the
Reformation ....- 35 -

CHAPTER IV Nuremberg and the Thirty
Years War Wallenstein—Gustavus
Adolphus—Kaspar Hauser. ....- 56 -

CHAPTER V The Castle, the Walls and
Mediæval Fortifications ....- 69 -

CHAPTER VI The Council and the Council
House—Nuremberg Tortures..- 89 -

CHAPTER VII...- 102 -

CHAPTER VIII The Meistersingers and
Hans Sachs ....- 129 -

CHAPTER IX The Churches of Nuremberg ....- 136 -

CHAPTER X The Houses, Wells, and
Bridges ....- 161 -

CHAPTER XI German Museum ....- 166 -

CHAPTER XII The Arms of Nuremberg ....- 180 -

CHAPTER XIII Itinerary, Places of Resort, Hotels ....- 184 -

PREFACE

I AM painfully aware of the defects of this little book, and still more painfully unaware of its errors. The best excuse for the mistakes that have surely crept in is the vast scope and variety of my subject—the story of the old mediæval town which was for long the centre of German industry and thought. But, for a guide-book, accuracy is above all things desirable, and I shall therefore be deeply grateful to the courtesy of any of my readers, who, having discovered any error or omission, will kindly point it out to me.

The sources from which I have drawn are far too numerous to acknowledge in detail. But in the matter of topography and architecture a more express note of indebtedness is due to the devoted labours of R. von Rettberg, A. von Essenwein, and Ernst Mummenhoff. Above all, I must pay my tribute of gratitude and acknowledgment to the enthusiastic erudition of Dr Emil Reicke,[1] whose mighty volume, Geschichte der Reichsstadt Nürnberg, is a mine of information from which I have freely quarried. Lastly, to those old chroniclers at whom I have sometimes laughed, but whose quaint phrases and legends may have saved these pages from too serious a dulness, I now hasten to make amends and to assure them that I am very conscious of my own inferiority as a storyteller.

The object of this book will have been in great part achieved if it succeeds in reviving the memories and quickening the affections of old lovers of Nuremberg; if it awakens a desire in those who have not yet known and loved her, to visit the old "White City," and join the band of her worshippers.

CHAPTER I
ORIGIN AND GROWTH

"In the valley of the Pegnitz, where across broad meadow-lands
Rise the blue Franconian mountains, Nuremberg the ancient stands."—
LONGFELLOW.

YEAR by year, many a traveller on his way to Bayreuth, many a seeker after health at German baths, many an artist and lover of the old world, finds his way to Nuremberg. It is impossible to suppose that such any one is ever disappointed. For in spite of all changes, and in spite of the disfigurements of modern industry, Nuremberg is and will remain a mediæval city, a city of history and legend, a city of the soul. She is like Venice in this, as in not a little of her history, that she exercises an indefinable fascination over our hearts no less than over our intellects. The subtle flavour of mediæval towns may be likened to that of those rare old ports which are said to taste of the grave; a flavour indefinable, exquisite. Rothenburg has it: and it is with Rothenburg, that little gem of mediævalism, that Nuremberg is likely to be compared in the mind of the modern wanderer in Franconia. But though Rothenburg may surpass her greater neighbour in the perfect harmony and in the picturesqueness of her red-tiled houses and well-preserved fortifications, in interest at any rate she must yield to the heroine of this story. For, apart from the beauty which Nuremberg owes to the wonderful grouping of her red roofs and ancient castle, her coronet of antique towers, her Gothic churches and Renaissance buildings or brown riverside houses dipping into the mud-coloured Pegnitz, she rejoices in treasures of art and architecture and in the possession of a splendid history such as Rothenburg cannot boast. To those who know something of her story Nuremberg brings the subtle charm of association. Whilst appealing to our memories by the grandeur of her historic past, and to our imaginations by the work and tradition of her mighty dead, she appeals also to our senses with the rare magic of her personal beauty, if one may so call it. In that triple appeal lies the fascination of Nuremberg. For this reason one may hope to add to the enjoyment of those who may spend or have spent a few days in the "quaint old town of toil and traffic, quaint old town of art and song," by recounting the tale of her treasures, and by telling, however imperfectly, something of the story of her rise and fall, and of the artists whom she cradled. Many shall go to and fro and their knowledge shall be increased. Is not that the justification of a guide-book?

The facts as to the origin of Nuremberg are lost in the dim shadows of tradition. When the little town sprang up amid the forests and swamps which still marked the course of the Pegnitz, we know as little as we know the origin of the name Nürnberg. It is true that the Chronicles of later days are only too ready to furnish us with information; but the information is not always reliable. The Chronicles, like our own peerage, are apt to contain too vivid efforts of imaginative fiction. The Chroniclers, unharassed by facts or documents, with minds "not by geography prejudiced, or warped by history," cannot unfortunately always be believed. It is, for instance, quite possible that Attila, King of the Huns, passed and plundered Nuremberg, as they tell us. But there is no proof, no record of that visitation. Again, the inevitable legend of a visit from Charlemagne occurs. He, you may be sure, was lost in the woods whilst hunting near Nuremberg, and passed all night alone, unhurt by the wild beasts. As a token of gratitude for God's manifest favour he caused a chapel to be built on the spot. The chapel stands to this day—a twelfth-century building—but no matter! for did not Otho I., as our Chroniclers tell us, attend mass in St. Sebald's Church in 970, though St. Sebald's Church cannot have been built till a century later?

The origin of the very name of Nuremberg is hidden in clouds of obscurity. In the earliest documents we find it spelt with the usual variations of early manuscripts—Nourenberg, Nuorimperc, Niurenberg, Nuremberc, etc. The origin of the place, we repeat, is equally obscure. Many attempts have been made to find history in the light of the derivations of the name. But when philology turns historian it is apt to play strange tricks. Nur ein Berg (only a castle), or Nero's Castle, or Norix Tower—what matter which is the right derivation, so long as we can base a possible theory on it? The Norixberg theory will serve to illustrate the incredible quantity of misplaced ingenuity which both of old times and in the present has been wasted in trying to explain the inexplicable. The Heidenthurm—the Heathen Tower of the Castle—is so called from some carvings on the exterior which were once regarded as idols. Wolckan maintains that it was an ancient temple of Diana. For those carvings, he says, represent the figures of dogs and of two male figures with clubs, who must be Hercules and his son Noricus. Hence Norixberg. After which it seems prosaic to have to assert that the "figures of dogs" are really lions, and the male figures are Saints or Kings of Israel, and certainly not heathen images. There is in point of fact no trace of Roman colonisation here.

THE HEATHEN TOWER

Other ingenious historians, not content with imaginary details of heathen temples and sanctuaries, hint darkly of an ancient God—Nuoro by name—who, they say, was worshipped here and gave his name to the locality, but "of whom nothing else is known." Some chroniclers drag in the name of Drusus Nero (Neronesberg) and refine upon the point, debating whether we ought not rather to attribute this camp to Tiberius Claudius Nero; and others, again, suggest that Noriker, driven out by the Huns, settled in this favourable retreat in the heart of Germany, and laid the foundations of Nuremberg's greatness. All we can say is that these things were or were not: but they have no history. After all, why should they have any? But those who prefer precision to truth shall not go empty away.

"The Imperial fortress of Nuremberg began to be built fourteen years before the birth of Christ, the 9th of April, on a Tuesday, at 8 o'clock in the morning; but the town only twenty-six years after Christ, on the 3rd of April, on a Tuesday, at 8.57 A.M."

Thus spake the Astrologer Andreas Goldmeyer, in his "Earthly Jerusalem." And yet, as Sir Philip Sidney sings, some "dusty wits can scorn Astrology!"

Be that as it may, the history of our town begins in the year 1050. It is most probable that the silence regarding the place—it is not mentioned among the places visited by Conrad II. in this neighbourhood—points to the fact that the castle did not exist in 1025, but was built between that year and

1050. That it existed then we know, for Henry III. dated a document from here in 1050, summoning a council of Bavarian nobles "in fundo suo Nourinberc." Of the growth of the place we shall speak more in detail in the chapter on the Castle and the Walls. Here it will suffice to note that the oldest portion, called in the fifteenth century Altnürnberg, consisted of the Fünfeckiger Thurm—the Five-cornered tower—the rooms attached and the Otmarkapelle. The latter was burnt

LUGINSLAND, KAISERSTALLUNG, AND THE FIVE-CORNERED TOWER

down in 1420, rebuilt in 1428, and called the Walpurgiskapelle. These constituted the Burggräfliche Burg—the Burggraf's Castle. The rest of the castle was built on by Friedrich der Rotbart (Barbarossa), and called the Kaiserliche Burg. The old Five-cornered tower and the surrounding ground was the private property of the Burggraf, and he was appointed by the Emperor as imperial officer of the Kaiserliche Burg. Whether the Emperors claimed any rights of personal property over Nuremberg or merely treated it, at first, as imperial property, it is difficult to determine. The castle at any rate was probably built to secure whatever rights were claimed, and to serve generally as an imperial stronghold. An imperial representative, as we have seen, took up his residence there.[2] Gradually round the castle grew up the straggling streets of Nuremberg. Settlers built beneath the shadow of the Burg. The very names of the streets suggest the vicinity of a camp or fortress. Söldnerstrasse, Schmiedstrasse, and so forth, betray the military origin of the present busy commercial town. From one cause or another a mixture of races, of Germanic and non-Germanic, of Slavonic and Frankish elements, seems to have occurred amongst the inhabitants of the growing village, producing a special blend which in dialect, in customs, and in dress was soon noticed by the neighbours as unique, and stamping the art and development of Nuremberg with that peculiar character which has never left it.

Various causes combined to promote the growth of the place. The temporary removal of the Mart from Fürth to Nuremberg under Henry III. doubtless gave a great impetus to the development of the latter town. Henry IV., indeed, gave back the rights of Mart, customs and coinage to Fürth. But it seems probable that these rights were not taken away again from Nuremberg. The possession of a Mart was, of course, of great importance to a town in those days, promoting industries and arts and settled occupations. The Nurembergers were ready to suck out the fullest advantage from their privilege. That mixture of races, to which we have referred, resulted in remarkable business energy—energy which soon found scope in the conduct of the business which the natural position of Nuremberg on the South and North, the East and Western trade routes, brought to her. It was not very long before she became the centre of the vast trade between the Levant and Western Europe, and the chief emporium for the produce of Italy—the Handelsmetropole in fact of South Germany.

Nothing in the middle ages was more conducive to the prosperity of a town than the reputation of having a holy man within its borders, or the possession of the miracle-working relics of a saint. Just as St. Elizabeth made Marburg so St. Sebaldus proved a very potent attraction to Nuremberg. We shall give some account of this saint when we visit the church that was dedicated to him. Here we need only remark that as early as 1070 and 1080 we hear of pilgrimages to Nuremberg in honour of her patron saint.

Another factor in the growth of the place was the frequent visits which the Emperors began to pay to it. Lying as it did on their way from Bamberg and Forcheim to Regensburg the Kaisers readily availed themselves of the security offered by this impregnable fortress, and of the sport provided in the adjacent forest. For there was good hunting to be had in the forest which, seventy-two miles in extent, surrounded Nuremberg. And hunting, next to war, was then in most parts of Europe the most serious occupation of life. All the forest rights, we may mention, of woodcutting, hunting, charcoal burning and bee-farming belonged originally to the Empire. But these were gradually acquired by the Nuremberg Council (Rat), chiefly by purchase in the fifteenth century.

In the castle the visitor may notice a list of all the Emperors—some thirty odd, all told—who have stayed there—a list that should now include the reigning Emperor. We find that Henry IV. frequently honoured Nuremberg with his presence. This is that

NÜRNBERGER ZEIDLER (BEE-FARMER) ARMED WITH CROSS-BOW

Henry IV. whose scene at Canossa with the Pope—Kaiser of the Holy Roman Empire waiting three days in the snow to kiss the foot of excommunicative Gregory—has impressed itself on all memories. His last visit to Nuremberg was a sad one. His son rebelled against him, and the old king stopped at Nuremberg to collect his forces. In the war between father and son Nuremberg was loyal, and took the part of Henry IV. It was no nominal part, for in 1105 she had to stand a siege from the young Henry. For two months the town was held by the burghers and the castle by the Præfect Conrad. At the end of that time orders came from the old Kaiser that the town was to surrender. He had given up the struggle, and his undutiful son succeeded as Henry V. to the Holy Roman Empire, and Nuremberg with it. The mention of this siege gives us an indication of the growth of the town. The fact of the siege and the words of the chronicler, "The townsmen (oppidani) gave up the town under treaty," seem to point to the conclusion that Nuremberg was now no longer a mere fort (castrum), but that walls had sprung up round the busy mart and the shrine of St. Sebald, and that by this time Nuremberg had risen to the dignity of a "Stadt" or city state. Presently, indeed, we find her rejoicing in the title of "Civitas." The place, it is clear, was already of considerable military importance or it would not have been worth while to invest it. The growing volume of trade is further illustrated by a charter of Henry V. (1112) giving to the citizens of Worms Zollfreiheit in various places subject to him, amongst which Frankfort, Goslar and Nuremberg are named as royal towns (oppida regis).

We may note at this point, however, that the Chroniclers declare that the town fell into the hands of the enemy, through the treachery of the Jewish inhabitants and was plundered and burnt. By this destruction they account for the absence of all earlier records, and are left at liberty to evolve their theories as to the history of previous days. They add that when the town was rebuilt (1120) the Jews chose all the best sites for their houses, and retained them till they were driven out. The first statement was an easy invention. The second, very probably true in effect, points to the reason—commercial jealousy—but does not afford an excuse for the shortsighted and unchristian persecution of the Jews which disfigures the record of the acts of Nuremberg.

With the death of Henry V., which occurred in 1125, the Frankish or Salic Imperial line ended. For the Empire, though elective, had always a tendency to become hereditary and go in lines. If the last Kaiser left a son not unfit, who so likely as the son to be elected? But now a member of another family had to be chosen. The German princes elected Count Lothar von Supplinburg, Duke of Saxony. This departure was not without influence on the fortunes of Nuremberg. The question arose whether Nuremberg had belonged to the late Imperial house as private or imperial property. Did it now belong to the heirs of that house or to the newly-elected Emperor?

In fact, part of the possessions, which had passed from the Salian Franks to the heirs, Conrad and Frederick, Dukes of Swabia, of the house of Hohenstaufen, was now demanded back by Lothar as being imperial property. Nuremberg was numbered among these possessions and became the head-quarters of the war which followed between the Kaiser and the two brothers. In 1127 the town had to stand another siege—this time of ten weeks' duration—whilst the Hohenstaufen brothers held it against Lothar. The siege was raised; but three years later the brothers had to give in. The Burg and town of Nuremberg were then given by the Emperor to Henry the Proud of Bavaria, a member of the great Wittelsbach family. He kept them till 1138, when Conrad having been elected King of the Germans, they went back in the natural course of things to the Hohenstaufen, who came once more to look upon the flourishing town as their own private property.

It was to the above-mentioned Kaiser Conrad that the chronicles attribute the foundation of the monastery of St. Ægidius, on the site of the chapel, St. Martin's, which Charlemagne was reputed to have built. To Conrad also, with less show of likelihood, they ascribe the widening of the city. Widened the city has been more than once, as we can tell by the remains of walls and towers.[3] But the earliest fragment of these now extant—the lower part of the White Tower—dates only from the thirteenth century.

It seems to have been the policy of the Hohenstaufen Kaisers to favour Nuremberg. They often held their court here. The greatest of them—the greatest and wisest of the Kaisers since Charlemagne—Frederick I. Barbarossa, to wit, lived in the castle in 1166. It was he, in all probability, who built the Kaiserliche Burg, and erected, over the Margaretenkapelle, the Kaiserkapelle, a grander and more splendid chapel of marble, which was certainly completed in the twelfth century. Of the remarkable Double Chapel thus constructed we shall have more to say later on. Meanwhile we must content ourselves with calling attention to the very similar Double Chapel at Eger in Bohemia.

It was through Barbarossa that Nuremberg became connected with another of the great ruling families of the world.

"It was in those same years," says Carlyle,[4] "that a stout young fellow, Conrad by name, far off in the Southern part of Germany set out from the old Castle of Hohenzollern (the southern summit of that same huge old Hercynian wood, which is still called the Schwarzwald or Black Forest though now comparatively bare of trees) where he was but a junior and had small outlooks, upon a very great errand in the world.... His purpose was to find Barbarossa and seek fortune under him. To this Frederick Redbeard— a magnificent, magnanimous man, holding the reins of the world, not quite in the imaginary sense; scourging anarchy down and urging noble effort up, really on a grand scale—Conrad addressed himself; and he did it with success; which may be taken as a kind of testimonial to the worth of the young man. Details we have absolutely none; but there is no doubt that Conrad recommended himself to Kaiser Redbeard, nor any that the Kaiser was a judge of men.... One thing further is known, significant for his successes: Conrad found favour with 'the Heiress of the Vohburg Family,' desirable young heiress, and got her to wife. The Vohburg family, now much forgotten everywhere, and never heard of in England before, had long been of supreme importance, of immense possessions, and opulent in territories, and, we need not add, in honours and offices, in those Franconian Nürnberg regions; and was now gone to this one girl. I know not that she had much inheritance after all: the vast Vohburg properties lapsing all to the Kaiser, when the male heirs were out. But she had pretensions, tacit claims: in particular the Vohburgs had long been habitual or in effect hereditary Burggrafs of Nürnberg; and if Conrad had the talent for that office, he now in preference to others might have a chance for it. Sure enough, he got it; took root in it, he and his; and, in the course of centuries, branched up from it, high and wide, over the adjoining countries; waxing towards still higher destinies. That is the epitome of Conrad's history; history now become very great, but then no bigger than its neighbours and very meagrely recorded; of which the reflective reader is to make what he can....

"As to the Office, it was more important than perhaps the reader imagines. In a Diet of the Empire (1170) we find Conrad among the magnates of the country, denouncing Henry the Lion's high procedures and malpractices. Every Burggraf of Nürnberg is in virtue of his office 'Prince of the Empire'; if a man happened to have talent of his own and solid resources of his own (which are always on the growing hand with this family), here is a basis from which he may go far enough. Burggraf of Nürnberg: that means again Graf (judge, defender, manager, g'reeve) of the Kaiser's Burg or Castle,—in a word, Kaiser's Representative and Alter Ego,—in the old Imperial Free-Town of Nürnberg; with much adjacent very complex territory, also, to administer for the Kaiser. A flourishing extensive city, this old Nürnberg, with valuable adjacent territory, civic and imperial, intricately intermixed; full of commercial industries, opulences, not without democratic tendencies. Nay, it is almost, in some senses, the London and Middlesex of the Germany that then was, if we will consider it!

"This is a place to give a man chances, and try what stuff is in him. The office involves a talent for governing, as well as for judging: talent for fighting also, in cases of extremity, and, what is still better, a talent for avoiding to fight. None but a man of competent superior parts can do that function; I suppose no imbecile could have existed many months in it, in the old earnest times. Conrad and his succeeding Hohenzollerns proved very capable to do it, as would seem; and grew and spread in it, waxing bigger and bigger, from their first planting there by Kaiser Barbarossa, a successful judge of men."

Nuremberg continued to receive marks of Imperial favour. The importance to which she had now grown is illustrated by the fact that Frederick II., son of Barbarossa, held a very brilliant Reichstag here in 1219, and on this occasion gave to the town her first great Charter.

The first provision of this Charter, by which the town is declared free of allegiance to anyone but the Emperor, is of special interest, seeing that it raises the question whether Nuremberg was really the private property of the Imperial family, or only owed allegiance to the Emperor as such. Probably Frederick did not intend to alienate Nuremberg from himself and his heirs as private individuals; but, regarding the empire as a permanent possession of his family, he intended by this clause to bind the burghers of

Nuremberg more closely to his own personal service by freeing them from all feudal obligations to others.

A few years later Frederick, in order to carry out his plans with regard to Italian lands, appointed his ten-year-old son as King of Rome and as his successor to the German Empire. Then leaving the young King in Germany under the guardianship of Bishop Engelbert of Cologne, he went to Italy, and was crowned Emperor by the Pope.

Young Henry held his court in Nuremberg in 1225. In the castle, in November, a double festival was celebrated—the marriage of the young King with Margaret, daughter of Duke Leopold of Austria, and of the brother of the bride, Duke Henry of Austria, with Agnes, a daughter of the Landgraf Hermann von Thüringen. At this double wedding, as some chroniclers aver, or at the wedding of Rudolph von Hapsburg (1284), as is more probable, a terrible catastrophe occurred. For just as the numerous assembly of nobles and ladies had begun to dance in the hall, the platform erected for spectators fell in, and about seventy nobles, knights, and girls were crushed to death.

It was certainly in the middle of this festival that the horrible news arrived that the Archbishop of Cologne, the young King's adviser, had been murdered, from motives of revenge, by his nephew, Duke of Isenburg. "Such deeds were then very frequent," says the Abbot Conrad von Lichtenau, "because the doers thereof hoped to obtain pardon by a pilgrimage to the Holy Land."

Three days after his marriage the young King had to sit in judgment on the culprit at the Kaiserburg. Deeply moved, he asked the noble Gerlach von Büdingen for his opinion. Ought the murderer to be outlawed, there and then? Gerlach answered yes, for the crime was patent. Friedrich von Truhendingen opposed him violently, however, maintaining that the accused man ought to be first produced, as justice and custom demanded. Gerlach became enraged. The argument grew hot, and presently, in spite of the King's presence, the supporters of either opinion seized their arms and came to blows. A fearful crush occurred on the stairs, which gave way under the weight of struggling humanity, and some fifty people were killed upon the spot. But the sentence of outlawry got itself pronounced, and a decree of excommunication followed from the Church.

This was but one example of the lawlessness of the times. Violence was not often so swiftly punished. Germany had fallen on evil days, and worse were in store for her. The absenteeism of her Emperors was producing its inevitable result.

One after another, the Emperors "had squandered their talents and wasted the best strength of their country in pursuit of a fancy, and never learned by the experience of their predecessors to desist from the dangerous pursuit. Instead of turning their attention to the development of their country, to the curtailment of the powers of the nobility, to the establishment of their thrones on enduring foundations, they were bewitched with the dream of a Roman-imperial world-monarchy, which was impossible to be realised when every nation was asserting more and more its characteristic peculiarities and arriving at consciousness of national and independent life. The Emperors were always divided between distinct callings, as Kings of Germany and Emperors of Rome. The Italians hated them; the popes undermined their powers, and involved them in countless difficulties at home and in Italy, so that they could not establish their authority as emperors, and neglected to make good, or were impeded in attempting to make good, their position as kings in Germany. The bat in the fable was rejected by the birds because he was a beast, and by the beasts because he had wings as a bird."[5]

So it came to pass that when the line of Hohenstaufen went miserably out on the death of the ill-fated Conradin (1268), Germany was already involved in times of huge anarchy; "was rocking down," as Carlyle puts it, "towards one saw not what—an anarchic Republic of Princes, perhaps, and of free barons fast verging towards robbery? Sovereignty of multiplex princes, with a peerage of intermediate robber barons? Things are verging that way. Such princes, big and little, each wrenching off for himself what lay loosest and handiest to him, found it a stirring game, and not so much amiss."

Towns like Nuremberg, on the other hand, found it very much amiss. Fortunately many of them were rich and strong, and took the task of preserving peace and order to some extent into their own hands.

During the period of the Interregnum, as it was called (1254-1273), "die herrenlose, die schreckliche Zeit" of disturbance and lawlessness, when the electors—the bishops and princes of the land—could only agree in giving the crown to foreigners who would leave them alone and unhindered in their efforts to enlarge their powers and territories by fair or foul means, some curious transactions took place with regard to Nuremberg. There exists a document by which, in 1266, Conradin pledged to his uncle, Duke Ludwig of Bavaria, a number of possessions to raise money in order to pay back the loan which his former guardian had advanced to him, and which was used to acquire the town and castle of Nuremberg. The transaction is obscure. Possibly after the death of Conradin's father, Conrad IV., Nuremberg was claimed by his executors as private property. In that case we may hazard the conjecture that the town resisted the claim, and that an appeal to arms was made. The money referred to may have been spent in conducting a siege.

This much is known for certain from a contemporary document, that when, in 1269, Duke Ludwig and his brother Henry, as heirs of Conradin, divided the Hohenstaufen inheritance between them, they took equal rights over Nuremberg. That may have been, however, merely a paper phrase. Imperial and private rights were apt to get confused in the minds of the Hohenstaufen. Nuremberg, at any rate, continues always to act as if she were a free town of the Empire. She was acutely conscious of the dignity of her charter. The great object for which the European towns, and Nuremberg among them, were all this time struggling was a charter of incorporation and a qualified privilege of internal self-government. Emperors and princes might try to get hold of a rich city like Nuremberg, and treat it as their private property, but, once she had won her charter, she was determined to remain a Reichstadt, and to enjoy all the privileges and liberties of a free city.

One interesting and important result this period of lawlessness had. The towns began to band themselves together in leagues—Der Rheinische Städtebund, 1254, was the first of these—for the purpose of defence against the plunder and rapine of the robber-knights, who had formerly been held in check to some degree by the sword and authority of the Emperors, but who now swooped down from their fortresses as they pleased on the merchants travelling from town to town, and robbed them or levied on them heavy tolls. Nuremberg joined this league: and it is in a document (1256) welcoming the entrance of Regensburg (Ratisbon) into the league that we first find mention of the Rat or Council of burghers joined to the chief magistrate as an institution representative of the community. Since the Charter of 1219, almost the whole administration of justice—government, police and finance—had been centred no longer in the Burggraf, but in the chief magistrate (Schuldheiss) of the town. But, by the same charter, Nuremberg was now to be taxed as a community. From the natural necessity and apprehensions of the situation, the burghers felt the need of a representative body to sit with and to advise the magistrate, who was, originally at any rate, a King's man and officer of the Burggraf. So it came to pass that the bench of judges who assisted the Schuldheiss in his judicial work, a bench composed of the most powerful and influential citizens, gradually acquired the further function of an advising and governing body, and finally became independent of the magistrate. Little by little, by one charter after another, by gradual and persistent effort, the Rat gained the position of landlords and Territoriiherren. But, as the Council gained power, the great families began to arrogate to themselves the sole right of sitting on it. A close aristocracy of wealth grew up more and more jealous of their fancied rights. Such was the origin of the constitution of Nuremberg—a constitution which in later times offers a striking resemblance to that of Venice.

At last the Interregnum came to an end. It was mainly through Burggraf Frederick III. of Nuremberg that Rudolph von Hapsburg succeeded to the Empire. For this and other service the Burggraviate was made hereditary in his family. Under Rudolph the strong and just, who, after the demoralising period of anarchy, worked wonders in the way of tightening, whether with gloved hand or mailed fist, the bonds of imperial unity, a brilliant gathering of princes assembled at Nuremberg for the Reichstag in 1274. The chronicles are full of stories to illustrate the character of their modern Solomon on this occasion. The following example will suffice:—

A merchant complained that he had given his host a purse of 200 silver marks to keep, but the host denied having received them. The Emperor thereupon summoned the landlord and several citizens. They all came, naturally enough, in their best clothes. The landlord, in particular, wore a costly cap, which, as he stood before the Emperor, he twisted nervously in his hand. Rudolph took it from him and, putting it on, exclaimed that it would become even an Emperor. Then he went into the next room—apparently forgetting all about the cap. The landlord meanwhile was detained. The Emperor sent the cap to the landlord's wife, with a request in her husband's name that she should give the bearer that sack of money she knew about. The ruse succeeded, and whilst the landlord was emphatically asserting his innocence to the Emperor, the sack of money was produced to confound him. The wretch had to atone for his crime by the payment of a heavy fine.

One other record of Kaiser Rudolph's presence at Nuremberg we have. It is illustrative of the violence of those times. In 1289 a grand tournament was held in honour of the King. In the course of it Krafft von Hohenlohe had the misfortune to run his spear through the neck of Duke Ludwig von Baiern, and the latter died of the wound. In consequence of this mischance such strife arose between the followers of the Duke and those of the Kaiser that the Council had to take measures for the defence of the town. They barred the streets with chains and garrisoned the Rathaus as well as the towers and walls. Luckily the quarrel was smoothed over and no further disturbance took place.

NASSAUER HAUS

A few years later Graf Adolph von Nassau succeeded Rudolph. Once in 1293 and twice in 1294 he held his court in Nuremberg and ratified all the privileges of the town. To him and to his race legend ascribes a great share in the building of the Lorenzkirche. "But," says Dr Reicke, "there is as little ground for this assertion as for the unfounded belief that the Schlüsselfelderische Stiftungshaus, so called because it belonged to the institution founded by Hans Karl Schlüsselfelder who died in 1709, and now known as the Nassauerhaus, was once in the possession of the Counts of Nassau." This house which stands at the corner of the Carolinenstrasse was built, according to Essenheim, at the beginning of the fifteenth century. According to the earliest existing records it belonged, with the house to the west of it, to a branch of the Haller family, long since extinct. The figure on the well at the east end of this house, which represents King Adolph of Nassau, belongs to the year 1824. To-day the crypt of the house has been turned into a Weinhaus, and there, in a vaulted cellar wreathed with yew, the diligent œnophilist will be rewarded by the discovery of some rare vintages.

The new King Albert held his court at Nuremberg in 1298. His arrival brought many days of splendour and festivity to the town. For the King had his wife Elizabeth crowned by the Archbishop Wigbold of Cologne in St. Sebalduskirche. Six thousand guests assembled on this occasion. There was no accommodation in the houses for so vast a gathering of strangers, many of whom, in spite of the wintry weather, had to camp out under canvas in the streets.

It was about this time that one of the fearful periodical persecutions of the Jews—persecutions as unchristian as uneconomical—broke out over all Franconia. It was said that in Rothenburg the Jews had pounded the Host in a mortar and that blood had flowed from it. On the strength of this fabulous sacrilege a fanatic, called Rindfleisch, led a "crusade" against the unfortunate people. In Würtzburg the Jews were burnt and massacred in crowds and utterly extirpated. Many from the surrounding country sought refuge in Nuremberg, where they were hospitably received by their fellow-believers and were at first protected by the Rat. Rindfleisch and his bands of murderous fanatics were then at a safe distance. But, as these drew near, the hatred of the Jews, which had long smouldered among the people, broke out into flame. The Jewish quarter was then in the centre of the town, a very advantageous position. Their houses reached from the market where their synagogue stood, on the site of the present Frauenkirche, to the Zotenberg, the present Dötschmannsplatz. Rich as a community, though they counted, then as ever, both the greatest and the least among their number, they were envied for their possessions and hated as people of a foreign faith. Nuremberg, like all the neighbouring towns except Regensburg, became the scene of murder and brutality. A hundred thousand Jews were the victims of a fearful death. The persecution continued till King Albert, in spite of the unpopularity of the proceeding, came to Franconia and put a stop to it, punishing the instigators and laying a heavy fine upon the towns.

In 1308 Albert was murdered by his nephew, John of Swabia—Parracida. The story of this murder is introduced, it will be remembered, at the end of Schiller's Wilhelm Tell. After seven months' interval, Henry VII., Count of Luxembourg, was elected king. He, in the following year, held his court in Nuremberg, before departing to be crowned Emperor at Rome, in the midst of battle and strife with the Guelphs. Dating from Pisa, 1313, Henry granted Nuremberg a very important charter. Here are some of its provisions:—

(1) The Imperial magistrate at Nuremberg shall protect the imperial or principal roads and have the right of way.

(2) Once a year the Magistrate shall pledge himself before the Council to exercise impartial justice towards rich and poor, to judge and to arrange all matters with the counsel of the Schöpfen (Bench of judges).

(3) The Burgomeister and judges are given complete control over the markets, trade, and means of preserving order.

(4) The Burg is not to be separated from the town.

Generally, one may say, this Charter confirms and extends the self-governing privileges of the town. The magistrate is still an imperial officer, but his position is in acknowledged dependence on the Council, into whose hands the regulation of trade and the preservation of order are entrusted. Moreover, in another provision, the citizens are clearly protected against trial by outside authorities, and against arbitrary imprisonment.

Scarcely had he marked his appreciation of Nuremberg in this way, when Henry was poisoned whilst besieging Siena. On his death, discord broke out in Germany. We will avoid, as far as possible, stepping on to the quaking bog of Reich's history. Suffice it to say that one party elected Frederick, the beautiful son of Albert, and grandson of Rudolph von Hapsburg. The other and stronger party chose Ludwig von Baiern, of the Wittelsbach family. Nuremberg stood by Ludwig. A long war ensued, till the great battle of Mühldorf ended the struggle. Ludwig's victory was in great part attributable to the timely arrival of the Nuremberg cavalry, under Burggraf Frederick IV.

"To us this is the interesting point: At one turn of the battle, tenth hour of it now ending, and the tug of war still desperate, there arose a cry of joy over all the Austrian ranks: 'Help coming! Help!'—and Friedrich noticed a body of horse in Austrian cognisance (such the cunning of a certain man), coming in upon his rear. Austrians and Friedrich never doubted but it was brother Leopold just getting on the ground; and rushed forward doubly fierce; and were doubly astonished when it plunged in upon them, sharp-edged, as Burggraf Friedrich of Nürnberg,—and quite ruined Austrian Friedrich! Austrian Friedrich fought personally like a lion at bay; but it availed nothing. Rindsmaul (not lovely of lip, Cowmouth so-called) disarmed him: 'I will not surrender except to a Prince!'—so Burggraf Friedrich was got to take surrender of him; and the fight, and whole controversy with it was completely won."—Carlyle.

It was after this battle that the Kaiser, when eggs were found to be the only available provision in a country eaten to the bone, distributed them with the legendary phrase that still lives on the lips of every German child—

"Jedem Mann ein Ey
Dem frommen Schweppermann zwey."

"To every man one egg and to the excellent Schweppermann two." Schweppermann was one of his generals, and it seems probable that he was a Nuremberg citizen.

The story of how Ludwig shared his kingdom with his noble prisoner and united with him in such cordial affection that they ate at the same table and slept in the same bed, forms one of the best known and most romantic episodes in German history.

Nuremberg, who had helped Ludwig with money and men, reaped her full reward. Ludwig showed great affection for her, staying continually within her walls (1320-1347), residing usually not in the castle, but with some distinguished citizen. Hence, and because the city stood by him throughout his quarrel with the Pope, he gave her many charters, confirming and increasing the rights and privileges of the burghers. He gave her permission, for instance, to hold a fair fourteen days after Easter for a month, and to issue her own decrees regarding it. From this arose the practice of the Easter Fair which still takes place. He granted her, also, freedom of customs in Munich, thus helping her trade. She already enjoyed a mutual Zollfreiheit with Berne and Heilbronn. All this amounts to evidence of the steadily increasing trade of Nuremberg. Already, in the beginning of the fourteenth century, her trade with Italy was considerable, in spite of the robber-knights and imperial requisitions. No paper privileges were, indeed, of much value, however often renewed, unless supported by power to resist the robber-knights who, from their castles, descended on the rich caravans of the peaceful merchants. That trade flourished now as it did, shows that the knights did not have matters all their own way. If the Emperors did little to preserve order in the empire, the towns were now fortunately strong enough and independent enough to protect themselves. When the knights proved too troublesome, the

THE PEGNITZ

citizens attacked their fortresses and burned them, and hanged the robbers from their own towers. There is, for instance, a document extant (1325) in which Ludwig grants immunity to the citizens of Nuremberg for having destroyed the castle "Zu dem Turm," which belonged to one Conrad Schenk von Reicheneck, a robber-knight, and promises the castle shall never be rebuilt. Nor did the towns despise the advantages of combination. In 1340 we find Nuremberg entering into a league, for mutual protection and the maintenance of peace, with the Dukes of Bavaria, with Würzburg, Rothenburg, etc., and a number of spiritual and temporal lords.

But if Nuremberg waxed in power and independence under the favour of Ludwig, the Burggraf also had claims on the King. To him therefore was given the office of Chief-Magistrate (Schuldheiss) and certain revenues from the town. This was not at all to the taste of the burghers. They grew restive under the Burggraf's abuse of justice, and finally managed to buy back the office from him through the agency of their rich citizen Conrad Gross, with whom the King often stayed. Conrad Gross was an early specimen of that fine type of merchant princes who contributed so much in later days to the glory of Nuremberg. Barter—trade in kind—was now giving place to trade done with money drawn from the German mines. The merchant prince began to raise his head. Whereas the trader had hitherto been despised as a shopkeeper by the free-knights, the merchant, who could indulge in luxury of dress and household furniture, now began to look down on the knights as impecunious robbers. The time was at hand when the Italian Æneas Sylvius could write:—

"When one comes from Lower Franconia and perceives this glorious city, its splendour seems truly magnificent. When one enters it, one's original impression is confirmed by the beauty of the streets and the fitness of the houses. The churches of St. Sebald and St. Laurence are worthy of worship as well as admiration. The Imperial castle proudly dominates the town, and the burghers' dwellings seem to have been built for princes. In truth, the kings of Scotland would gladly be housed so luxuriously as the ordinary citizen of Nuremberg."

It was Conrad Gross who, "longing to change his worldly goods for heavenly ones," founded, in 1333, the "New Hospital of the Holy Ghost." Within the church is the tomb of the founder. Additions were made to the hospital and church at the end of the fifteenth century. What is called the south building was erected on two arches over the water. In the courtyard of the hospital is a little chapel of the Holy Sepulchre, founded by George Ketzel in 1459. The church itself was restored in the seventeenth century, from which period dates the stucco work of the chancel. These things the visitor will see and appraise for himself. Meantime the following beautiful legend concerning the founder is worth recording:—

A man of the family of Heinzen, afterwards called "Great" (Gross), fell asleep one day in his garden beneath the shade of a lime tree. He dreamed that he found a large treasure there, but had no spade with which to dig for it. To mark the place, therefore, he took a handful of leaves and laid them on the spot where the treasure was buried. When he awoke and walked round the garden, he came to a spot where it seemed that someone had purposely scattered lime leaves on the ground. Then he remembered his dream, and, since he thought the dream had not come to him without some reason, he called his men to help him, and vowed that if he found anything he would help the poor and sick with it. And indeed he found so great a treasure of silver and gold that he became very rich, and founded therewith the Hospital of the Holy Ghost.

Ludwig had been a good friend to Nuremberg, and therefore when Karl IV.,[6] the enemy of Ludwig and friend of the Pope, succeeded him, the new Kaiser was regarded with some apprehension. Karl, however, was very gracious to Nuremberg, and gave her new privileges, for he was eager to secure the loyalty of her citizens. He confirmed the rich burghers in their offices, and succeeded in winning over the patricians to his side. But it was at this time that a desire for a more democratic form of government began to manifest itself throughout the towns of Germany. The lower classes showed signs of restiveness, and evinced a desire to have a voice in the counsels of their town. The patrician families had engrossed all the rights. The proceedings of the Council were secret, and no account of the money which passed through their hands was forthcoming. The administration of justice rested entirely with them. Complaints were loud that the rights of the poor and the artisans did not receive proper attention. The pride of the hereditary patrician Councillors had become notorious. The sturdy independent craftsmen began to murmur against this state of affairs. They felt they were entitled to a place in the government of the town, which they supported by their industry and, in war, with their arms. They were ready at last to take steps to secure that place. When their demands were refused by the patricians, bloodshed and strife resulted. In Rothenburg, Regensburg, and Munich the patricians were successful in retaining the Council in their own hands. And so it was with Nuremberg. But of the details of the great revolution which broke out there at the beginning of Karl's reign little is known. The artisans, it seems, were staunch and faithful to the memory of Ludwig. He had, says one of the chroniclers, won their adherence by his popular manners and by giving them the right of having their own drinking clubs. The change of policy on the side of the Council who embraced the cause of the Luxembourg (Caroline) party enabled the artisans, who were loyal to the Bavarian (Wittelsbach) family, to make a bid for a share in the government of their town. The Council, with promises of redress of grievances, tried to stem the revolt. But it was too late. In alarm they called in the aid of Karl, and Karl sent a peace-maker who came and went in vain. Some of the Council then fled the town. The chroniclers go so far as to say that a surprise of the Council—a regular coup d'état—was planned for a particular day, but that the Council was warned in time. Though the Rathaus was stormed and the gates of the town occupied, "the birds had flown." They had escaped from the town by all sorts of curious devices.

This story may have sprung from the unchastened imagination of the chroniclers, but we know as an historical fact that on June 4, 1348, the rebels opened the gates to soldiers of Ludwig, Markgraf of Brandenburg, eldest son of the late Emperor. He was excommunicated (for Karl was the Papal nominee) as his father had been. The city when it received him shared in his excommunication. The clergy tried to escape from the tainted city, but the people, having shut the gates, compelled them to read mass. A copy of a certificate from the Bishop of Clure to the clergy, testifying that they had only held mass under compulsion, is still extant.

The rebels, then, were for the moment successful: the old Council was abolished and a new one chosen, which was composed mainly of artisans, but did not exclude all the old Councillors. Their chief work of innovation was to allow the artisans to form Guilds. On the whole the new Council was not a success. Prosperity is a cynical but convincing test of a government. Confusion and disorder obtained, and commerce was affected by the lack of police and the little real power of the Council. The finances of the town suffered accordingly. The partisans of the old régime refused to contribute.

It was therefore a good thing for Nuremberg when, in 1349, the opposition of the Wittelsbach party broke down, and terms were made which left Karl master of the situation. Nuremberg passed into his hands, and he proceeded to restore the status quo ante there. A new Council[7] was elected, and the ringleaders of the conspiracy were banished with their families.

CHAPTER II
DEVELOPMENT OF NUREMBERG

"Nürnberg's Hand
Geht durch alle Land."
—Old Proverb.

KARL IV. proceeded to confirm the privileges of the town for a cash consideration. That was the way of mediæval monarchs. We have seen that the finances of Nuremberg were not at this moment in a very flourishing condition. There is little doubt that the heavy payment she was called upon to make to the King was one of the chief causes which led to the great persecution of the Jews which soon broke out.

The Jews are first mentioned in Nuremberg in 1288. They were then personally free. They could hold land and live after their own laws. Medicine was their chief profession; for money-lending—at first without interest—was originally the business of the monasteries. It was one of the most unfortunate results of the Crusades that they stirred up feeling against the Jews. Persecutions began, and a change took place in the personal position of the Jews. They had now to wear a special dress and to cut their beards, whilst the Christians luxuriated in beards as long as they could possibly grow them. When the Christians were no longer allowed to take interest for money lent, the Jews stepped in, being under their own laws, as money-lenders. In many places they were forbidden to follow any other profession than that of usury. By a charter of the Hohenstaufen another important change was wrought in their condition. They were made directly subject to the King and Empire (Königliche Kammerknechte). For this protection they had to pay a tax direct to the Imperial treasury. Their riches grew in spite of all sorts of commercial disabilities, and with them grew the value of this tax. One good result of this was that it interested the King in their favour. He did not care to see his golden geese slain, and their property confiscated by the towns. In Nuremberg it was possible for the Jews to become citizens on the payment of a certain sum of money. In 1338, it appears from an old Burgher list, there were 212 Jewish citizens. Ten years later, when the Black Death was devastating Europe, it was said that the Jews had poisoned the wells and purposely propagated the plague in order to annihilate the Christians. They were accused of all sorts of sacrilege and unnatural crimes. A frightful persecution broke out. All along the Rhine thousands of them were burnt at the stake.

The Austrian poet Helbing echoed the public sentiment, during a later persecution, when he exclaimed, "There are too many Jews in our country. It is a shame and a sin to tolerate them. If I were King, if I could lay my hand on you, Jews, I tell you in truth I would have you all burnt." And this is the opinion of the humanist, Conrad Celtes, in his praise of Nuremberg:—

"Exscindenda protecto gens aut ad Caucasum et ultra Sauromatas perpetuo exilio releganda, quæ, per universum orbem in se totiens iram numinum concitat, humani generis societatem violans et conturbans."

At Nuremberg there were other reasons for the outbreak. In old days the Jews had been told to build their houses in the modern Dötschmannsplatz. Their synagogue stood on the site of the present Frauenkirche. Hence the space between the Rathaus and the Fleischbrücke was all the market-room the Christians had. The increasing numbers and prosperity of the Jews, in this, the best site of the town, was very distressing to observe. So it came to pass that in 1349, on the strength of a document signed by Karl, in which he undertakes to ask no questions if anything should happen to the Jews at the hands of the people or the Council, the Christians pulled down the Jewish houses, and made the two large market-places, called to-day the Hauptmarkt and the Obstmarkt. Between these they built, to the glory of God, the beautiful Frauenkirche. As for the Jews, "The Jews were burnt on St. Nicholas' Eve, 1349," is the laconic report of Ulman Stromer, chronicler.[8] The modern Maxfeld is supposed to have been the scene of this atrocity. Such is the origin of those picturesque market-places, where to-day beneath the shadow of St. Sebald's shrine, St. Mary's church and the stately Rathaus, the Beautiful Fountain pours its silvery waters, and the peasants sell the produce of the country, sitting at their stalls beneath huge umbrellas, or leading the patient oxen which have drawn their carts to the city.

We have mentioned above the grievances of the artisans at this period. It must not be supposed that they were altogether down-trodden and miserable. Pecuniarily they must have been comparatively well off. For from this time, up to the middle of the Thirty Years War, the Nuremberg workmen flourished in reputation and execution. Their numbers were large; their work was distinguished for its beauty and durability. Their metal work in particular was famous; and they maintained its excellence for a long while, fostered by the system of masters and apprentices, which in this case led to a real desire to reach or improve upon a high standard of sound and artistic work. Even to-day you can hardly walk ten yards in Nuremberg without coming upon some perfect piece of ironwork, such as the railings round the wells or in front of the Frauenkirche. In the German Museum[9] there are two rooms full of locks and hinges, which, if once seen and studied by the modern manufacturer of inferior wares, should almost certainly make him cease from his evil ways. Or, if the reader wish for an example of the wide gulf which separates the good from the indifferent, let him secure a genuine specimen of those old waterpots (Butte), in which women so picturesquely carry water on their backs from the wells, and compare it with a modern imitation. These old workmen took a pride in their work. They were not, however, for that reason contemptuous of a little relaxation. They had their general holidays. We know Victor Hugo's description of All Fools' Day in Notre Dame de Paris. And here, in Nuremberg, we find the butchers and cutlers asking and obtaining from Karl the right to hold a carnival, and to dance in silks and velvets like the great families. This right was afterwards extended to all the trades. Schembartläufer the carnival was called. Every year the dance took place. By degrees the great people began to take part in it. The good burghers were very fond of dancing, as we shall have further occasion to notice. In time all sorts of rites and ceremonies grew up round the celebration of this holiday, which not even the presence of the enemy or the plague could induce the artisans to omit. Like Don't-care Hippocleides, they would dance. Masks were worn, spears and crackers carried, and a special costume designed for each year. Popular songs and pasquinades were sung and published. Personalities of course were rife. In 1523, for instance, a man appeared dressed in "Indulgences." Not a little rough buffoonery of one sort or another found place. To conclude the proceedings, a so-called "Hell," made of fireworks, was let off in front of the Rathaus. And so to bed, as Pepys would have written.

The influence of the Reformers proved fatal to indulgence in this sort of wild hilarity. The celebration of the carnival was finally forbidden in 1539, much to the annoyance of the people.

In 1349 Karl issued from Nuremberg the declaration of public peace (he was always an eager promoter of Landfrieden—public peaces) for Franconia—to last for two years. In this arrangement Nuremberg was accorded the same standing as other Imperial cities and received, under Karl, equal political rights with the princely and other communities. A board of representatives of each town or district was to sit periodically at Nuremberg and see to it that the peace was kept. Whilst the King tried to preserve order in this way, peace leagues were also common in these times of feuds. So we find Nuremberg joining the league of the Swabian towns.

It was at Nuremberg that Karl, when he returned from being crowned at Rome (1356), held a famous Reichstag and issued the Golden Bull, so-called from the golden seal, or bulla, appended to the deed, which determined the method of electing the emperors and reduced the number of electors to seven. The place where the first twenty-three articles of this important law were published is still known as the house "Zum Goldenen Schild," in the Schildgasse. The old custom by which the newly chosen Kaiser held his first Reichstag at Nuremberg was made law by the Golden Bull—a law in later times frequently ignored. By the Golden Bull, also, towns were forbidden to league together, which was a very burdensome provision secured by the influence of the princes, but, luckily for the towns, not able to be enforced.

The Golden Bull, acknowledging, as it did, the power and increasing the territorial rights of the great princes, and rousing the envy of those who were not made electors, held in it the seeds of the dissolution of the Empire. It encouraged, in effect, all the petty princes to exceed their powers and to encroach on the rights of the towns. The Nuremberg Burggraf was no exception to this rule. From this time forward he is continually coming into conflict with the town. The quarrel began over the Geleitsrecht, right of convoy and customs. The Emperor in 1357 gave to the Burggraf certain rights of way which enabled him to exact toll from the merchants on their way to Frankfort. Now this was a direct infringement of the charter given them a few years before forbidding all unjust or unusual taxes. They appealed on the strength of this and the Kaiser revoked the right. But the question crops up again and again. A little later we find the Kaiser, in recognition of his indebtedness to the Burggraf for past services, giving him the office of Chief Magistrate of the town together with large revenues therefrom. The town, anxious to have the magistracy under its own control, wished to buy it from the Burggraf. The Kaiser, with a view to sharing the proceeds, raised the price at which it was to be sold, so that in 1385 the town had to redeem the magistracy and taxes for the exorbitant sum of 8000 gulden.

Karl, as far as one can make out, tried to hunt with the hounds and run with the hare, first helping the town and then the Burggraf, partly because he was indebted to both for their aid, and partly because the issue of a new charter was a proceeding which brought cash into the Imperial treasury. For directly or indirectly charters were always paid for. This accounts to some extent for the mass of contradictory decrees which survive to perplex the modern historian. Such a little compliment as the following, for instance, which we find at the end of a charter dated 1366, had doubtless its origin in a cash transaction:—

"The Emperor is accustomed to live and to hold his court in his Imperial town of Nuremberg, as being the most distinguished and best situated town of the Empire here in the land."

The relations between the Burggraf and the town continued to be so strained that they almost came to blows in 1367 over the building of a wall.

This wall was run up in forty days by the citizens, completely cutting off the approach from the castle to the town, and thus protecting the town from all hostile attacks of the Burggraf. The quarrel thereby occasioned dragged on for ten years before it was settled by an Imperial decree. Much to the chagrin of the Burggraf, the Kaiser, in deciding the dispute, unexpectedly favoured the town. We can hardly be surprised that the Burggraf, still smarting from this humiliation, was inclined to interpret as an act of aggression the building by the citizens of the tower "Luginsland" (1377),[10] which, besides commanding, as its name implied, a wide view of the surrounding country, would serve also as a watch-tower whence the actions of the Burggraf might be observed and forestalled. "Man pawet in darümb das man darauf ins marggrafen purk möcht gesehen," says one chronicler.

Before all this, the future King Wenzel had been born in Nuremberg and baptised in St. Sebalduskirche. The chronicles say that at the baptism of the Imperial child—with whose birth Karl was so pleased that he remitted the Imperial taxes of the town for a year—the font was not clean, and that, as the baptismal water was being warmed in the Parsonage, a fire broke out and the whole of the choir adjoining it was burnt down. Only the beautiful (fourteenth century) oriel window remained uninjured by the flames.[11] The present parsonage was built by Pfinzing, the author of the Theuerdank, of whom more anon.

ORIEL WINDOW OF THE PARSONAGE

On the day of the baptism it is recorded that the Emperor displayed to the people from the gallery over the door of the church the Imperial insignia and relics which he had brought from Prague to the new Frauenkirche.

This Wenzel, or Wenceslas, of whom we have spoken, succeeded his father when he was but seventeen. Half-idiot, half-maniac, addicted to drunkenness and hunting, he was not the man to restore order in an Empire which had already fallen into a state of chaos. He was one of the worst Kaisers and the least victorious on record. He would attend to nothing in the Reich, "the Prague white beer and girls of various complexions being much preferable," as he was heard to say. The result was that his reign was a period of feuds, the golden era of free or robber knights. Club-law, or Faustrecht, as it was called—the right of private warfare—was the order of the day. The history of Nuremberg resolves itself into the police-news of the period, the record of the sallies and outrages of such knights as Ekkelein von Gailingen, whose headquarters were at Windsheim, some thirty miles off, and who was the Götz von Berlichingen of the fourteenth century. The old castles which the traveller sees from time to time on the banks of the Rhine, or on the ravines and large brooks which flow into it, were then no picturesque ruins, rendered interesting by the stories which were told about their former inhabitants, but constituted the real and apparently impregnable strongholds of this robber-chivalry.

On the east wall of the castle, near the Five-cornered Tower, they will show you to this day two hoof-shaped marks, which are said to be the impressions left there by the hoofs of Ekkelein (or Eppelein) von Gailingen's gallant steed. For this freebooter, Ekkelein, who had long been feared, admired, and even credited with magical powers, was at length captured by the Nuremberg burgher-soldiers and condemned to death. Shut up in the castle, he pined in the dungeon until the day arrived on which he was to expiate his crimes with his life. When he was brought out into the yard for execution, he begged, as a last request, that he might be allowed to say farewell to his favourite horse and his servant Jäckel. The beautiful charger, neighing with pleasure, was brought. Ekkelein put his arm round its neck and embraced it lovingly.

"If only, before I die, I might once more feel myself on his back!"

So natural and so harmless did the request seem that his wish was granted. His groom placed the saddle and bridle on the horse, who, when his master mounted, shook his mane for joy. At first the faithful creature moved gently and proudly in the circle of the guard, looking round him and snorting. When Ekkelein patted his powerful, smooth neck, the muscles of the noble animal grew larger and the veins of his flanks swelled at the touch of the master's hand. He spurned the ground, raised his fore-feet and threw himself forward into a thundering gallop. Lightly and gently the spur of the rider touched his sides: he rushed furiously round the court. Guards and jailors shrank back before the stones which his hoofs threw high into the air. But the gate was secure and escape not to be thought of. Then, whoever is able to read the eyes of dumb beasts might have seen flaming in those of Ekkelein's charger a lament like this: "How, my noble master? Shalt thou die here? Shall thy knightly blood flow ignominiously in this miserable place! Shall I never again carry thee into the battle, or bear thee through the defiles and the forests, and never more eat golden oats out of thy brave hand! O my master, save thyself! Trust in me and my strength and the impossible shall become possible." The horse raised himself. The knight struck both spurs into his sides, held breath and, stooping low, embraced with both arms the neck of the faithful steed, from whose hoofs showered sparks of fire. Before the burghers could stay them, before the guards could lift a finger, before breath could be drawn, the desperate spring was made and man and horse were over the parapet which overhung the moat 100 feet below. They leaped not—as it appeared to the incredulous eyes that peeped at them from the top of the battlements—to their destruction; for, after a huge splash and struggle in the waters of the fosse, horse and rider rose again to the surface, and, long before the drawbridge could be let down and his captors could pursue him, Ekkelein was away in the deep forest, galloping on his brave steed, well on the road to the impregnable castle of Gailingen. The dent made by the horse's hoofs in the stones below is there to this day. Can we wonder if the story went round that it was his Satanic majesty who had presented the bold knight with this wondrous steed, the better to facilitate the various little errands with which he had entrusted him?

Fortunately for the burgesses of Nuremberg not every free-knight could rely on such diabolic means of succour, so that they were able to defend themselves with energy and success against the noble and aggressive freebooters. The Council saw to it that the fortifications were continually strengthened and they did not despise the aid of the newly-introduced blunderbuss.[12] Indeed, even in the field the burgesses and their mercenaries showed themselves a match for the free-knights. So confident was Nuremberg in her own resources that at first she refused to join the great league of all the Rhenish towns founded in 1381, but three years later she came in. Though the great princes of the Empire were very jealous of such leagues, the Kaiser managed to patch up a union, with himself at the head, between this league and the princes, and called it the "Heidelberg Union" for the maintenance of peace. However a year or two later the Dukes of Bavaria, jealous as ever of the towns, broke loose, and seized the Archbishop Pilgrim von Salzburg, a friend of the towns, and some

Nuremberg merchants. The Kaiser, instead of taking strong measures at once, pursued his usual policy of shilly-shally. But in January 1388 a strong army of the League started from Augsburg, ravaging all Bavaria with fire and sword. To this army Nuremberg contributed some mounted mercenaries, and at the same time marched an army of her own—8000 strong, a very large army for those days—against Hilpoltstein, but without success. The war resolved itself into a struggle between the interests of the princes and of the towns. The towns failed to hold together, and paid the penalty in failure. They had commenced hostilities vigorously, but Nuremberg set the example of wavering. In a year or so she made peace on no very favourable terms, consenting to pay heavy indemnities. Still, the general result of the war, though the towns were not successful, was not to lower the status of the towns. So far as Nuremberg was concerned the administration of the war had been carried on by a Committee of the Rat—the Kriegsrat, which henceforth became permanent. As to the expenses, they were in part defrayed by a wholesale seizure of Jews and confiscation of their property. This disgraceful proceeding was done by the League in general (1385, and again in 1390), and countenanced by the Kaiser. Here is a characteristic story of that very feckless Kaiser, which will show how fit he was to govern the German Empire.

Wenzel, the story runs, demanded from the Nuremberg Council the key of the Stadtthor. The Council, though very loth to do so, gave him the key, on condition that he would grant them a request in return. The Kaiser consented. When he graciously inquired what it was they demanded, the Burgomeister asked for the key back again! The Kaiser was so enraged that he slapped the Burgomeister on the cheek, and rode off in a royal huff to Rothenburg. In revenge, on St. Margaret's Day, when the consecration of the Schlosskapelle was celebrated, he allowed his followers to plunder the booths of the fair held round about the castle.

Wenzel, in fact, let things go their own gait in the Empire. Knights plundered and traders quarrelled as they would. The Kaiser indulged in bouts of drinking, in long hunting forays, and in insane fits of rage. At last the princes began to dispense with his presence. They called a Reichstag at Frankfort and sent to him demanding a regent. Then Wenzel roused himself, returned to Nuremberg, and proclaimed a public peace (1397). A crusade against the turbulent knights in the valley of the Pegnitz was undertaken and proved successful. Their castles were taken and Wenzel forbade them to be rebuilt. This was but a momentary outburst of energy on his part. He soon resumed his old indifference. In 1400 the discontent of the princes came to a head. Wenzel was deposed: Ruprecht von der Pfalz was chosen King and, after some cautious hesitation, was finally accepted by the towns.

In a charter confirming her privileges Ruprecht granted to Nuremberg the care of the Reichsburg at all times, and made the town independent of the Burggraf in the time of feud,—excused them, that is, from assisting him in his little wars. Nuremberg gave Ruprecht active support in the proceedings against Wenzel; her chief exploit being the capture of Rothenburg after a siege of five weeks. When Ruprecht died (1410) Jobst and Sigismund were competitors for the Kaisership, Wenzel too striking in with claims for reinstatement. Both the former were elected, so that Germany rejoiced in as many Kaisers as Christianity had Popes. Happily Jobst died in three months, and Sigismund, chiefly through the faithful and unwearied diligence of Burggraf Frederick VI. of Nuremberg, became Kaiser, "an always hoping, never resting, unsuccessful, vain and empty Kaiser. Specious, speculative, given to eloquence, diplomacy, and the windy instead of the solid arts: always short of money for one thing." This last fault affected Nuremberg in more than one way. In the first place it necessitated the borrowing of heavy loans from her. Throughout the fourteenth century and onwards the Kaisers asked and received very large loans (pleasantly so-called) from Nuremberg. Wenzel, Ruprecht and Sigismund demanded ever larger and increasingly frequent donations. Sometimes, but not very often, the citizens were rewarded by the concession of a charter or the ratification of some procedure on their part. But the price was, of course, out of all proportion to the value of the thing purchased. As an example of these dealings we may instance the "loan" exacted by Sigismund in 1430, which amounted to 9000 gulden, besides other requisitions in the same year. One sees, at any rate, that Nuremberg must have been sufficiently full-blooded to endure being bled in this manner. But it was this same impecuniosity on the part of the Kaiser which led him to sell outright, for a total sum of 400,000 gulden, the Electorate of Brandenburg, with its land, titles and sovereign electorship and all to Burggraf Frederick, who already held it in pawn. This step was, in its immediate results at least, distinctly advantageous to Nuremberg. Clever and energetic, the Burggraf set about suppressing the robber-knights and establishing order.

Burggraf Frederick on his first coming to Brandenburg found but a cool reception as Statthalter. He came as a representative of law and rule; and there had been many noble gentlemen of the Turpin profession helping themselves by a ruleless life of late. Industry was at a low ebb, violence was rife; plunder and disorder everywhere; trade wrecked, private feuds abounding; too much the habit of baronial gentlemen to live by the saddle, as they termed it; that is by highway robbery in modern phrase. At first the Burggraf tried gentle methods, but when he found the noble lords scoffed at him, calling him a "Nürnberger Tand" (Nuremberg Toy), and continued their plunderings and other contumacies, then with the aid of his Frankish men-at-arms, neighbouring potentates and artillery—one huge gun, a twenty-four pounder, called Lazy Peg (Faule Grete), is mentioned—he set to work, and in a remarkably short period established comparative peace and order.[13]

That was a piece of work highly acceptable, we may be sure, to the merchants of Nuremberg. Were they not concerned in bringing fish and wool from the North, to exchange them in Italy and Venice for the silks and spices of the East?

In 1414 we catch a glimpse of the sombre figure of John Huss, the reformer, the Bohemian successor of Wiclif, passing through Nuremberg. The people here seem to have sympathised with his views. He explained his position to the clergy and council, and they invited him to return to them if he fared successfully at Kostnitz. But there he met his martyrdom. His supporters, the down-trodden peasantry of Bohemia, thereupon rose in a revolt, which Empire for a long while utterly failed to suppress. Nuremberg had exhibited no great enthusiasm against heretics. Though, in 1399, she had burnt six women and a man for heresy, yet she had given Huss a warm welcome. But the devastation wrought by the Hussite army alienated all sympathy, and on the suppression of the "heretics," Nuremberg joined in the universal rejoicings of all steady-going merchants. She had taken occasional part in the Hussite wars; but chiefly through paying money instead of sending a proper contingent of men—a fact which illustrates the narrow, selfish and lazy policy of the town communities where the Empire was concerned. It was impossible for the Emperor to keep order with insufficient means of police. For the Emperor got not a foot of German territory with his Imperial crown. He was merely the feudal head, and as such found it very hard to get troops or money from the German people. Most of the members of the Empire—petty princes and Imperial towns alike—were concerned chiefly not with the ordering of the Empire but with becoming sovereign in their own territories. There was very little feeling of Imperial unity. If the Empire did not do its duty by the towns, the towns did very little for the Empire, beyond supplying money.

The Nurembergers were energetic enough when it came to fortifying their town on the approach of the victorious Hussites (1430). The grim heretics advanced ravaging and destroying the country, depopulating the towns. Night and day, men, women and children worked at the walls, striving to render the place impregnable. But the danger passed away. Thanks to the Markgraf Frederick, who bought them off very cheaply, the Hussites returned, for the time, in peace to their homes.

Sigismund succeeded in being crowned at Rome in 1433, and on this occasion he knighted Sebald Behaim, of the great Nuremberg family of that name, and gave to Nuremberg a charter confirming her privileges and giving her the right to keep the Imperial jewels, insignia, and sacred relics for ever. These were brought with great pomp and rejoicing to the Church of the Holy Spirit (Neuenspital) and there they were kept and jealously guarded till 1796. They were shown with much ceremony once a year to the people. This occasion was a very popular festival down to the Reformation days. But in 1523 the relics were shown for the last time.

Frederick the Third we shall only mention for the sake of the picturesque ceremonial which occurred when he held his first Reichstag at Nuremberg, at Easter 1442. The Kaiser rode in at the Spittlerthor. In the middle of the street where he had to pass St. Jakobskirche a table was spread on which, besides a crucifix, were placed the heads of St. Sebald and St. Cyprian. The Kaiser dismounted, took the cross from the Abbot of St. Ægidius and kissed it.

Thereupon one of the holy skulls was placed on the Kaiser's head, whilst the priests and choristers in surplices and birettas sang responses. The Kaiser and his retinue and all the priesthood then made a solemn procession to the Sebalduskirche. Here the Kaiser worshipped on his knees before the altar. The priest read the special collect over him, and, taking a handful of flax and tow, lighted it and, as it burnt, exclaimed in a loud voice, "Most illustrious Kaiser, sic transit gloria mundi." Then the chorus of priests burst out into the strains of the Te Deum, and the Kaiser went his way in the world—a compromising Emperor who slept through a long reign to the no small detriment of Germany.

We must not think of the Nurembergers as altogether given up to trade and merchandise. They were capable of being stirred up into the deepest religious enthusiasm. I know not what reception they gave to the Cardinal Nicholas of Cusa, who (1451) came preaching through Germany, and passed through Nuremberg selling "Indulgences" like a cheap-jack, lowering his price from time to time to get rid of his stock. But the monk, Capistranus, a great preacher, who came in the following year, created so tremendous a sensation by his eloquence and by miracles which he wrought that the people, we are told, flocked in crowds, laden with their new-fashioned pointed shoes, their Schlitten (sledges—harmless enough one would have thought—but they were regarded as extravagant luxuries), and thousands of dice and cards, and burnt them all in the market-place.

Next year they were stirred again by the terrible news that the Turks had taken Constantinople. Eleven hundred burghers seized their arms and went as Crusaders to help the Hungarians in Belgrade against the infidel Turk.[14] But they did not do great deeds. Scarce a third of them returned at Christmastide. The rest had died of hardship or of disease. This gave the Council a distaste for Crusades. They took to discouraging the preachers who came to beat up recruits against Hussites or Turks. The town, it was found, had to support the widows and children of the dead Crusaders.

The preachings of the firebrand Johannes Capistranus had another evil result. The Jews since the persecution in 1349 had not been much molested, though continually squeezed for money by both Kaiser and Council. But the increase in their numbers, the riches they had accumulated through usury, and the eloquence of this monk all tended to rouse religious hatred.

"The hatred against the Jews is so general in Germany," writes Froissart in 1497, "that the calmest people are beside themselves when the conversation turns on their usury. I should not be surprised if on a sudden a bloody persecution broke out against them all over the country. They have already been forcibly expelled from many towns."

After many half resolves, the Council determined to ask Maximilian to drive these "sucking leeches" from the town. Reluctantly he consented.

"Their numbers have increased too much. Under pretext of loans they have given themselves up to a dangerous and detestable traffic of usury. Many honourable citizens, deceived by their devices, are so deeply in debt that they see their private honour and their very means of existence threatened. For these reasons the Jews are invited to quit the town altogether within a period fixed by the Council. They are permitted to take with them their moveable property, but henceforth none of them shall have the right to reside in Nuremberg."[15]

On the 10th of March 1499, driven from their homes amid the curses of the Christians, the Jews left Nuremberg with groans and lamentations, never to dwell there again till 1850. Maximilian sold their houses to the Council. Their churchyard was built over, their tombstones used for building the Corn Exchange—(die Waage). But no persecution, no repression, no laws forbidding commercial transactions between Christian and Jew, could ever subdue that despised but indomitable race. Most of them found refuge in Frankfort; but some years later, with the encouragement of the Markgrafs of Brandenburg, many of them settled at Fürth, which speedily became a serious commercial rival to Nuremberg, and remains to this day as prosperous as her neighbour.

One curious and interesting result this expulsion had. In order to supply the place of the money-lenders the Emperor ordered a Leihaus or State Pawnshop to be built, where money was to be advanced at a moderate percentage on property to people in difficulties. It was to be run at cost price, or, if there were any surplus, it was to go to the State. This was an imitation of the Italian system (Monte di Pietà) already in vogue at Augsburg—a system not without interest to the Englishman of to-day.

During the Thirty Years War, the Jews in Fürth, oppressed by the Imperial troops, asked to be received back into Nuremberg. Some of the Council were ready to comply, on the receipt of a large payment, but the majority refused to have the "damaging rascals" within their walls.

So long did the hostility towards the Jews survive here that it was not till 1800 that the regulation was done away with by which, in order to stop a day in Nuremberg, a Jew had to pay a personal tax of 45 kreuzer, and, in addition, had to be accompanied by a guard, for he was not allowed to walk in the streets alone. This guard was usually an old woman, who followed her Jew everywhere for the consideration of 15 kreuzer.

CHAPTER III

NUREMBERG AND THE REFORMATION

"Trading Staple of the German World in old days, Toyshop of the German World in these new, Albert Dürer's and Hans Sachs' City."—CARLYLE.

WE have watched the dawning sun of Nuremberg's greatness rise over the forest till now it has reached the Mittags-quarter. We have seen, to change the metaphor, the little foundling of the swamps grow year by year till at last she has arrived at the full strength and beauty of womanhood. For it was under Maximilian that Nuremberg reached her prime: it was under him and his successors that the greatest of her sons flourished. She was lavish as a princess in the adornment of her person. Once in 1447, and again in 1491, for instance, we find her voting some 500 florins to gild the Beautiful Fountain (Schöner Brunnen), which had been placed in the Hauptmarkt 1385.[16] She was already adorned with those churches which in her old age are still her brightest jewels.

Once completed, these churches were not regarded merely as houses of prayer, but rather as the books of God, where the divine history of the Redemption might be read and illustrated. The Christian fervour of the artists led them to give their best and sincerest work to the decoration of them. So that in the course of time the churches came to represent for the people museums constantly open, historic galleries of sacred art, to which one masterpiece after another was added.

"From daily admiration of them an æsthetic sense was formed in the minds of the young, and thanks to them the artists found repeated opportunities for exercising their art. Orders from private individuals or public bodies abounded. Every well-to-do family, every corporation was eager to do honour to God by the presentation of some gift to his holy dwelling-place: some offered a picture, a statue, a window, or an altar-piece; the portraits of the families themselves,[17] as portraits of the donors, were placed at the feet of the saints. When the artists represented themselves in paint, bronze, wood, or stone, they gave themselves the humble attitude of suppliants: in those of their compositions which contain numerous personages they always choose the humblest place for themselves; often, like Adam Krafft in the tabernacle in the Church of St. Lorenz, they appear in their working clothes, tools in hand, in the attitude of servants."[18]

Whilst such men as Adam Krafft and Peter Vischer were giving their lifework to the beautifying of the churches, sculpture and painting also were turned to the adornment of domestic and public life. The mansions of the merchant princes still bear witness to the wealth of the burgesses, and to the vigour of the artistic impulse of this period. Every house, apart from architectural splendour, was decorated with a painting, whether of some symbol or the patron saint of the family. The very aspect of the streets spoke to the importance of the rôle which art played in the life of the town. The influence of the town reacted no less surely on the art of the period. Albert Durer, for instance, in spite of his wide experience always speaks in his art, like his master Wolgemut, in the Nuremberg dialect. The intense patriotism and the deep religious feeling which formed so intimate a part of the lives of the citizens are reproduced in their art and literature,

SCHÖNER BRUNNEN

giving the greatest examples of them the added charm of locality. Their love of science was no less genuine than their love of art. In June 1471, a few weeks after the birth of Albert Durer, Johannes Muller, (surnamed Regiomontanus in allusion to Königsberg, his native village) the great mathematical genius, "the wonder of his generation," took up his abode at Nuremberg, making her the true home of physical and mathematical science and contributing mightily to her reputation as "the capital of German art, the most precious jewel of the Empire, the meeting-place of art and industry." "I have chosen Nuremberg for my place of residence," he writes, "because there I find without difficulty all the peculiar instruments necessary for astronomy, and there it is easiest for me to keep in touch with the learned of all countries, for Nuremberg, thanks to the perpetual journeyings of her merchants, may be counted the centre of Europe." Inspired with the eager desire to know everything, so characteristic of his age, he was equally desirous to impart his knowledge. We may trace to his influence Durer's book on geometry and his beautiful chart of the heavens. Muller introduced popular science lectures, and organised the manufacture of astronomical and nautical instruments. His most famous pupil was Martin Behaim the constructor of the first globe and the adventurous navigator, whose monument (1890) may be seen in the Theresien Platz. Behaim in 1492 indicated on his terrestrial globe the precise route followed six years later by Vasco da Gama when he doubled the Cape of Good Hope. It was Behaim, too, who suggested to Magellan the first idea of the strait which bears his name. Behaim's famous globe is kept in the Behaim House, which is in the Ægiden Platz, next to the house of Koberger, the printer, and opposite the statue of Melanchthon (by Burgschmiet, 1826).

Maximilian, "the last of the knights," had taken a considerable part in the government before he succeeded his father in 1493. The Nurembergers, who always had an eye for a strong man, had already shown their loyalty to him. He had stayed amongst them at the house of Christopher Scheurl (father of the famous Dr Scheurl), and whilst there would seem to have amused himself light-heartedly enough. When about to depart, we are told, he invited twenty great ladies to dinner; after dinner, when they were all in a good humour, the Margraf Frederick asked Maximilian in the name of the ladies to stay a little longer and to dance with them. They, it is said, had taken away his boots and spurs, so he had no choice. Then the whole company adjourned to the Council House, several other young ladies were invited, and Maximilian stayed dancing all through the afternoon and night and arrived a day late at Neumarkt where the Count of the Palatinate had been expecting him all the preceding day.

As Emperor, Maximilian stayed at the Kaiserburg. A brilliant assembly attended his first Reichstag. Masques, dances, tourneys and so forth are recorded with gusto by the chroniclers. The Emperor, they say, entertained all the ladies of the town at dinner and provided them with two hundred and forty sorts of dishes. No wonder he was popular!

Nuremberg was not allowed to be content with supplying Maximilian with partners in the ball-room. In 1499 she had to support him in his disastrous war with Switzerland. The Nuremberg contingent was under Willibald Pirkheimer and Wolf Pömer. Beautifully dressed in red and white uniforms these soldiers earned the reputation of cowardice and treachery. Such imputations were, let it be confessed, not unfrequently cast upon

Nuremberg courage; but on this occasion the Emperor took their part and refuted the charge.

Nuremberg knew at any rate how to fight her own battles. Throughout this period we find her engaged in continual quarrels with the Markgrafs of Brandenburg. The Burggraf Frederick once made Elector, had parted with the Burggrafship, sold it, all but the title, to the burghers in 1427. But principalities and territories were retained in that quarter, and about these, and their feudal rights and boundaries and tolls, endless trouble arose. Some fifty years later actual furious war resulted between the Elector Albert Achilles and the jealous citizens—a war in "which eight victories are counted on Albert's part—furious successful skirmishes they call them; in one of which Albert plunged in alone, his Ritters being rather shy, and laid about him hugely, hanging by a standard he had taken, till his life was nearly beaten out. Eight victories, and also one defeat wherein Albert got captured and had to ransom himself. The captor was one Kunz of Kauffungen, the Nürnberg hired General at the time, a man known to some readers for his stealing of the Saxon princes (Prinzenraut, they call it), a feat which cost Kunz his head."[19] Such quarrels continued, for the Markgrafs did not relinquish their efforts to extend their powers. Details it would be wearisome to give, but they illustrate the general family tendency of the Hohenzollern. It is characteristic that they were generally successful in their claims (all cases, it was now decided, arising from Nuremberg property outside the walls were to be tried by the Landgericht, of which the Markgraf was president), and based on this success still greater claims in the future.

The memoirs of Götz von Berlichingen furnish us with an interesting account of the Battle of the Forest of Nuremberg (1502), which affords a good example of the sort of thing continually occurring in those days.

Towards the end of May it was rumoured in the town that warlike preparations were being made in Ansbach, the headquarters of the Markgraf. The feelings of the citizens were still further roused by the fact that the Markgraf had taken under his protection an enemy of Nuremberg. The day of the Affalterbacher Fair was at hand. The prospect seemed so threatening that the Council sent a specially large contingent—2000 men, with a "Wagenburg" and cannon under the command of the Magistrate Hans von Weichsdorf, Wolf Haller, and Wolf Pömer—to escort their citizens who went to attend the fair. An accidental explosion of powder when they were starting seemed ominous. At home they kept a small force under Ulman Stromer, who drew up between the Frauen- and Spitler-Thor. On the day of the fair, the Markgraf appeared with a large force of knights, Swiss and local soldiery. Amongst them was Götz von Berlichingen, who was only twenty-two years of age. The following manœuvers then took place. In the morning some sixty horsemen were seen driving off the cattle about a quarter of a mile south of Nuremberg. Ulman Stromer thereupon marched out and took up a strong position, under protection of his guns, and drove the horsemen back into the woods, "for they did not find it very amusing: it is not everybody who likes to hear the cannon roar," says Götz. The retreat of the enemy enticed Ulman Stromer to follow them with his carts and cannon into the wood. Suddenly he came upon the Markgraf Casimir with his main army. Though outnumbered, the Nurembergers did not lose their courage, but fired with such effect that the riff-raff of the enemy

FRAUEN THOR

cleared off, leaving the knights and Switzers to do battle. Under cover of a strong fire, "so that nothing could be seen for smoke," Stromer tried to form a "Wagenburg" (waggon fortress), by having the carts driven round so as to form a circle about the men and guns, hoping to be able to wait in this extemporised fort till reinforcements should arrive from Affalterbach. Götz boasts that it was he who prevented this manœuvre from being executed. For he killed one of the drivers, and so interrupted the completion of the circle. The Brandenburgers were thus enabled to rush in, and compelled the citizens to take to flight. At this juncture the reinforcements came up, but it was too late. A general rush for safety to the town took place. On the bridge over the moat there was so great a crush of refugees that many were forced over into the water. Luckily the cannon on the Frauen Thor kept the Markgraf at a safe distance. Within the town a terrible panic had occurred. Götz, indeed, says that the place could easily have been taken—a statement not very easy to believe. At any rate, the Markgraf did not attempt it, but marched back to Schwabach to hold a service of thanksgiving, whilst the

Nurembergers revenged themselves on the peasants whom they had taken prisoner. Intense indignation was felt and expressed against the Markgraf: prisoners were torn to pieces in the streets. At last a curious peace was arranged, to begin on July 1st, but not before. Each side tried to damage the other as much as possible before that day came, and the Council, in order to get in a good final blow, burned the Markgraf's castle of Schönberg at the last moment. A peace thus inaugurated did not, as may be imagined, produce any lasting good feeling between the two parties. In the very next year fresh trouble arose over one Heinz Baum, a Nuremberg citizen who had come down in the world and been put into prison by his creditors. As soon as he was released, he left the town, threw up his citizenship, and, after writing various threatening letters to the Council, he surprised Hans Tucher, a Nuremberg patrician, when riding out to his country seat, and kept him prisoner till he was ransomed. With the Markgraf's secret support, Baum proceeded to seize and keep in the stocks till ransom was paid all the citizens he could lay his hands on. Though the Emperor outlawed him, he pursued his way unhindered, protected by the Markgraf, till 1512, when Nuremberg bought off his chief supporter, and Heinz Baum retired to Bamberg, where he died poor but unpunished.

The importance of Nuremberg was still further enhanced by the part she took in the war of the Bavarian Succession. In 1503 George the Rich of Bavaria had died without male issue. According to the feudal right, his lands ought to have gone to the male heir, but, hating as he did his natural successors, his cousins Albrecht of Bavaria and Wolfgang, he had made his daughter his sole heiress, and married her to her cousin Ruprecht (third son of the powerful Philip, Elector of the Palatinate), whom he adopted as his son and made governor of a great part of the country. On the death of Duke George, Ruprecht succeeded, but Albrecht and Wolfgang raised such strenuous protest that the Emperor, after repeated attempts to arrange a compromise, was obliged to outlaw Ruprecht and all his supporters, his father the Elector Philip included. War was the inevitable result. The Emperor and other princes, amongst whom was the Markgraf of Brandenburg, gave their support to Albrecht, who promised them a share in what was conquered. Many of Philip's possessions were close to Nuremberg. Albrecht was therefore able to entice her to fight for him, promising her in return for her aid 40,000 gulden, with all the Palatinate towns and the value of all George's towns that she might manage to take. With the aid of three special cannon, called the Owl, the Falcon, and the Fishermaid, capable of shooting balls of 263 pounds weight, the Nuremberg army captured a considerable number of Palatinate towns. But even after the deaths first of Ruprecht and then of his brave widow, who had carried on the struggle like another Margaret of Anjou, the war still dragged on on behalf of their little sons, and the Palatinate party were actually getting a little the best of it when, at a Reichstag in Cologne, Maximilian at length arranged a successful compromise.

Nuremberg was allowed to keep what she had taken, and now had more land than any other free town in the Empire. It was a doubtful blessing. She was involved in constant wars to keep it, in further quarrels with the Markgraf over the rights of Fraisgericht,—of jurisdiction in matters of life and death in the newly acquired towns, and she had to pay largely increased contributions to the Empire. Altogether she was impoverished rather than benefited by her new property.

We have now to trace the story of the celebrated feud with Götz von Berlichingen—the warrior knight, the chivalrous and charitable, the brave, free-booting noble, Götz of the Iron Hand. Such is the character Goethe gave him when he centred in him, as the heroic champion of the privileges of the Free Knights, the interest of his Shakesperian drama. Truth, however, compels us to declare, that though men like Götz or Franz von Sickingen, the Robin Hoods of Germany, had the qualities of a certain rough justice and courage, they were, for the rest, wholly undeniable brigands. The love of destruction, disorder, and rapine, and the hatred of authority were their chief motives. They used their rights as pretexts for violence and devoted themselves to brigandage as to a legitimate vocation and organised industry. They were, indeed, little better than leaders of bands of robbers, the wolves of civilisation.

"One day," says Götz, "as I was on the point of making an attack, I perceived a pack of wolves descending on a flock of sheep. This incident seemed to me a good omen. We were going to begin the fight. A shepherd was near us, guarding his sheep, when, as if to give us the signal, five wolves threw themselves simultaneously on the flock. I saw it and noted it gladly. I wished them success and ourselves too, saying, 'Good luck, dear comrades, success to you everywhere!' I took it as a very good augury that we had begun the attack together!"

It was in 1495 that Maximilian, ever anxious to promote peace and order within the borders of his Empire, abrogated by edict the right of private war under the penalty of the ban of the Empire—a penalty which involved the dooms of outlawry and excommunication. Thus the "last of the Knights" gave the death-blow to the chivalry of the Middle Ages. Hitherto every German noble holding fief directly from the Emperor had been on his own property a petty monarch, as it were, subordinate to the Imperial authority alone. These proud military barons,—an ever-increasing host of petty lords, since the rule of inheritance in Germany was division among the male heirs—esteemed above all other privileges the right of making war on each other, or on the towns, with no other ceremony than that of three days' notice in writing (Fehdebrief). The evils and dangers of this privilege are clear, but they were left untouched by the Golden Bull. With the advance of civilisation, which was ever opposed to the feudal system, this Faustrecht had come to be regarded as intolerable by such princes, bishops and free towns as suffered from the consequent disorder of the country and the marauding expeditions of the free-knights. For the residence of every baron had become, as we have seen, a fortress from which, as his passions or avarice dictated, a band of marauders sallied forth to back his quarrel or to collect an extorted revenue from the merchants who presumed to pass through his domain. Princes and bishops, abbots and wealthy merchants of the towns banded together, therefore, to enforce the new ordinance and to suppress the petty feudatories, who, like Götz, struggled to maintain their privilege and independence. Under Sigismund various efforts had been made to suppress the harrying of the knights and many robber-nests on solitary rocks were taken. When taken the robbers, especially those of the lower class, were made short work of and dealt with in various ways—ways best illustrated by a visit to the torture chambers of the castle. There was one Hans Schuttensamen, for instance, on whose head the Council put a price. A citizen of Bamberg came forward and claimed the reward, saying he had shot him. After he had received the money his story was found to be a stretch of the imagination and he was burnt accordingly. Ten years later (1474) the robber also got burnt.

So bitterly were these knights hated and feared that even the great tourneys, such as the one recorded in 1446,[20] when all the neighbouring nobles came in from the surrounding country and tilted and displayed their skill and valour in the market-place, were very unpopular with the peace-loving burghers.

Nuremberg, then, joined the Swabian League to suppress such knights as chose still to indulge in the forbidden Club Law or Faustrecht. It was not long before she came into direct collision with Götz von Berlichingen of the Iron Hand. Götz, who had a fine gift for chastising the gutter-blooded citizens of a free town, had long been anxious to try conclusions with the men of Nuremberg. He carried out his intention on a very futile pretext. The Nurembergers, it seems, had pursued and fought in the adjacent woods some unknown knights, who had refused, when challenged, to give their names as honest knights and fled. Now, some years after, Hans von Geislingen, brother of one George, who was the Squire of Eustace of Lichtenstein and was killed on this occasion, demanded blood-money for his brother, and on being refused, he seized some Nuremberg citizens and merchants' caravans. He was outlawed, but this did not prevent Götz von Berlichingen from helping him. George, he declared, had been his page (a statement that had the defect of being untrue), and he demanded a large sum of money in compensation. When this was refused Götz did not send an Absagebrief, or letter of notice of war, but merely a note saying that he was considering, with his friends, how to get compensation. His bitterness was further increased by the action of the Council, who shortly afterwards decapitated Sebastian von Seckendorf, a knight who had long been a source of annoyance, and whom they had at last been successful in catching. Suddenly, and without warning, Götz and his friends swooped down on a party of fifty-five Nuremberg merchants who were travelling back from the fair at Leipzig, under the escort of the Bishop of Bamberg. These he plundered and took prisoners as they were crossing the Rednitz, near Forcheim. Götz did not treat his prisoners too gently, but used the art of torture to persuade them to offer huge ransoms. The news of this seizure caused consternation and surprise in Nuremberg. Götz's letter of notice came only nine days later to the Council. Spies were sent out to discover his whereabouts: the town was prepared for a siege, and 800 mercenary soldiers were hired. Götz was outlawed. But the Council were accused of being slack to avenge, what they called "a handful of small merchants, not of patrician families," and Maximilian was not willing to be plunged into an Imperial war "to recover a merchant's sack of pepper." What he did do was to attempt to bring about one of his favourite compromises. The Markgraf was appointed to arbitrate, and his award was that Nuremberg should pay a certain sum. As is not unusual in the case of arbitrations, the money was not paid. Götz, laughing at the sentence of outlawry that had been passed upon him, protected by the princes who resented peace and order in an Empire, continued to ravage, burn and pillage, until the Swabian League was renewed, at the end of 1512, to keep the "eternal peace," at which Maximilian aimed. Nuremberg once more joined the League, on Maximilian's injunction, though she distrusted the alliance with the Markgraf thereby involved. The League, however, decided in January 1513 to take strong measures to repress the outlawed nobles and to destroy the castles of the robber-knights. But the Emperor objected, and said that he wanted to arrive at a peaceful compromise with Götz. The Nurembergers replied that they would be content if the latter paid over a sum of money sufficient to compensate the merchants for the losses they had suffered. At the same time they took prisoner a robber-knight who was a friend of the Markgraf, and to procure his release the Markgraf promised to arrange peace for them with Hans von Geislingen. This he succeeded in doing. Götz, however, remained at war, proud and obstinate in spite of all mediation. Again and again the League threatened war, the Emperor temporised, and Götz plundered, until at last Maximilian got it arranged that Götz should pay 14000 florins damages. These were subscribed chiefly by his supporters, such as the Bishop of Würzburg, who also persuaded him to cease from his career of robbery.

Maximilian died in 1519. He had shown himself a good friend to the Nuremberg artists. No doubt his patronage and his keen interest in art and literature had been partly responsible for the good work of this period. He was himself an author, for he had a considerable share in the Weisskunig and the Theuerdank—the latter, a poem which describes allegorically the private life and ideals of the Emperor, being chiefly executed by Melchior Pfinzing, his secretary, the Provost of St. Sebald's and builder of the Parsonage. Of the artists, he frequently employed Peter Vischer and Veit Stoss, whilst he showed the greatest appreciation of Albert Durer, to whom he gave a pension of 100 florins. When at Nuremberg in 1512 Maximilian with the aid of Willibald Pirkheimer and others, planned a colossal Holzschnittwerk, or wood-cut picture, "The Triumph," in which he himself was, as usual in the works of art he inspired, to be idealised as the greatest of princes. Durer was to draw part of it. Ninety-two blocks did Durer design for the Triumphal Arch in the course of the next two years. Amongst other works for this patron we may mention The Triumphal Car, the Crucifixion, and the ornamental borders of the famous Book of Hours. Finally when Maximilian held the diet at Augsburg in 1518, Durer, who was one of the commissioners sent by the town of Nuremberg, drew the Emperor's portrait from the life, "in the little room upstairs in the palace." From this sketch he painted the picture now at Vienna, another version of which is in the German Museum at Nuremberg. Durer was as good a courtier as artist. Melanchthon tells us how Maximilian was endeavouring to draw a design which he wished Durer to carry out, but kept breaking the charcoal in doing so. Durer took the charcoal and, without breaking it, easily finished the drawing. Maximilian, somewhat vexed, asked how this was, to which the artist replied, "I should not like your Majesty to be able to draw as well as I. It is my province to draw and yours to rule." Aliud est plectrum, aliud sceptrum. The hand that wields the sceptre is too strong for the brush.

Maximilian was, in many aspects of his character, a typical product of the Renaissance. Nuremberg had felt the full force of the revival of learning, the new stimulus in art and literature which was being brought to the West from Constantinople by the Jews and Greeks who had been driven out by the Turks. Not a few of the knights and pilgrims, too, must have passed through Nuremberg on their return from the Crusades, and her growing commerce with the East and West and Italy would tend to keep her in touch with the developments which were taking place in the world of ideas, and which were tending inevitably towards the Reformation. She had been among the first to welcome and to practise the new "German art" of printing. Between 1470, when Johann Sensenschmidt had brought Gutenberg's invention to Nuremberg, and the end of the century, twenty-five printers received the rights of citizenship. Johannes Regiomontanus printed here in 1472 his Kalendarium Novum. But Anthoni Koberger was the most celebrated man in the trade. Over two hundred different works, mostly in large folio, were issued from his twenty-four printing presses before 1500. The "prince of booksellers," as one of his contemporaries calls him, he had agents in every country, and sixteen depôts in the principal towns in Christendom. The first work of art which left his presses was a magnificent illustrated Bible, published in 1483, and printed from blocks he had obtained from Henry Quentel of Cologne. But, besides the Bible and theology, the press poured forth a stream of literature of every kind, spreading new ideas with unexampled rapidity, and giving expression to thoughtful criticism or popular satire of established abuses. Under such influences as these it was felt that a new era of progress was at hand. Nuremberg, stimulated by the education of self-government and of commercial intercourse, did not fail to produce such independent humanists as Conrad Celtes, Dr Scheurl, Lazarus Spengler, Albert Durer, Willibald Pirkheimer, who could write as well as read, and preach as well as applaud the doctrines of necessary reform. She was, in fact, one of the first towns to express sympathy with Martin Luther, when he nailed his ninety-five theses on the church door of Wittenberg, in protest against what Erasmus had called "the crime of false pardons," the sale of Indulgences, to which Leo X. had resorted in order to raise money for a little war.

Luther came to Nuremberg in the course of the next year (1518) and stayed in the Augustinerkloster. His friend Leirck, we are told, had to buy him a new cowl, in order that he might appear in fitting costume before the Cardinal Cajetan at Augsburg, where he was summoned to answer for his heresies. None the less the Cardinal received at Nuremberg a great welcome next year, and Luther's followers continued at present to perform the rites and cling to the old forms of the Church. Reform, not revolution, was what they still hoped for. But the stream of events carried them rapidly with it. Willibald Pirkheimer, thanks to a satire against Eck, the bitter opponent of Luther, was included in 1519 in the Papal Bull, by which Luther was excommunicated. The Council, annoyed by the excommunication of Pirkheimer and Lazarus Spengler (Clerk of the Council), refused to interfere with the printing and publishing of Luther's works, and gradually passed over to his side. To show how little they respected this decree of excommunication, they actually sent Spengler to represent the town at the Diet of Worms. For Charles V. held his first Reichstag (1521) at Worms, and not at Nuremberg, because of an outbreak of plague there. (Outbreaks of plague were not uncommon at Nuremberg, nor were they surprising. For all refuse was always thrown into the Pegnitz on the understanding that "the river would eat up all the dirt.") It was at this Diet of Worms that Luther made his Confession of Faith, and fought single-handed against Pope and Emperor the great battle for the right of freedom of conscience.

When, as the result, the ban of the Empire had been passed upon him and all his works, and the report was abroad that violent hands had been laid on him, Albert Durer, who had followed him from the first, wrote in his diary, expressing at the same time the opinion of the nation; "Whether he lives or whether he has been murdered, I know not; but he has suffered for the Christian faith and has been punished by the unchristian Papacy." That, too, was the opinion of all the more important men in Nuremberg. Cautious in expressing their feelings at first, after a time the people boldly showed their dislike of monasteries and their approval of the new movement.

"Wake up! Now may the dawn be seen;
And singing in a thicket green
I hear a tuneful nightingale,"

wrote Hans Sachs, in a poem which had no small influence in forwarding the reformation movement. So, in many of his later prose dialogues, he upholds liberty of conscience and freedom of opinion in religious matters. The Council, in deference to the Emperor, made a bare pretence of stopping the publication of Lutheran writings. So half-hearted were they that the Papal Legate demanded that stronger measures should be taken, and that Lutheran preachers should be imprisoned. But the Council pursued its policy of keeping the peace between both parties, taking a middle course and siding with neither reactionary nor revolutionary. That policy could not be pursued for long. The Council had to yield, not unwillingly, to public opinion. At a meeting of representatives of the towns at Rothenburg, held there in 1524 because forbidden by Imperial edict to meet at Spires and to discuss religious matters, Nuremberg was very bold and "gave three brave Christian reasons" why they should not obey this edict. She organised a further meeting of the towns at Ulm, and for herself began to determine on a new form of worship. The Sacrament was now administered in both kinds, and Mass was read in German, with Lutheran omissions, by the Prior of the Augustin Monastery. Both the Parish Churches followed his example. The Council excused themselves for allowing this by saying that they did it to avoid an uproar among the people. The Bishop of Bamberg held an inquiry, and summoned the officiating priests before him. They denied his power to judge them, and his sentence of excommunication was practically ignored. Other towns followed the example of Nuremberg, and imitated her Lutheran services. Meanwhile the dislike of the people for monasteries and nunneries broke out more vehemently. The air was full of satires and cartoons directed against nuns and monks. Hans Sachs was not silent on this point. At last the Council ordered these institutions to be handed over to the guidance of the

Lutheran preachers. Charitas Pirkheimer, the virtuous and accomplished abbess of the Klarakloster, friend and correspondent of Durer and sister of Willibald, has left us in her memoirs a touching account of the manner in which she was torn from her beloved convent, over which no breath of scandal had ever passed, and which contained many of the daughters of the best families in Nuremberg. These memoirs are well worth looking at by those who care to see the other side of the question, and to make the acquaintance of a beautiful and fascinating character. Unfortunately we have no space in this little book to deal with them here.

Shortly after this an organised discussion between the representatives of the old and new orders of religious belief was held before the Council. One by one, twelve points of doctrine were put to the heads of the Lutheran, Carmelite, Augustin and Dominican bodies, and each answered after his kind. The Catholic party finally claimed that the decision between them should be referred to the University; but Osiander, declaring that God's word was the only salvation, wound up the discussion with a bold and eloquent speech, and called upon the Council for an immediate decision. The Council gave their vote for the Lutheran case, and thus formally threw in their lot with the Reformation. The following year saw a whole series of decrees from the Council carrying out Lutheran principles. Thus, chiefly no doubt in deference to the popular demand—for these were the days of the terrible Peasant wars—the property of the priests was ordered to be taxed. There was little violence. The influence of the gentle Melanchthon, who came to Nuremberg in 1525, did much to smooth down any tendency to brutality, or harsh treatment of the monks and nuns. Even in the first flash of religious excitement education was not neglected. The educational movement inaugurated by Luther's letter to the towns asking them to found schools, met with eager support at Nuremberg. Through the agency of Hieronymus Paumgärtner and Spengler, Philip Melanchthon was induced to come and assist at the founding of a new gymnasium for secondary education. No expense was spared, and Melanchthon brought a brilliant staff of teachers with him. The institution was established in the buildings of the Ægidienkloster. But the school languished. Nuremberg, after all, was a town of shopkeepers, and, though some were ready to pay for masters, few were ready to pay, or spare the time, for their sons' higher education. The school was at last moved to Altdorf, and grew into the University there. The present gymnasium was refounded in 1633. Melanchthon's statue, mentioned above, stands in front of the building erected in 1711 on the site of the old monastery which together with the church was burnt down in 1699. Conrad III. is said to have built the church for the Benedictine Order in 1140. Three chapels remain—the Eucharius, the Wolfgang, and the Tetzel chapels, of which the first is the oldest, and affords an interesting example of the transition style (see p. 260).

The Council all this time had a difficult part to play: it had to show itself both strong and conciliatory. When the Peasants' War broke out, Nuremberg, the capital of Franconia, was not unaffected by it though

ROTHENBURG

she suffered less than her neighbours—Rothenburg for example. But the new-found spiritual freedom preached from Lutheran pulpits was likely to be misinterpreted by the lower classes in the town, as it had been by the peasants outside, and construed into temporal licence. The Council, therefore, whilst striving not to cause any irritation, had to take strong measures to repress the outbreaks which occurred within the walls, when the peasants, whom Götz von Berlichingen had joined, were ravaging and rioting through the country in their barbarous struggle for emancipation. First of all the Council very wisely expelled Thomas Münzer, the mad, well-meaning fanatic and agitator, and then promised the peasants to remain neutral, as long as they did not ravage her territory or tamper with her citizens. Still, for a few months, Nuremberg was in imminent danger. She might have fallen into the hands of the rebels at any moment in the May of this year (1525). The Council, realising the peril, remitted some of the tithes, as a sop to the peasants, and sent urgent appeals for aid to the Swabian League. But the thunder-cloud passed by without breaking over Nuremberg, and she, to her credit be it recorded, when the revolt was crushed, was not slow to speak on behalf of towns like Rothenburg which had taken the side of the peasants. The result of her intervention was to preserve for us the walls and fortifications of Rothenburg. The illustration shows the towers and gateways there which recall the White Tower and Lauferschlagthurm at Nuremberg.

In the later developments of the Protestant revolution, we find Willibald Pirkheimer warmly supporting Luther with his pen, when Zwingle, denying the Real Presence, treated the Sacrament as symbolic, and was violently denounced by Luther for this view. Pirkheimer, however, was no blind follower of Luther. He, remembering his sister's case, thought the monasteries and convents too hardly treated, and he saw, what Luther failed to see, that the peasant risings were the inevitable results of such times of upheaval and repression. He grew soured and disappointed with Luther. Like Scheurl, and, as he says (1528)—

"Like Durer, I was at first a good Lutheran. We hoped things would be better than in the Roman Church, but the Lutherans are worse. The former were hypocrites: the latter openly live disgraceful lives. For Justification by Faith alone is not possible. Without works faith is dead. Luther, with his bold, petulant tongue, has either fallen under a delusion, or else is being led astray by the Evil One."

However, in spite of splits, the wave of Protestantism was not diminishing. The answer to the Emperor's order that stringent measures should be taken against the Lutheran heresy, and that the Edict of Worms should be carried out, was, that the towns, under the leadership of Nuremberg, banded themselves together with the Lutheran princes, and at the Diet of Spires (1526) it was decreed that "Each State should, as regards the Diet of Worms, so live, rule, and bear itself as it thought it could answer to God and the Empire."

From this decree, which was an acknowledgment of the temporary breakdown of Roman Catholicism, resulting from the Emperor's quarrel with the Pope, came the division of Germany into Catholic and Protestant States. Next year, when the Bishop of Bamberg commanded the priests of Nuremberg to observe the Roman Catholic ceremonies, the Council, whom he asked not to interfere with the carrying out of his order, were able to point to this Edict. In order, however, to be secure from the Swabian League, which was hostile to the new teaching, Nuremberg, Augsburg, Ulm, and other towns, bound themselves together and protested against any interference, on the part of the League, in religious matters.

But in 1529 the Emperor had settled his quarrel with the Pope and returned to his loyalty to Rome. Taking advantage of this, the Papal party succeeded in passing a decree in the Reichstag confirming the Edict of Worms. The Lutheran princes protested against the decree, and so earned the name of "Protestants." The Protestant communities assembled in Nuremberg, and sent a representative to the Emperor, who was in Italy, to complain. The Emperor, however, took a firm tone with them and declared the dispensation of Spires at an end. Philip von Hessen and other zealous leaders were now very eager to make a firm stand and to form a Protestant union against this fresh attempt to suppress the new teaching. But the

Lutherans could not bring themselves to work with the Zwinglians. The influence of Luther and Osiander was sufficient to deter Nuremberg from joining in such a scheme. Wisely or not, she refused to belong to any union which might bring her into conflict with the head of the Empire. But, though she said she would not take up arms, she knew her own mind in religious matters. At a Reichstag held at Augsburg (1530) the Emperor was to be present. Owing to the exertions of the Nuremberg Council, the Evangelical party united to send the celebrated "Confession," or statement of Lutheran doctrines, which was drawn up by Luther and Melanchthon, signed by Nuremberg and Reutlingen, and read to Charles. The representatives of Nuremberg also took with them a confession of faith, drawn up under the direction of the Council by Nuremberg theologians. A peaceful solution of the question was what they aimed at: a recognition of religious freedom brought about by argument, not by arms. For this reason, and because she had a great distrust of the Protestant princes ("The princes are princes," it was said, "and if anything happens they will withdraw their heads out of the noose and leave the towns in the lurch") Nuremberg would not join "the league of Schmalkalden," formed by the Protestant princes to defend themselves from that crushing of the Lutheran heresy by the Imperial power, which the Diet now threatened. This league, in spite of Luther's protest against opposition to the civil power, would have led at once to war, had not a Turkish invasion of Austria diverted Charles' attention. Something like a religious truce was proclaimed, and Nuremberg sent a double contingent of men to help Charles.

It was, perhaps, in recognition of this proof of loyalty that Charles, on his way to Regensburg in 1541, held the Reichstag at Nuremberg for the first time. The town on this occasion was in a great state of festivity. The roads were strewn with sand; festoons and hangings brightened the streets which were lined by 5000 armed citizens. Bells were rung and cannon fired as Charles, clothed in black, with a felt hat on his head, rode into the town, beneath a magnificent red velvet canopy held by eight members of the Council in turn. He passed beneath a triumphal arch which had been erected near Neudörfer's house, in the Burgstrasse. In the Rathaus a solemn act of homage was performed, and the Emperor confirmed all the privileges of the town. Costly gifts were lavished on him; fireworks were let off from the bastion then being built (see p. 115). The Council, in fact, though they would concede nothing, even at the Emperor's request, on the religious question, showed themselves loyal and conciliatory. The bells of the principal churches were ordered to be rung at noon, to remind all good Christians to pray for protection against the Turks, the arch-enemies of Christianity. This ringing, called Betläuten, still takes place.

The Civil War, which was the inevitable result of the formation of the Schmalkalden League, had only been postponed. The Emperor and the Catholic princes tried to reduce the Protestant princes to obedience, with the aid of Spanish soldiery, soon after the death of Luther. Though Charles had said he was going to attack the princes and not the towns, the northern towns promised help to the princes. Nuremberg, however, determined to obey the Emperor; she strove, in fact, to pursue, so far as possible, her usual policy of inactive neutrality. Money was paid to the Emperor: but, when urgent appeals for help came from the princes, the Council sent them privately a sum of money, but would take no further step for the Evangelical cause at present. The sympathy of the majority was, indeed, with the League, but they shrank from risking all the great wealth and privileges of the town for the common welfare and for the freedom of religious belief. Nürnberg trage auf beiden achseln was the bitter sneer of the day. The temper of her citizens was sorely tried when the Emperor's ill-behaved Spanish troops were quartered on them. Still, money was supplied loyally enough to the Imperial treasury. In religious matters they remained steadfast, politely but firmly forbidding the Emperor's Confessor to read Mass to the nuns in the Katharinenkirche.

The result of Charles' campaigns against the princes was to leave him apparently more powerful than any Emperor since Charlemagne. We can hardly wonder if, in the Reichstag of 1547, he tried to get himself recognised as supreme head of the Empire, not only in political, but also in religious matters. A year later he appointed a Commission which published the "Interim," establishing a half-and-half religion for all not of the Roman Catholic faith. It was called the strait-waistcoat of German Protestantism. Papacy was thereby almost reintroduced. The work of Luther seemed entirely undone. This attempt at repressing Evangelical teaching roused the Nurembergers. Sermons thundered from the pulpit, and the Council was severely criticised. None the less they accepted the "Interim." Osiander resigned his post and shook the dust of Nuremberg from off his feet. Others followed his example. But, in spite of protest, the Catholic reaction was, for the moment, successful. It could not last. The Spanish yoke was in itself intolerable. In 1552 the revolt of the princes, in alliance even with France, began. The Council pursued its old policy of neutrality—a policy destined this time not to pay. Money was contributed to the princes: devotion to the Emperor was expressed. So they thought they were safe. But the Markgraf of Brandenburg, Albert Alcibiades, who had declared for the Protestant cause, held only to the princes' manifesto, that those who were not for them were against them. He turned his eyes on his old enemy, and seized the merchant-trains that were leaving the city in fancied security. Then, suddenly in May, he appeared with a strong force before Lichtenau— a castle and mart belonging to Nuremberg. The place fell into his hands, was burnt and razed to the ground. Next day he sent a message, bearing the Bourbon arms, to express his surprise that he had received no help from Nuremberg. In the name of the King of France and of the allied princes who "purposed to bring back and keep liberty in the dear Fatherland, and to establish a right and true Christian religion," he demanded whether the town intended to join the league against the Emperor or not. She referred to her dealings with the princes. But the Markgraf, ignoring this subterfuge, moved on the city, and the Council, seeing that he was set on war, determined to stand a siege, and strained every nerve to strengthen the fortifications. The princes, indeed, remonstrated with the Markgraf; but in vain. He advanced, ravaging the villages, taking castles, burning and plundering all he could lay his hands on in his drunken and murderous march. When he arrived beneath the walls of Nuremberg, a truce of eight days was arranged till the Markgraf could hear from Francis I. of France. Meanwhile he busied himself with throwing up entrenchments. But before the eight days had expired, he opened fire on the city. Some cannon-shots struck the Ægidienskirche, in which a service was being held. One house in the Ægidiensplatz still bears the marks of shot that struck it on this occasion, says Dr Reicke. Meanwhile Nuremberg was not slow to defend herself. Her citizens returned the fire with energy, and made some successful sallies. Gold they seem to have used as well as steel; for the Markgraf, after one or two experiments, declared that he would hold no more parleyings with the Nurembergers, for that they had tried to corrupt one of his commanders.

The position of Nuremberg was now very serious. No help was to be expected from any quarter. When, therefore, the towns of Franconia and Swabia came forward at last to act as intermediaries, she welcomed them with every feeling of relief, and was easily persuaded to join, nominally, at any rate, the league against the Emperor. The Markgraf's casus belli was now gone; but his demands knew no bounds. He insisted on a huge indemnity and the right to garrison the town. In face of this, continued resistance was the only course for Nuremberg. The siege began again with renewed vigour. The Markgraf, who boasted, between his curses, that murder and burning were his favourite pastimes, now thoroughly enjoyed himself. He destroyed, in this war, 3 monasteries, 2 small towns, 170 villages, 19 castles, 75 estates, 28 mills, and 3000 acres of wood. The position of Nuremberg thus became more and more difficult. Her trade and buildings were suffering severely: the forest was being burnt down. The lukewarmness with which she had espoused their cause made it not worth while for the princes to relieve her. The Markgraf, on the other hand, had received numerous reinforcements, and had won over the neighbouring towns to his side. At last, therefore, Nuremberg yielded on these terms (June 9, 1552):—

(1) She was to join the League on the same terms as Augsburg and the other towns.

(2) She was to demand no compensation for injuries inflicted.

(3) She was to pay a large indemnity in cash and war material.

(4) The Markgraf was to give back all the castles, etc., which he had taken.

(5) Matters in dispute between the two parties were to be decided by a commission of princes.

So, for a moment, ended this disastrous war, only to break out again with variations in the following year, until the Emperor, who had entered into treaty with the League, declared the Markgraf outlawed and bade the four Rhenish electors to carry out the sentence. For the Markgraf had refused to enter into this treaty, which, seeing that the money and lands he had won in the name of religion and liberty were not guaranteed to him by it, he denounced as a betrayal of the German nation and carried on the war on his own account. His power was broken at last in a battle with the allies near Schwarzach.

Nuremberg paid a douceur to the Emperor and was excused from her obligations to the Markgraf, whose lands were sequestered. It is amusing to find that, in spite of this, the Markgraf's rightful heir, George Frederick, succeeded him and actually obtained through the Emperor compensation from the allies for the damage done to his property. Hence arose a fresh series of quarrels with Nuremberg.

The hatred of Nuremberg for the Elector Albert is expressed in the unsparing satire of Hans Sachs, in which the full bitterness of ruthless patriotism finds vent. This poem is of so violent a nature that the Council suppressed it, but a copy is still preserved in the library. It was written in 1557 after the Markgraf's death, and describes the descent into hell of this "blütiger Kriegsfürst." A spirit appears to Hans and bids him accompany him for the purpose of seeing how the soul of a bloodthirsty warrior goes to—heaven,

"Ich will dir zeigen ein Kriegsfürsten
Den allezeit hart nach blut ward dürsten
Welcher schier das ganze Deutschland
Mit Krieg erweckt—hat durch sein hand
Wollauf rund kom bald mit dar
Schan wie sein sel gen Himmel far,"

and shows the reception the Markgraf gets there from the soldiers he has not paid, the citizens and peasants, with their wives and children, whom he has robbed and ruined, and the wretched men whom he has forced to murder the helpless and innocent.

The result of the treaty we have mentioned above was that the "Interim" was revoked. Religion was declared free. Three years later came the peace of Augsburg, with its legal recognition of the Protestant States and its system of toleration—cujus regio, ejus religio—not of the sort to avert the evils of the Thirty Years War.

PELLERHOF

Nuremberg was now at last at peace and kept on good terms with the new Emperor. But the Hapsburg emperors seldom visited her. In 1570, however, the Emperor Maximilian II. was welcomed with such pomp and jubilation as had greeted Charles V. On this occasion the records mention the novelty of an elephant bearing a gold and grey canopy with a Moorish mahout. Again we are told that when the Emperor Matthias, then King of Bohemia, stayed in the town in 1612, on his way to be crowned King of Rome, he was lodged, not in the Castle but in the Ægidienplatz. The house of Martin Peller was intended for his residence, but to this the King's chamberlain objected on the ground that the Queen did not care for that style of architecture and decoration. This house, on the north side of the Ægidienplatz, is a very fine specimen of rich Florentine, Renaissance building. It is interesting to observe how the façade has been adapted to the old German high-pitched roof. It was built in 1605 by Jakob Wolff, and is now used for the art and furniture show-rooms of Herr J. A. Eysser. Within will be found a grand hall, court and staircase, carved and decorated in the same rich style, and upstairs a beautifully panelled room.

The policy of the town during this period was purely defensive. The wars with the Markgraf had cost Nuremberg dear, and she now set herself to recover from their disastrous effects. Her history for the next few years is a record of peace and of commercial and architectural activity. The great new building of the Rathaus was begun in the year 1622 by Jakob Wolff, the younger. The outbreak of the Thirty Years War prevented it from ever being really completed.

With regard to religious matters peace was preserved outwardly. Whilst the struggles between the Catholics and Protestants and Lutherans and Calvinists and various other sects were being stubbornly fought out elsewhere, the Nuremberg Council was content to forbid the propagation of false doctrines by word or writing. Cujus regio, ejus religio. They rejected the Konkordienformal drawn up at Magdeburg and directed against Melanchthon and his followers. And in 1573 they, in conjunction with the Markgraf, published a sort of Confession of Faith, consisting of various Lutheran and other theological works, which was signed by the clergy and accepted as a sort of rule for the churches. It was called the Nuremberg Konkordienbuch—Libri Normales—and every priest was required to swear to conform to it.

Perhaps one of the most important occurrences for Nuremberg, in connection with these theological matters, was the founding of the University of Altdorf (south-west of Nuremberg). Joachim Camerarius, we are told, suggested to Joachim Haller, the superintendent of the Nuremberg schools, that he should form a new school on the pattern of the monastic schools in Saxony, at which youths were prepared for the University. This school was to be outside the town, so that there should be no distractions to interfere with the work of the students. The Council approved of the scheme. The school was founded and endowed, and Melanchthon's institution at St. Ægidien's was moved there. In 1622 the Emperor raised it to the rank of a University. Among the most famous of its alumni was Goethe's grandfather. Leibnitz received his degree as doctor-of-law, and Oberst von Pappenheim and the great Wallenstein matriculated there. But whilst Pappenheim became rector for a short period, Wallenstein, by reason of his wild excesses, was requested to leave after a residence of five months. The University, however, after a chequered career, fell at last on evil days: the new University of Erlangen proved too powerful a rival on her borders, and in 1809 the old University of Altdorf was by royal order abolished.

CHAPTER IV
NUREMBERG AND THE THIRTY YEARS WAR WALLENSTEIN—GUSTAVUS ADOLPHUS—KASPAR HAUSER.

THE Catholic Reaction was now in full swing. With the determination of Catholicism to regain her ancient dominion came the Thirty Years War, the last and cruellest of the religious wars, which deprived Germany of, some say, half her population, and turned a comparatively rich and prosperous country into a barren desert.

The violence of Duke Maximilian of Bavaria towards the town of Donauwörth (1607), "which had been put under Ban of the Empire for some fault on the part of the populace against a flaring Mass-procession which had no business to be there," filled the free-towns and Protestant communities with dark forebodings of approaching disturbance. An Evangelical League, "The Union," was formed by the towns and princes for the purposes of self-defence against any attacks on religious freedom. Nuremberg joined it in 1610. This step was, of course, distasteful to the Emperor, but Nuremberg was left no choice in the matter. For the bishops of Bamberg and Eichstätt had forced the Nuremberg Evangelical subjects, living in their dioceses, to revert to the old religion. The Catholic communities formed a counter-league. Only a signal was wanted to make the opposing parties draw swords; and in 1618 the Bohemian resistance to the suppression of the Evangelical religion gave the signal for that bloody war, in which Nuremberg was to endure her full share of suffering. But, first, for a long time she endeavoured to pursue her old policy of neutrality, keeping peace with both parties and remaining subject to the Emperor. Meantime, as one after another of the Catholic generals passed through, men were quartered on Nuremberg in ceaseless relays, and she was bled of money and provisions. The treasury was depleted; trade disorganised; and the peasantry suffered cruelly.

In 1629 Ferdinand II. thought the time had come to strike a determined blow for Catholicism, and he published an Edict of Restitution, giving back to the Roman Catholics all the ecclesiastical property and institutions which had been handed over to the Evangelists by the Treaty of Passau and the Peace of Augsburg. This brought matters to a crisis. But even yet Nuremberg did not follow the example of Magdeburg and make a firm stand against religious aggressions. Even when Gustavus Adolphus, the Protestant champion, the Lion of the North, had landed on the

Pomeranian coast, and made secret proposals of union with her, she turned a deaf ear to him, and received, with princely honours, Wallenstein, Duke of Friedland, the Catholic General, when on his way to Memmingen. But at a convention of the Evangelical communities at Leipzig, called together by the Elector of Saxony, she did sign a complaint to the Emperor with regard to religious oppression, and also an agreement of the communities to help each other in case of need, and to prevent the unbearable quartering of troops and other exactions of the Emperor. Then in 1631 came the fall of Magdeburg. The subsequent horrors of that two-days' sack struck terror into the hearts of Protestant Germany. Nuremberg gave in at once to the demands of the Emperor. She denounced the Leipzig Convention, dismissed her soldiers, and paid the money required of her. In spite of these concessions, she had reason to fear that the freedom of the town would be forfeited. Tilly's defeat at Breitenfeld, however, prevented the Emperor from carrying out his expressed intention. Inspired by that victory of the Swedes, the Council plucked up courage to refuse almost all Imperial contributions. If they had consulted the wishes of the citizens, they would have joined Gustavus Adolphus forthwith. They still hankered after neutrality, however, and even when Gustavus Adolphus informed them that he would treat neutrals as enemies, they would only promise to be true to the Evangelical faith. The Swedish King continued to press them, and, still in the hope of being able to keep in favour with the Emperor, they sent a sum of money. But Gustavus Adolphus demanded their full and open support. They were still torn between the fear of offending the Emperor and the desire of securing Gustavus' aid. A sharp and menacing letter arrived. At last it was decided to send envoys to Würtzburg with instructions to draw up a treaty, if there was no help for it. The result was that Nuremberg and Bayreuth drew up a treaty with Gustavus Adolphus (October 1631), in which money was promised, and it was arranged that a special alliance should be concluded in two months' time. They agreed to put their resources at his disposal, and to stand by him to the last, whilst he on his side promised to succour them in all danger, and to relieve them if besieged. In November they renounced their allegiance to the Emperor, and lost not a moment in arming themselves. It was not too soon, for the cloud of war which had long been hanging over Franconia broke at last. Tilly took Rothenburg on October 30th, and on the 8th of November Lichtenau surrendered. Negotiations with him were opened by Nuremberg, to gain time, but, when he found how strongly fortified and garrisoned the town was, he drew off. He returned next year, but attempted nothing, for Gustavus Adolphus was now drawing near, to whom Nuremberg, after much shilly-shallying, was persuaded, by dint of threats, to send 1500 men with arms and ammunition. In March 1632, the King, leaving his army near Fürth, entered the town by the Spittlerthor amidst the heart-felt enthusiasm of the people, who had never approved of the pusillanimous policy of the Council. The Defender of the Protestants received a splendid and affecting welcome. The Patricians rode out to meet him before the gates. They presented him with four cannons and, amongst other works of art, two silver globes supported by figures of Atlas and Hercules respectively, which are still to be seen in the Museum at Stockholm. "Tears of joy streamed down the cheeks of bearded men as they welcomed the deliverer from the north, whose ready jest and beaming smile would have gone straight to the popular heart even if his deserts had been less. The picture of Gustavus was soon in every house, and a learned citizen set to work at once to compose a pedigree by which he proved to his own satisfaction that the Swedish King was descended from the old hereditary Burggrafs of the town."[21] The same day, with further reinforcements from Nuremberg, he went on his way south to deliver Donauwörth.

Three months later Wallenstein, breaking up from Bohemia, directed his whole force upon Nuremberg, which thus became the chief scene in that drama immortalised by Schiller in his trilogy of plays. For no sooner did Gustavus hear that Wallenstein with the Imperial army was marching against her than, mindful of his pledge and eager not to sacrifice so valued an ally, he summoned all his reinforcements and set out to the relief of Nuremberg. Thus beneath her walls the Protestant King and the inscrutable Catholic general were to be brought face to face at last. The citizens had for some time past been anxiously increasing their fortifications, storing provisions, and enlisting soldiers. Now, between June 21st and July 6th, under the direction of Hans Olph, the Swedish engineer, and with the aid of Gustavus' army, an entirely new ring of earthworks was constructed enclosing the suburbs. Men and women, soldiers, burghers and peasants, laboured night and day at these entrenchments, which were provided with many small bastions and redoubts, and defended by over 300 cannon. Round them was dug a moat eight feet deep and twelve feet wide. Very few traces of these fortifications, which were removed soon after 1806, can be found to-day. In the Swedish camp lay some 20,000 veterans, for whom 14,000 pounds of bread were supplied per diem. Within the city was a population of at least 65,000, of whom 8000 were fighting men, 3000 of these being armed citizens. Such were the resources with which Gustavus hoped to do battle with Wallenstein's gigantic army of 60,000 men and 13,000 horse. His preparations were not yet complete when Wallenstein appeared, July 1, at Schwabach. Had he consulted the wishes of Gustavus or listened to the advice of the Elector of Bavaria, Wallenstein would have attacked the Swedes at once. But, though superior in numbers, he would not pit his newly enrolled troops against the veterans of the Swedish King. He preferred to entrench himself in a strong position on the hills above Fürth, and to starve his enemy out. By the 6th of July he had completed a camp, which, if not so skilfully engineered as that of the Swedes, was, thanks to the natural advantages of the ground, almost impregnable. This vast camp, nearly eight miles round, stretched from the left banks of the Rednitz, from Stein, over the stream of the Biebert, and enclosed the villages of Zierndorf, Altenberg, Unterasbach, and Kreutles. Every house and village and advantage of the ground was turned to account and utilised for defence. The ruin of an old Burgstall—the Alte Veste—a castle which had been destroyed in 1388 during the great Städtekrieg by the Nurembergers, formed the most important outwork. Here, where the hill is at its highest, was the northernmost point of the camp, and from this fortress on the steep, wooded ridge across four miles of clear plain, through which the little Rednitz winds its course, Wallenstein gazed sternly on the climbing roofs and splendid mansions, the gabled houses and innumerable turrets of the beleaguered city. To-day, a modern tower, some eighty feet high, rears its head above the woods that crown the hill, and the adjoining inn is a favourite place of resort with the inhabitants of Fürth and Nuremberg. But some few traces of the old fortress and of Wallenstein's entrenchments may yet be found, and he who loves "to summon up remembrance of things past" will find food enough for his imagination when he attempts to reconstruct the scene of that terrible encampment.

For terrible it was both to besiegers and besieged. Gustavus was cut off from his base of supplies in the Upper Danube and Rhine by this great entrenched camp south-west of Nuremberg, and all the roads leading into Franconia were scoured by Wallenstein's light Croatian cavalry. Though provisions had at first been plentiful, the resources of the city were soon strained to the uttermost by the influx of peasants who had fled for refuge from the country. The mills and bakeries were unable to supply bread fast enough to the starving inhabitants, so that mobs fought outside the bakers' shops in their desperate haste for food. Famine laid hold of the city first, then of the Swedish, and finally of the Imperial camp. And in the path of famine followed, as ever, pestilence. Pestilence in July, in a mediæval city, crowded with grim soldiers, grown shrunken and meagre, with starving women and whitefaced children—it would require the pen of a Flaubert or a Zola to describe. Worse than all for Gustavus to bear, when want came to be felt in the army, there came the relaxation of that discipline on which he had prided himself. The citizens complained that his Swedish troops were behaving like Austrian banditti. Sending for the chief Germans in his service, the King rated them soundly in a famous oration. Never was his Majesty seen before in such a rage.

"They are no Swedes who commit these crimes," he said truly enough, "but you Germans yourselves. You princes, counts, lords, and noblemen, are showing great disloyalty and wickedness on your own fatherland, which you are ruining. You colonels and officers, from the highest to the lowest, it is you who steal and rob everyone, without making any exceptions.

"You plunder your own brothers in the faith. Had I known that you had been a people so wanting in natural affection for your country, I would never have saddled a horse for your sakes, much less imperilled my life and my crown and my brave Swedes and Finns. It is your inhumanity towards your mother-country that has tarnished the glory of my victorious subjects. My heart is filled with gall when I see anyone of you behaving thus villainously. For you cause men to say openly, 'The King, our friend, does us more harm than our enemies.' If you were real Christians you would consider what I am doing for you, how I am spending my life in your service. I came but to restore every man to his own, but this most accursed and devilish robbing of yours doth much abate my purpose. I have given up the treasures of my crown for your sake, and have not enriched myself so much as by one pair of boots since my coming to Germany, though I have had forty tons of gold passing through my hands.

"Enter into your hearts, and think how sad you are making me, so that the tears stand in my eyes. You treat me ill with your evil discipline; I do not say with your evil fighting: for in that you have behaved like honourable gentlemen, and for that I am much obliged to you. Take my warning to heart, and we will soon show our enemies that we are honest men and honourable gentlemen."

Again when informed that a soldier had stolen a cow, he turned a deaf ear to him as he pleaded for his life, for

"My son," he said, "it is better that thou shouldst expiate thy offence by the sacrifice of life than that thy crime should draw down the vengeance of the Almighty upon me and thy gallant comrades; for though I consider every soldier in the light of a child, yet I am destined to perform the duties of a judge, no less than those of a parent."

So for two weary months plague, famine and wounds did their fell work inside and out. The hospitals were full to overflowing. The graves could not be dug fast enough to hold the dead. The countless victims of hunger and pestilence lay for days in the trenches, poisoning the air. In the streets were strewn the half-decayed bodies of men and horses, eaten of pigs. But if the Protestants suffered so did the Imperialists. And always Wallenstein sat implacable on the height refusing to join battle, waiting grimly till starvation should have done its work and the sack of Magdeburg could be repeated. For Gustavus must either attack Wallenstein in his impregnable position or march away the city to its fate. The arrival of reinforcements, which increased the King's army to 50,000 men, determined him to make a general assault on the Alte Veste and the northern side of the camp. It will be clear to anyone who examines the ground that this was an almost impossible undertaking, the forlornest of forlorn hopes. What desperate courage could do was done. For ten hours the Swedes stormed undaunted against fearful odds and with fearful losses. Three times they got actual footing in the Burgstall itself; three times they were hurled back. At last Gustavus, who had had a piece of the sole of his right boot shot off, and had always been in the thickest part of the fight, dragging the cannon to points of vantage and aiming them with his own hands, was obliged to relinquish the desperate enterprise. "We have done a stupid thing to-day," was his comment. For the first time in his life, indeed, he was conquered, because he was not conqueror. But Wallenstein's claws were cut: he had suffered little less than Gustavus in the fight round the Alte Veste. Nuremberg was saved for the present, for Wallenstein was in no condition to prosecute a siege. After fifteen days, therefore (September 8), Gustavus, unable to stay for lack of supplies, and failing to entice the enemy into battle on the plain, marched away into Thuringia, and two months later, on the field of Lutzen, he fell in the moment of victory when he had defeated his old enemy. Before that, however, ten days after he had departed, and a week after Wallenstein had broken up his camp, Gustavus came back to Fürth and looked at what had been the enemy's position. It is said that he had breakfast on the round stone table still to be found at the Alte Veste, and known as the Schweden Tisch. Once more, in October, he returned, drove the Imperial troops out of the Nuremberg territory, and took his last farewell of the town.

The Treaty of Westphalia brought the Thirty Years War to an end in 1648, but not before the interruption of commerce and the extraordinary exertions she had made had reduced the resources of Nuremberg to a very low ebb, and saddled her with a load of debt from which she never recovered. When at last peace was announced, the festivals with which she celebrated it reflected the last splendour of the once prosperous city. Karl Gustav, as representative of the crown of Sweden, gave a magnificent dinner—the "Friedensmal"—in the Rathaus to celebrate this occasion. The Council ordered a Neptune with nymphs and dolphins, designed by Christoph Ritter, and figures modelled by Georg Schweigger, to be placed in the middle of the market-place. It was, for some reason, placed in the Peünt-hof. It was sold in 1797 to Paul of Russia to raise money.

Another incident which is recorded of these days of rejoicing is as follows: When peace was proclaimed with France, Octavio Piccolomini was staying in the Pellerhaus, and he gave a dance to the peasants. Now a rumour was circulated that all the boys who appeared on hobby-horses before his house on the following Sunday would get a silver coin. They assembled accordingly, and when he heard the reason of this extraordinary parade, he told them to come next Sunday, and then gave them each a four-cornered medal—still to be seen in numismatic collections—with a picture of a hobby-horse, and the date 1650 on it.

Through the peace of Westphalia Nuremberg with the other free towns obtained full political equality with the princes of the Empire. Their representatives, who before only had a voice in the discussions, now enjoyed the full right of voting. But, in spite of this, the political importance of Nuremberg began to disappear. Her sovereignty, her right of peace and war, were recognised. But she became a quiet and obedient attendant of the Reichstag in Regensburg, paying her quota of men and money, and supporting the Hapsburg interests.

Her energy, in fact, had been exhausted. The census of her citizens in 1622 amounted to 40,000; in 1806 to 25,000. With the decrease in her population, her prosperity decreased. The load of debt accumulated during the Thirty Years War weighed her down. Her trade, like that of Augsburg and all the other German towns, went from bad to worse. Dislocated during the war, it could not recover now. Chief among the causes of decay must be counted the circumnavigation of the Cape of Good Hope. Prior to that, all merchandise from the East was obliged to travel overland into Europe and came for distribution by way of Germany. Nuremberg then naturally became the chief entrepôt. Now she suffered, with Venice, from the discovery of this new channel of commerce. The Venetians had boasted that thanks to them Nuremberg had come from nothing to be the richest town in Germany. The Fondaco dei Tedeschi, the German quarter in Venice since the days of the Crusades, still bears witness to their connection with the German traders, and, in Nuremberg, winged lions on many of the houses still record the same fact.

Other and more avoidable causes contributed to the decrease of Nuremberg trade. She adopted an exaggerated system of protection, and levied exorbitant taxes on goods brought into or through the country.

In the old days every good thing had been said to come out of Nuremberg (Was gut sein sollte, wurde aus Nürnberg verschrieben); now the output of her manufactures was foolishly limited by rules. In some trades, for instance, only the son or the husband of a widow of a master might become a master craftsman. Hence many failed to find employment, and set up in the surrounding country as competitors. The selfish and misguided prejudices of the trades led also to the exclusion of the Protestant weavers who had been exiled from France or Flanders, and who, finding asylum elsewhere, soon became rivals of the shortsighted Nurembergers.

The Council, too, suffered and aided the common degeneration. A narrow, effete, and selfish oligarchy, it became more tyrannical as it became more incompetent. The authors of libels and satires, criticising it, were rewarded with lifelong imprisonment. More and more the patrician families drew together and separated themselves from the common people. They clung closer to their exclusive privileges as they became less worthy of them. Endeavouring to become more like the landed nobility, they began to abandon business, and withdrew from the State the capital and brains which had formerly made it prosperous. They grew, indeed, in their false pride, so ashamed of trade that they said that no Nuremberg patrician had ever had to do with business! So a proud and poor nobility came to take the place of rich and patriotic merchant princes. Some even gave up their rights of citizenship and went to live on their property outside Nuremberg, thus still further weakening the Council and quarrelling with it over rights of taxation.

From war, also, Nuremberg suffered. Besides her own private bickerings with the Markgraf, she felt the wars with France, the war of the Austrian succession, and suffered still more in the Seven Years War.

In 1786 a fresh struggle arose between the Council and the town over a new tax which it was sought to impose without consultation. The citizens made a fruitless complaint to the Imperial Court. Then the Council appealed to the Diet, saying that the town was overtaxed. An inquiry into her finances showed that Nuremberg was heavily in debt and practically bankrupt. There had been a large yearly deficit since 1763. A commission to economise and to govern was appointed from both Councils, and in 1794 an arrangement was confirmed by the Emperor by which the larger Council was to consist of 250 members (70 of whom were to be patricians), chosen by the smaller Council. The citizens, however, were not contented, complaining that they were still not properly represented.

Meanwhile an event had occurred which drove another nail into the coffin of the free Imperial city. In 1791, Charles Alexander, Markgraf of Brandenburg, Ansbach and Bayreuth, died childless, and the government of his principalities passed to Prussia, together with the old claims of the Franconian line of the Brandenburg house. A minister, Graf Karl August von Hardenberg, the famous chancellor, was appointed to rule these lands. In the name of the King of Prussia he asserted his right of supremacy over all the territory up to the gates of the town itself. The oldest claims of the Burggräflichen times were reasserted by the Prussians. Nuremberg was powerless to resist. Even so her troubles were not yet ended. A Prussian army had occupied Fürth on July 4, 1796, and in August a vanguard of the French victorious army, which was swarming over South Germany, entered Nuremberg on the 9th of August. The scenes of the Thirty Years War were repeated. The country was ravaged, and the town called upon for contributions. It was impossible to comply at once with these demands. Eighteen citizens were therefore taken away to France as hostages. When, a few weeks later, the French army withdrew, after the Archduke Karl's victory, a fresh contribution was demanded. In despair the town almost unanimously decided to seek union with their old enemy, the King of Prussia. But he refused this Grecian gift, for the debt of the town was enormous. Then the Council turned to the Emperor and offered to accept an Imperial commission, which introduced some financial reforms. But the year 1800 brought more French troops into Nuremberg, who were a further strain upon her resources.

Even after the Peace of Pressburg the long agony of the Imperial free city was continued, till in 1806 by a decree of Napoleon, in the 17th article of the Rheinbund Act, it was laid down that "the town and territory of Nuremberg be united to Bavaria with full sovereignty and possession." On the 6th of August 1806, Emperor Francis abdicated, and the Holy Roman Empire, "which was a grand object once, but had gone about in a superannuated and plainly crazy state for some centuries back, was at last put out of pain and allowed to cease from the world."

Since then the story of Nuremberg is swallowed up in the history of United Germany. She has shared and still shares in the growing prosperity of the new Empire. The first railway in Germany was opened in 1835 between Nuremberg and Fürth. Her hops, her toys, her cakes, her railway-carriages, her lead-pencils, are they not known the world over? New buildings have sprung up on every side of her: the suburbs are themselves great manufacturing towns. The population has grown to 170,000. These are all things on which she may most sincerely be congratulated; but whatever her prosperity in the present or the future, her golden age, we feel, is in the past. She is Albert Durer's and Hans Sachs' city.

. . . .

We began by hinting that the atmosphere of Nuremberg is mediæval, that of a city of legend. We will close this account of her history with the brief narration of her last, her nineteenth century myth. For we cannot pass over in silence the curious case of Kaspar Hauser.

At a time when Europe was still dripping from the douche of sentimentality in which it had been bathed by the sorrows of Werther and the romanticism of Byron, Kaspar Hauser appeared suddenly in Nuremberg. His astonishing story achieved a European celebrity. The history of this impostor has recently been placed once more before the public by the Duchess of Cleveland,[22] with the object of clearing her father from imputations which would have been ridiculous if they had not been so impudent. Charity, and the facts of the case, enable us to add with regard to Kaspar himself, that if he was an impostor he was also half a lunatic; for we can trace in the records of his career, among other symptoms of a diseased brain, the mania of persecution, an over acute and perverted sense of smell, a restless love of notoriety, and an ineradicable habit of lying.

On Easter Monday, May 1828, a lad of seventeen, dressed like a countryman, appeared outside the Neue Thor, and asked, in the low Bavarian dialect, his way to the Neue Thor Strasse.

He had with him two letters in one envelope addressed to "The Captain of the 4th Squadron of the Schmolischer Regiment, Neue Thor Strasse, Nuremberg." They ran as follows, in handwriting exactly similar to Kaspar's:—

"HONORED SIR,—I send you a lad who wishes to serve his King truly; this lad was brought to me on Oct. 7, 1812. I am a poor day labourer, with ten children of my own; I have enough to do to get on at all. His mother asked me to bring up the boy. I asked her no questions, nor have I given notice to the county police that I had taken the boy. I thought I ought to take him as my son. I have brought him up as a good Christian, and since 1812 I have never let him go a step away from the house, so no one knows where he has been brought up, and he himself does not know the name of my house or of the place; you may ask him, but he can't tell you. I have taught him to read and to write; he can write as well as myself. When we ask him what he would like to be, he says a soldier, like his father. If he had parents (which he has not) he would have been a scholar: only show him a thing and he can do it.

"Honoured Sir, you may question him, but he don't know where I live. I brought him away in the middle of the night; he can't find his way back."

Dated, "From the Bavarian Frontier; place not named."

The second letter ran thus:—

"The boy is baptized, his name is Kaspar; his other name you must give him. I ask you to bring him up. His father was a Schmolischer (trooper). When he is seventeen send him to Nuremberg to the 6th Schmolischer Regiment; that is where his father was. I beg you to bring him up till he is seventeen. He was born on April 30, 1812. I am so poor, I can't keep the boy; his father is dead."

In answer to the Captain's questions the lad would only reply: "My foster-father bade me say, 'I don't know, your honour.'" The result was that he was placed in a prison cell in the castle. That was neither a fair nor a judicious proceeding. The garbled story of a wild man, a wronged man, quickly spread through the town. Feigning at first an intense fear and animal stupidity, it seems probable that Kaspar picked up from the visitors who discussed his history in his presence the suggestion of the marvellous tale which he presently told, and which made so tremendous a sensation. It was a tale demonstrably false on the face of it—of a life spent in close and solitary confinement in a cell, without knowledge of his kind or acquaintance with the outside world.

Here is his story as he told it to the Nuremberg magistrates, and as it found acceptance in credulous quarters.

"All his life," he said, "had been spent in a cell 6 or 7 feet long, 4 feet wide, and 5 feet high, and always in a sitting posture; the only change in which was that when awake he sat upright, but leant back on a truss of straw when he slept. There were two small windows, but they were both boarded up, and as it was always twilight he never knew the difference between day and night. Nor did he ever feel hot or cold. He saw no one, and no sound of any kind ever reached his ear. Each morning, when he awoke, he found a pitcher of water and a loaf of rye bread by his side. He was often thirsty, and when he had emptied his pitcher, he used to watch to see whether the water would come again, as he had no idea how it was brought there. Sometimes it tasted strangely and made him feel sleepy. He had toys to play with—two wooden horses and a wooden dog, and he spent his time in rolling them about, and dressing them up with ribbons.

"One day a stool was placed across his knees, with a piece of paper upon it: an arm was stretched out over his shoulder, a pencil put into his hand, which was taken hold of, and guided over the paper. 'I never looked round to see whom the arm belonged to. Why should I? I had no conception of any other creature beside myself.' This proceeding was repeated seven or eight times: the arm was then withdrawn, but the stool and paper left behind. He tried to copy the letters he had been made to trace, and pleased with this new occupation, persevered till he had succeeded. Thus it was that he learned to write his name. About three days afterwards—as far as he could judge—the man came again and brought a little book (a prayer-book which was found on him). This was placed on his knees and his hand laid upon it; then, pointing to one of the wooden horses, the man kept on repeating the word 'Ross' (horse) till he had learned to say it after him. According to his own account, this was the first time in his life he had ever heard a sound of any kind, as the man came and went noiselessly. Then, in the same fashion, he was taught two sentences—'In the big village, where my father is, I shall get a fine horse.' 'I want to be a trooper as my father was'—which he repeated by rote, of course without understanding them. When his lesson was learnt the man went away, and he began playing with his toys, making so much noise that the man returned and gave him a smart blow with a stick, which hurt him very much.

"'After that I was always quiet.' The last time the man came it was to take him away. His clothes had been changed while he slept; a pair of boots were now brought and put on; he was hoisted up on the man's shoulders, and carried up a steep incline into the open air. It was night-time and quite dark. He was laid down on the ground, and fell asleep at once. When he awoke, he was lifted upon his feet, and placed in front of the man, who, holding him under the arms, pushed forward his legs with his own, and showed him how to walk. But the pain and fatigue were very great, and he cried bitterly. The man said impatiently, 'Leave off crying at once, or you shall not get that horse;' and he thereupon obeyed. Then he was again lifted up and carried; again dropped asleep, and again he woke to find himself lying on the ground. This was repeated over and over again. There were the same painful attempts to walk; the same floods of tears, checked by the same threat; and then the same rest on the ground, with 'something soft' under his cheek. By degrees he began to walk alone, supported by the man's arm, though at first only six steps at a time. The sunshine and fresh air together dazzled and bewildered him, and he scarcely took note where they went. They never travelled on a beaten track, but generally on soft sand; never went up or down hill, or crossed a stream. Sometimes he attempted to look about him; then the man instantly desired him to hold his head down. His clothes were once more changed; but the man, even while dressing him, stood behind him, so that he might not see his face. The two sentences he had learned were again and again impressed on his memory as he went along, the man always adding impressively, 'Mind this well.'

"He also said, 'When you are a trooper like your father, I will come and fetch you again.'"'The journey cannot have been a long one, as he only took food once; he himself computed it had lasted a day and a night.

"Finally the letter was put into his hands with the words: 'Go there—where the letter belongs;' and the man suddenly vanished from his side. He found himself alone in the street of Nuremberg—having never till then perceived that he had entered the town, or, in fact, seen it at all. He was quite dazed and helpless, but someone kindly came and took charge of him and his letter." ...So great was the interest caused by this story, which easily roused the sympathy of the illogical—people are always readier to sympathise than to inquire—that Kaspar was (July 1828) formally adopted by the town of Nuremberg. An annual sum of 300 florins was voted for his maintenance and education. He became the idol of society. It was openly hinted that he was the legitimate son of the reigning House of Baden, who stood in the way of the next in succession, and would have been long since in his grave had he not been rescued by a faithful retainer, who kept him in close confinement to conceal him from his pursuers. In the course of a year or so, however, the interest in him began to wane. His tutor, who had at first been delighted with him, was beginning to find him out. Kaspar, in fact, was both cunning and untruthful. One day a particularly gross instance of his deceitfulness came to his tutor's knowledge. The same morning Nuremberg was electrified by the news that Kaspar's life had been attempted in broad daylight, and actually under his tutor's roof. A man, he said, with a black handkerchief drawn across his face, had suddenly confronted him, and aimed at him a blow with a heavy woodman's knife, crying, "After all, you will have to die before you leave Nuremberg." The voice was the voice of the man who had brought him to the town. He described him accurately. But no such man could be traced. The wound was very slight. Almost certainly it was self-inflicted, with the object of stimulating the flagging public interest by a new and romantic incident. That at any rate was its effect. Pamphlets by the dozen appeared, and in 1832 President von Feuerbach published his "History of a Crime against a Human Soul," which moved all hearts by the pathos and eloquence with which it pleaded the cause of the mysteriously persecuted "Child of Europe."But the Nurembergers were no longer eager to continue their allowance to the boy, so Lord Stanhope, who had always befriended him, now came forward, and made himself responsible for his education and maintenance. The rest of Kaspar's life is somewhat dismal reading. He had to endure the process of being found out by successive people at successive places, for he had all the astuteness but also all the vanity of a lunatic. Once again, it appears, he attempted to reawaken the flagging interest of the public. At Ansbach he tried to repeat his Nuremberg success, and to confirm the existence of the mysterious persecutor who was supposed to haunt him. But this time he failed. Once more he got stabbed, but instead of a slight, he inflicted on himself a deadly wound. Now though he had taken much trouble to make the conditions of the affair as mysterious and misleading as possible, a long judicial investigation resulted in the irresistible conclusion that "no murder was committed." At Ansbach stands the tomb of the poor deluded and deluding "Child of Europe," a monument of folly not all his own.

> "Hic jacet
> CASPARUS HAUSER
> Ænigma sui temporis
> Ignota Nativitas
> Occulta Mors,
> 1833."

CHAPTER V
THE CASTLE, THE WALLS AND MEDIÆVAL FORTIFICATIONS

"Aufwärts Ich mit dem Alten ging
Nach einer königlichen Veste,
Am Fels erbauet auf das Beste;
Manch Thurm auf Felsvorsprüngen lag,
Darin ein kaiserlich Gemach.
Geziert nach meisterlichen Sinnen
Die Fenster waren und die Zinnen;
Darum ein Graben war gehauen
In harten Fels."
—HANS SACHS.

NUREMBERG is set upon a series of small slopes in the midst of an undulating, sandy plain, some 900 feet above the sea. Here and there on every side fringes and patches of the mighty forest which once covered it are still visible; but for the most part the plain is now freckled with picturesque villages, in which stand old turreted châteaux, with gabled fronts and latticed windows, or it is clothed with carefully cultivated crops or veiled from sight by the smoke which rises from the new-grown forest of factory chimneys.

The railway sets us down outside the walls of the city. As we walk from the station towards the Frauen Thor, and stand beneath the crown of fortified walls three and a half miles in circumference, and gaze at the old grey towers and picturesque confusion of domes, pinnacles and spires, suddenly it seems as if our dream of a feudal city has been realised. There, before us, is one of the main entrances, still between massive gates and beneath archways flanked by stately towers. Still to reach it we must cross a moat fifty feet deep and a hundred feet wide. True, the swords of old days have been turned into pruning-hooks; the crenelles and embrasures which once bristled and blazed with cannon are now curtained with brambles and wallflowers, and festooned with virginia creepers; the galleries are no longer crowded with archers and cross-bowmen; the moat itself has blossomed into a garden, luxuriant with limes and acacias, elders, planes, chestnuts, poplars, walnut, willow and birch trees, or divided into carefully tilled little garden plots. True it is that outside the moat, beneath the smug grin of substantial modern houses, runs that mark of modernity, the electric tram. But let us for the moment forget these gratifying signs of modern prosperity and, turning to the left ere we enter the Frauen Thor, walk with our eyes on the towers which, with their steep-pitched roofs and myriad shapes and richly coloured tiles, mark the intervals in the red-bricked, stone-cased galleries and mighty bastions, till we come to the first beginnings of Nuremberg—the Castle. There, on the highest eminence of the town, stands that venerable fortress, crowning the red slope of tiles. Roofs piled on roofs, their pinnacles, turrets, points and angles heaped one above the other in a splendid confusion, climb the hill which culminates in the varied group of buildings on the Castle rock. We have passed the Spittler, Mohren, Haller and Neu Gates on our way, and we have crossed by the Hallerthorbrücke the Pegnitz where it flows into the town. Before us rise the bold scarps and salient angles of the bastions built by the Italian architect, Antonio Fazuni, called the Maltese (1538-43).

Crossing the moat by a wooden bridge which curls round to the right, we enter the town by the Thiergärtnerthor. The right-hand corner house opposite us now is Albert Durer's house. We turn to the left and go along the Obere Schmiedgasse and the row of houses labelled Am Oelberg, till we arrive at the top of a steep hill (Burgstrasse). Above, on the left, is the Castle, and close at hand the "Mount of Olives" Sculpture (see p. 201).

We may now either go through the Himmels Thor to the left, or keeping straight up under the old trees and passing the "Mount of Olives" on the left, approach the large deep-roofed building between two towers. This is the Kaiserstallung, as it is called, the Imperial stables, built originally for a granary. The towers are the Luginsland (Look in the land) on the east, and the Fünfeckiger Thurm, the Five-cornered tower, at the west end (on the left hand as we thus face it). The Luginsland was built by the townspeople in the hard winter of 1377. The mortar for building it, tradition says, had to be mixed with salt, so that it might be kept soft and be worked in spite of the severe cold. The chronicles state that one could see right into the Burggraf's Castle from this tower, and the town was therefore kept informed of any threatening movements on his part. To some extent that was very likely the object in view when the tower was built, but chiefly it must have been intended, as its name indicates, to afford a far look-out into the surrounding country. The granary or Kaiserstallung, as it was called later, was erected in 1494, and is referred to by Hans Behaim as lying between the Five-cornered and the Luginsland Towers. Inside the former there is a museum of curiosities (Hans Sachs' harp) and the famous collection of instruments of torture and the Maiden (Eiserne Jungfrau), to which we shall refer at greater length in the next chapter. The open space

THE CASTLE FROM THE HALLERTHORBRÜCKE
adjoining it commands a splendid view to the north. There, too, on the parapet-wall, may be seen the hoof-marks of the horse of the robber-knight, Ekkelein von Gailingen, whose story we have already narrated (p. 43). Here for a moment let us pause, consider our position, and endeavour to make out from the conflicting theories of the archæologists something of the original arrangement of the castles and of the significance of the buildings and towers that yet remain.

Stretching to the east of the rock on which the Castle stands is a wide plain, now the scene of busy industrial enterprise, but in old days no doubt a mere district of swamp and forest. Westwards the rock rises by three shelves to the summit. The entrance to the Castle, it is surmised, was originally on the east side, at the foot of the lower plateau and through a tower which no longer exists.

Opposite this hypothetical gate-tower stood the Five-cornered tower. The lower part dates, we have seen, from no earlier than the eleventh century. It is referred to as Alt-Nürnberg (old Nuremberg) in the Middle Ages. The title of "Five-cornered" is really somewhat a misnomer, for an examination of the interior of the lower portion of the tower reveals the fact that it is quadrangular. The pentagonal appearance of the exterior is due to the fragment of a smaller tower which once leant against it, and probably formed the apex of a wing running out from the old castle of the Burggrafs. The Burggräfliche Burg stood below, according to Mummenhof, south-west and west of this point. It was burnt down in 1420, and the ruined remains of it are supposed to be traceable in the eminence, now overgrown by turf and trees, through which a sort of ravine, closed in on either side by built-up walls, has just brought us from the town to the Vestner Thor. The Burggrafs' Castle would appear to have been so situated as to protect the approach to the Imperial Castle (Kaiserburg). The exact extent of the former we cannot now determine. Meisterlin refers to it as parvum fortalitium—a little fort. We may, however, be certain that it reached from the Five-cornered tower to the Walpurgiskapelle. For this little chapel, east of the open space called the Freiung, is repeatedly spoken of as being on the property of the Burggrafs. Besides their castle proper, which was held at first as a fief of the Empire, and afterwards came to be regarded as their hereditary, independent property, the Burggrafs were also entrusted with the keeping of a tower which commanded the entrance to the Castle rock on the country side, perhaps near the site of the present Vestner Thor. The custodia portæ may have been attached to the tower, the lower portion of which remains to this day, and is called the Bailiff's Dwelling (Burgamtmannswohnung). The exact relationship of the Burggraf to the town on the one hand, and to the Empire on the other, is, as we have already observed, somewhat obscure. Originally, it would appear, he was merely an Imperial officer, administering Imperial estates, and looking after Imperial interests. In later days he came to possess great power, but this was due not to his position as castellan or castle governor as such, but to the vast private property his position had enabled him to amass and to keep.

As the scope and ambitions of the Burggrafs increased, and as the smallness of their castle at Nuremberg, and the constant friction with the townspeople, who were able to annoy them in many ways, became more irksome, they gave up living at Nuremberg, and finally were content to sell their rights and possessions there to the town. Besides the custodia portæ of the Burggrafs, which together with their castle passed by purchase into the hands of the town (1427), there were various other similar guard towers, such as the one which formerly occupied the present site of the Luginsland, or the Hasenburg at the so-called Himmels Thor, or a third which once stood near the Deep Well on the second plateau of the Castle rock. But we do not know how many of these there were, or where they stood, much less at what date they were built. All we do know is that they, as well as the Burggrafs' possessions, were purchased in succession by the town, into whose hands by degrees came the whole property of the Castle rock.

Above the ruins of the "little fort" of the Burggrafs rises the first plateau of the Castle rock. It is surrounded by a wall, strengthened on the south side (l) by a square tower against which leans the Walpurgiskapelle.

The path to the Kaiserburg leads under the wall of the plateau, and is entirely commanded by it and by the quadrangular tower, the lower part of which alone remains and is known by the name of Burgamtmannswohnung (r). The path goes straight to this tower, and at the foot of it is the entrance to the first plateau. Then along the edge of this plateau the way winds southwards (l), entirely commanded again by the wall of the second plateau, at the foot of which there probably used to be a trench. Over this a bridge led to the gate of the second plateau. The trench has been long since filled in, but the huge round tower which guarded the gate still remains and is the Vestner Thurm (r).[23] The Vestner Thurm or Sinwel Thurm (sinwel = round), or, as it is called in a charter of the year 1313, the "Turm in der Mitte," is the only round tower of the Burg. It was built in the days of early Gothic, with a sloping base, and of roughly flattened stones with a smooth edge. It was partly restored and altered in 1561, when it was made a few feet higher and its round roof was added. It is worth paying the small gratuity required for ascending to the top. The view obtained of the city below is magnificent. The Vestner Thurm, like the whole Imperial castle, passed at length into the care of the town, which kept its Tower watch here as early as the fourteenth century.[24]

VESTNER THURM

The well which supplied the second plateau with water, the "Deep Well," Tiefer Brunnen, as it is called, stands in the centre, surrounded by a wall. It is 335 feet deep, hewn out of the solid rock, and is said to have been wrought by the hands of prisoners, and to have been the labour of thirty years. So much we can easily believe as we lean over and count the six seconds that elapse between the time when an object is dropped from the top to the time when it strikes the water beneath. Passages lead from the water's edge to the Rathaus, by which prisoners came formerly to draw water, and to St. John's Churchyard and other points outside the town. The system of underground passages here and in the Castle was an important part of the defences, affording as it did a means of communication with the outer world and as a last extremity, in the case of a siege, a means of escape.[25]

Meanwhile, leaving the Deep Well and passing some insignificant modern dwellings (r), and leaving beneath us on the left the Himmelsthor, let us approach the summit of the rock and the buildings of the Kaiserburg itself. As we advance to the gateway with the intention of ringing the bell for the castellan, we notice on the left the Double Chapel, attached to the Heidenthurm (Heathen Tower, see page 3), the lower part of which is encrusted with what were once supposed to be Pagan images. The Tower protrudes beyond the face of the third plateau, and its prominence may indicate the width of a trench, now filled in, which was once dug outside the enclosing wall of the summit of the rock. The whole of the south side of this plateau is taken up by the Palas (the vast hall, two stories high, which, though it has been repeatedly rebuilt, may in its original structure be traced back as far as the twelfth century), and the Kemnate or dwelling-rooms which seem to have been without any means of defence. This plateau, like the second, is supplied with a well. But the first object that strikes the eye on entering the court-yard is the ruined lime-tree, the branches of which once spread their broad and verdant shelter over the whole extent of the quadrangle.

The Empress Kunigunde planted it, says the legend, some seven hundred years ago. For once, when King Henry was a-hunting, he came in the pursuit of a deer to the edge of a steep precipice, and this in the heat of the chase he did not perceive, but would have fallen headlong had not a lime-branch, at which he grasped in his extremity, stopped and saved him. And he, recognising the special protection of the Most High, broke off a twig of the lime-tree in remembrance of his wonderful preservation, and brought it to his anxious wife, who planted it at once with her own hands in the earth, and it soon grew into a beautiful tree.

A modern staircase leads from the court to the rooms of the Castle. They have been much spoilt by being rebuilt in modern Gothic style by Voit (1856) and being furnished as a royal residence. Some objects of considerable interest, however, may still be seen here. In the great hall and in the bedrooms will be found some magnificent old stoves by Augustin Hirschvogel and others; whilst in the various rooms may be seen some fine stained glass and some heraldic paintings of Albert Durer's time. The single large spread-eagle on the ceiling of the writing-room (which was discovered in 1833 after two other ceilings had been removed) is especially remarkable.

The windows command splendid views of the surrounding country. There are a few pictures in the hall of unequal interest. They are mostly copies of Italian painters; but we may mention the Venus and Cupid by Lucas Cranach, the Mocking of Christ by Hans Schäuffelein, Durer's favourite pupil, and others by artists of the old Nuremberg and Flemish schools.

A narrow staircase leads from the dining-hall to the Emperor's Chapel (Kaiser-kapelle). It was built in the twelfth century by one of the Hohenstaufen emperors, very likely by Frederick Barbarossa himself, when the growing favour with which Nuremberg was regarded gave rise to the need of a larger and more splendid building than the primitive St. Margaret's Chapel and fort which already existed. A rebuilding and enlarging of the Imperial castle then took place, and the beautiful Emperor-Chapel was superimposed on the Margaret-Chapel, thus forming the two-storied or double chapel. Romanesque in style, it is comparatively uninjured, and resembles the Double Chapel of Eger, where the lower chapel is also attributed to Barbarossa. The two chapels are very different in character. The lower, which was used as a Gruftkapelle[26] or place of sepulture, is solemn and almost gloomy in effect; the upper, whilst harmonising with the lower, is in a much lighter and more charming style. The plan of the lower chapel is rectangular with an extension into the Heathen Tower in the shape of a rectangular choir, lighted by a romanesque window.

The low, round vaulting of this, the St. Margaret's Chapel, rests on two low four-cornered pillars and on four columns, the capitals of which, hewn from great blocks, are richly sculptured, one with four eagles, two with foliage, and the fourth with masks. They were, according to the manner of construction customary at Nuremberg, set up unwrought and only carved afterwards, as may be seen from the capital of the south-west column, which is only decorated on the two inner sides, the other two being unfinished. From the walls spring heavy brackets to receive the plinths of the arches which support the cross-vaulting.

The two low pillars mentioned above divide the main body of the chapel from an irregular intermediate building adjoining the Castle.

Entrance to the upper, or Kaiser, Chapel is only possible from the lower rooms of the Castle, whence, above the flight of steps already referred to, a Gothic doorway now leads to the chapel, by way of a vestibule or entrance hall. This hall is situated exactly over the western irregular section of the lower chapel. The low stout pillars which support the vaulting correspond in their ornamentation with that of the lower chapel. On the hexagonal capitals of one we find four of the familiar mediæval masks, whilst on both of them the sculptured foliage and basket-work recall that of the Margaret Chapel.

In the wall which separates the vestibule from the Castle a small connecting staircase leads up to a platform, which opens out in two arches towards the chapel and probably formed the Imperial oratory. It is in immediate connection with the upper rooms of the Castle by means of a Gothic door which has replaced a romanesque gateway. Thus the Emperor could easily reach his seat in the chapel from the Castle.

Ascending three steps, one arrives through a broad archway at the raised choir, which also resembles the Margaret Chapel in its ornamentation. But the most striking and distinctive feature of the Kaiserkapelle, which gives it its characteristically light and graceful appearance, is the four slender columns of white marble, with richly decorated capitals and bases, which support the vaulting. One of the columns is built of two pieces. An unwrought ring covers the seam. Hence arose the legend that, at the time when the chapel was building, the Devil, who lusted after the soul of the Castle chaplain, wagered him that he would bring these four pillars from Milan sooner than the priest could read the Mass. The priest, who had a glib tongue, cheerfully undertook the wager. The Devil was quick, but the chaplain was quicker. The Devil had already brought three columns, and the fourth was close at hand, when the nimble priest said "Amen." So infuriated was the Devil at losing his wager that he flung down the pillar. It fell so heavily on the floor that it broke in two, and had to be bound together with the ring. The coloured stone head above the choir-arch is supposed to be a memorial of this castle chaplain, who so cleverly obtained cheap transport for the Church!

Without taking this legend altogether au pied de la lettre, we may think it likely from the style and material that these pillars were brought from some Italian building.

On the north-east wall of the chapel is an altarpiece with wings by Wolgemut—SS. Wenceslaus and Martin, and SS. Barbara and Elizabeth on the reverse. The carved figures in the centre of the altarpiece on the south-east wall are by Veit Stoss, and the wings are of the school of Wolgemut. On the south wall are two pictures by Burgkmair (?) and a relief after designs by Adam Krafft. On the west wall are a picture by Kulmbach and a remarkable relief by Krafft, and on the north wall two pictures by Strigel, and one by Holbein the elder.

The quadrangular aperture,[27] which occupies the entire space between the four pillars and allows a full view of the lower chapel, was for a long time walled up. This was done after the chapel had been plastered over, probably towards the end of the fifteenth century. Ably restored in 1892 the chapel is now very much in its original state. The plaster, repeated layers of which had covered the capitals and ornaments with a thick crust, preventing their shape from being any longer recognisable, has been removed. The missing parts of the ornaments have been very skilfully replaced. The original red stone flooring was laid bare and the aperture reopened. There is some disagreement as to the purpose of this opening. We are usually told that it was made for a united church service of the Emperor and Castle retainers: the Emperor taking his seat in the upper, the retainers in the lower chapel. It may be so: but one would rather believe that it was intended to enable the Castle dignitaries, when the service was held in the upper chapel, still to obtain a view of the niches where the mortal remains of their ancestors rested, and to reflect upon the virtues and the end of their mighty dead, remembering the while that they too were mortal.

On leaving the Castle we find ourselves in the Burgstrasse, called in the old days Unter der Veste, which was probably the High Street of the old town. Off both sides of this street and of the Bergstrasse ran narrow crooked little alleys lined with wooden houses of which time and fire have left scarcely any trace.

As you wander round the city tracing the line of the old walls, you are struck by the general air of splendour. Most of the houses are large and of a massive style of architecture, adorned with fanciful gables and bearing the impress of the period when every inhabitant was a merchant, and every merchant was lodged like a king. The houses of the merchant princes, richly carved both inside and out, tell of the wealth and splendour of Nuremberg in her proudest days. But you will also come upon a hundred crooked little streets and narrow alleys, which, though entrancingly picturesque, tell of yet other days and other conditions. They tell of those early mediæval days when the houses were almost all of wood and roofed with straw-thatching or wooden tiles; when the chimneys and bridges alike were built of wood. Only here and there a stone house roofed with brick could then be seen. The streets were narrow and crooked, and even in the fifteenth century mostly unpaved. In wet weather they were filled with unfathomable mud, and even though in the lower part of the town trenches were dug to drain the streets, they remained mere swamps and morasses. In dry weather the dust was even a worse plague than the mud. Pig-styes stood in front of the houses; and the streets were covered with heaps of filth and manure and with rotting corpses of animals, over which the pigs wandered at will. Street police in fact was practically non-existent. Mediævalism is undoubtedly better when survived.

As to the original extent of the city walls there are many theories. Most likely they embraced a very small district. According to Mummenhoff the first town wall ran from the west side of the Castle in a southerly direction over the modern Weinmarkt. (To reach it go straight down the Albert Durer Strasse, starting from Durer's house.) Further on the wall struck eastwards (l) to the river, either leaving the swampy meadowland near the river free, or, as others hold, coming right down to the river banks. Then, leaving the river again near the Spitalplatz, it stretched northward, apparently from the Malerthor which was then in existence, to the Romer Tower in the Tetzelgasse.[28] This tower was probably not actually part of the wall but a fortified house, such as may be seen in many German and Italian towns, built by the dwellers in it for their own especial protection. A noble family of the name of Romer lived there in early times and gave their name to the house. But popular tradition has forgotten this fact and asserts that the tower dates back from Roman times.

From this spot the wall made a distinct bend to the east, ran over the Ægidien hill through the Wolfsgasse, where we may perhaps still recognise in one of the houses an old tower of the wall, and so on to the Fröschturm, or Frog's Tower near the Maxthor of to-day.

A glance at the map will show us that Nuremberg, as we know it, is divided into two almost equal divisions. They are called after the names of the principal churches the St. Lorenz, and the St. Sebald-quarter. The original wall which we have just described included, it will be seen, only a small portion of the northern or St. Sebald division. With the growth of the town an extension of the walls and an increase of fortification followed as a matter of course. It became necessary to carry the wall over the Pegnitz in order to protect the Lorenzkirche and the suburb which was springing up around it. The precise date of this extension of the fortifications cannot be fixed. The chronicles attribute it to the twelfth century, in the reign of the first Hohenstaufen, Konrad III. No trace of a twelfth-century wall remains; but the chroniclers may, for all that, have been not very wide of the mark. The mud and wood which supplied the material of the wall may have given place to stone in the thirteenth and fourteenth centuries. However that may be, it will be remembered that the lower part of the White Tower, which is the oldest fragment of building we can certainly point to dates from the thirteenth century. All other portions of the second wall clearly indicate the fourteenth century, or later, as the time of their origin. What, then, was the course along which ran this second line of fortifications?

Assuming that the reader has accompanied us on our short circuit of the imaginary first town wall—(there is no better way of acquainting oneself with the topography of the place and of coming upon the most picturesque bits of old Nuremberg than to work round the three lines of fortifications sketched here)—we will start again from the Maxthor, the nineteenth-century gateway on the north side of the town. From the Froschturm, which is near at hand, the wall ran alongside of the seven rows of houses

(Zeilen) which were built by the Council in 1488 (on the old moat which had been filled in) for the immigrating Swabian weavers; and then from the Webersplatz by the Landauerkloster (used at the present time as a polytechnic school) straight down to the Lauferschlagturm. This tower, also called the inner Lauferturm, dates in its present form from the fifteenth century and in part from the sixteenth century. It derives its name from the striking clock which was put up in 1478, at a period when clocks with bells to mark the hours were still rare. Proceeding past the Lauferschlagturm we can trace clearly enough the shooting-trench, which was assigned to the cross-bowmen in 1485 and runs on to the former foundry of the coppersmiths "Auf dem Sand." Presently before reaching the Pegnitz the wall made a sharp turn to the west: it is uncertain whether the present Neuegasse (which we must follow) ran inside or outside of it; at any rate the Mohler or Mahler Thor (Müllerthor) stood at the spot where the Heugässchen and Neuegasse run into the Spitalplatz. Leaving the Mohlerthor the wall crossed the Spitalplatz (l) and ran in a straight line, strongly protected by towers, across the two arms of the Pegnitz which encircle the Schütt Island. In the northern arm of the river, near the Synagogue (l), you may still distinguish a bit of ruined wall overgrown by alders, rising out of the water. This is the remains of the pier which once buttressed the town-wall against the current of the Pegnitz. On the island there are still two towers, the larger of the two being the Schuldturm or Debtor's Tower for men (Männereisen) which bears the date 1323. Originally a corresponding tower for female debtors stood on the south bank of the river. But this, together with the connecting walls and the arch over the Pegnitz, was demolished in 1812. The bridge, which joined the two debtors' towers, was called the Schuldbrücke, and the whole probably resembled the Henkersteg group at which we shall presently arrive. At any rate it is recorded that towards the end of the fifteenth century "they built dwellings for the townspeople on the old arch by the Debtors' Towers, through which the Pegnitz formerly flowed into the town."

We have now reached the South or Lorenz-quarter of the town. From the river the wall ran straight on along the Nonnen-gasse to the inner Frauenthor, which was destroyed in 1499. Cross the Lorenzer Platz and go down the Theatergasse opposite. Behind the theatre there is still a piece of open ditch—the old Lorenzer shooting-trench, and near the old inner Frauenthor is the entrance to the Herrenkeller, which goes under the Königstrasse to beneath the Great Hall. The old moat was converted into this cellar, which is 447 feet long, and supported by twenty-six pillars. Over it the architect Hans Behaim erected the Neue Kornhaus and the Great Hall or Grosse Wage, a deep-roofed building, also called the Mauthaus, because it is now used as a Custom House. Going straight on down the north side of this hall we come to the Frauengässlein, a fascinating old street, which stretches behind the old arsenals (r) (now used as storehouses for hops) to the Färbergasse, and marks the further course of the walls, which, from the arsenals to the White Tower (Weissturm) is easily traced. For a considerable part of the old moat (Färbergraben) and a piece of the old wall, with its large curved blocks of sandstone black with age, are still visible. At the end of the Frauengasse turn first to the right and then to the left into the Breitegasse, when the White Tower will confront you. The lower portion of the White Tower, or inner Spittlerthurm as it used to be called (a name, like that of the modern Spittlerthor, derived from the St. Elizabethspital), is, as we have noted, thirteenth-century work. The tower was renovated in the fifteenth century and fitted, like the Lauferschlagturm, with a chiming clock. The outer gate (Vorthor) is still preserved. Keeping on the inside of the White Tower cross the Ludwig Strasse and go down the Waisen Strasse, which brings you to the Brewery. Keep on down the same street with first the Brewery and then the Unschlitthaus on the right till you reach the river.

Beyond the White Tower the moat was long ago filled up, but the section of it opposite the Unschlittplatz remained open for a longer period than the rest, and was called the Klettengraben, because of the burdocks which took root there. Hereabouts, on a part of the moat, the Waizenbräuhaus was built in 1671, which is now the famous Freiherrlich von Tuchersche Brewery. Here, too, the Unschlitthaus was built at the end of the fifteenth century as a granary. It has since been turned into a school.

We have now reached one of the most charming and picturesque bits of Nuremberg. Once more we have to cross the Pegnitz, whose banks are overhung by quaint old houses. Their projecting roofs and high gables, their varied chimneys and overhanging balconies from which trail rich masses of creepers, make an entrancing foreground to the towers and the arches of the Henkersteg. The wall was carried on arches over the southern arm of the Pegnitz to the point of the Saumarkt (or Trödelmarkt) island which here divides the river, and thence in like manner over the northern arm. The latter portion of it alone survives and comprises a large tower on the north bank called the Wasserthurm, which was intended to break the force of the stream; a bridge supported by two arches over the stream, which was the Henkersteg, the habitation of the hangman or Löb as he was called, of whom and of whose duties we shall have to speak in the next chapter; and on the island itself a smaller tower, which formed the point of support for the original, southern pair of arches, which joined the Unschlitthaus, but were so badly damaged in 1595 by a high flood that they were demolished and replaced by a wooden, and later by an iron bridge.

After the great Wasserthurm, all trace of the old wall is lost. Probably it stretched in a straight line across the Weintraubengässlein, along the back of the houses of the Karlstrasse, and across the Irrergasse to the Lammsgasse. Mummenhoff fancies that he can recognise one of the towers of it in an exceptionally high house on the north side of this latter street. There too stood the inner Neuthor. The houses at the back of Albrecht-Dürerstrasse show pretty clearly the further course of the wall until at the Thiergärtnerthurm it finally joined the fortifications of the Castle.

Thus we have completed the second circuit of the old Imperial town as it was in the thirteenth and most of the first half of the fourteenth centuries. It was then a city of no mean size for the middle ages, but it was far from having attained its full development. New monasteries and churches and new suburbs sprang up outside the new line of fortification. As usually happens, the majority of the dwellers outside the walls were of the lower class: but, besides their houses, there were, especially towards the east, splendid gardens and properties belonging to the patrician families and also several large buildings, including the Katherine and Clara Convents, the Mary Hospital, and the Carthusian Monastery (now part of the German Museum). Buildings of this kind, close to and outside of the gates of the old town, would, if they fell into the hands of an enemy, be a continual menace to the peace and safety of the burghers. Hardly, therefore, was the second line of fortifications completed when it became necessary to protect the new suburbs with wall and ditch like the old town. It may be noted that even when the new enceinte, that is the third or outer town wall, was finished, the second wall was still carefully preserved as a second line of defence. This was directly contrary to the advice of Macchiavelli "not to establish within the circuit of a city fortifications which may serve as a retreat to troops who have been driven back from the first line of entrenchments ... for there is no greater danger for a fortress than rear-fortifications whither troops can retire in case of a reverse; for once a soldier knows that he has a secure retreat after he has abandoned the first post, he does, in fact, abandon it and so causes the loss of the entire fortress." The Nurembergers, however, never favoured any policy that could even remotely suggest that of burning their boats. For a long time they kept their second line of defence. Thus in 1509 it came to the notice of the authorities that "the inner moat near the arsenals and granaries were filled up with dirt and rubbish, which at some future time might do harm to the town, and the neighbours were forbidden to empty any more rubbish into the moat, and the town architect was ordered to see to it that what had been thrown into it was either levelled or taken out and that the parapet was renewed." Similarly and in the same year the inhabitants of the neighbourhood of St. Katherinagraben (the present Peter Vischerstrasse) were refused leave to build a bridge over the existing moat.

That part of the town which lay between the second and third lines of fortification continued for a long time to retain something of a suburban character. People of small fortunes who came to settle in Nuremberg were at first admitted only into the district outside the older wall and were only allowed to move into the inner town after they had been domiciled in the outer town for several years. The suburban character of the outer town was and is still in some degree apparent also from the large open spaces there and, especially on the eastern side, from the extensive farms and gardens belonging to the richer citizens, such as the Holzschuhers, the Volkamers and the Tuchers.

Somewhere in the second half of the fourteenth century, then, in the reign of Karl IV., they began to build the outer enceinte, which, although destroyed at many places and broken through by modern gates and entrances,[29] is still fairly well preserved, and secures to Nuremberg the reputation of presenting most faithfully of all the larger German towns the characteristics of a mediæval town. The fortifications seem to have been thrown up somewhat carelessly at first, but dread of the Hussites soon inspired the citizens to make themselves as secure as possible. In times of war and rumours of war all the peasants within a radius of two miles of the town were called upon to help in the construction of barriers and ramparts. The whole circle of walls, towers, and ditches was practically finished by 1452, when with pardonable pride Tucher wrote, "In this year was completed the ditch round the town. It took twenty-six years to build, and it will cost an enemy a good deal of trouble to cross it." Part of the ditch had been made and perhaps revetted as early as 1407, but it was not till twenty years later that it began to be dug to the enormous breadth and depth which it boasts to-day. The size of it was always a source of pride to the Nurembergers, and it was perhaps due to this reason that up till as recently as 1869 it was left perfectly intact. On the average it is about 100 feet broad. It was always intended to be a dry ditch, and, so far from there being any arrangements for flooding it, precautions were taken to carry the little Fischbach, which formerly entered the town near the modern Sternthor, across the ditch in a trough. The construction of the ditch was provided for by an order of the Council in 1427, to the effect that all householders, whether male or female, must work at the ditch one day in the year with their children of over twelve years of age, and with all their servants, male or female. Those who were not able to work had to pay a substitute. Subsequently this order was changed to the effect that every one who could or would not work must pay ten pfennige (one penny). There were no exemptions from this liturgy, whether in favour of councillor, official, or lady. The order remained ten years in force, though the amount of the payment was gradually reduced.

Whilst the enceinte was in course of erection the Burggraf Frederic VI. sold (1428) to the town the ruins of his castle. Steps were immediately taken therefore to fortify the whole of the Castle grounds with ditch and large revetted circular bastions. Paul Stromer was the director of the works. At this time we first find distinct mention of the Vestner Thor, and the Vestnerthorbrücke. The other main gates, the Neue Thor, the Spittler Thor, the Frauen Thor, and the Laufer Thor had begun to be built about 1380.

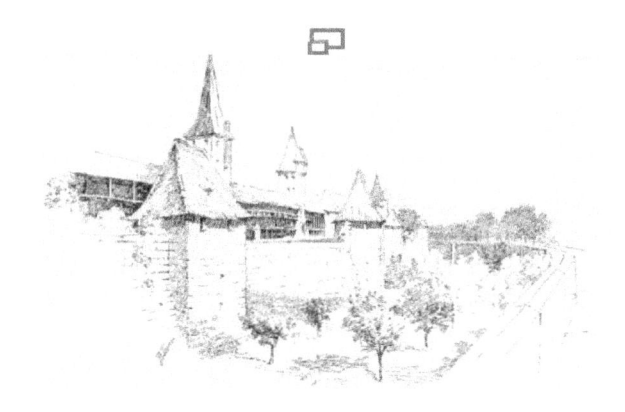

WALLS AND DITCH

The Wührderthürlein and the Hallerthürlein were constructed probably about the same time as the Vestnerthor—i.e. circ. 1430. It was against the gates that the main attacks of the enemy were usually delivered, and they were therefore provided with the most elaborate means of defence. Each principal gate in fact was an individual castle, a separate keep: for it was defended by one of those huge round towers which still help to give to Nuremberg its characteristic appearance. The Laufer, Spittel, and Frauen towers, and the tower near the new gate were built in the above order in their present cylindrical shape (1555-1559) by the architect George Unger, on the site of four quadrilateral towers that already existed. The towers are about 60 yards in diameter. They are furnished on the ground story with one or two gun-casemates, which would command the parapet wall if that were taken. Above, beneath the flat roof, is fixed a platform blinded with wood relieved by embrasures capable of receiving a considerable number of cannon. Guns indeed were in position here as recently as 1796, when together with all the contents of the arsenal they were removed by the Austrians.

At the time of the construction of these and the other lofty towers it was still thought that the raising of batteries as much as possible would increase their effect. In practice the plunging fire from platforms at the height of some eighty feet above the level of the parapets of the town wall can hardly have been capable of producing any great effect, more especially if the besieging force succeeded in establishing itself on the crest of the counterscarp of the ditches, since from that point the swell of the bastions masked the towers. But there was another use for these lofty towers. The fact is that the Nuremberg engineers, at the time that they were built, had not yet adopted a complete system of flank-works, and not having as yet applied with all its consequences the axiom that that which defends should itself be defended, they wanted to see and command their external defences from within the body of the place, as, a century before, the baron could see from the top of his donjon whatever was going on round the walls of his castle, and send up his support to any point of attack. The great round towers of Nuremberg are more properly, in fact, detached keeps than portions of a combined system, rather observatories than effective defences.[30]

They were perhaps the last of their kind. Tradition has quite incorrectly ascribed them to Albert Durer. Not only were they built thirty years after his death, but they are in principle entirely opposed to the views expounded in his book on the "Fortification of Towns." This book, which appeared in 1527, broke completely with the old mediæval art of fortification (the theory of which may be said roughly to have consisted in an extensive use of towers), and recommended the construction of such bastions as the Köcherts-zwinger, or that in the neighbourhood of the Laufer Thor (1527) which form the starting-point of modern fortification.

The round towers, however, were not the sole defences of the gates. Outside each one of them was a kind of fence of pointed beams after the manner of a chevaux-de-frise, whilst outside the ditch and close to the bridge stood a barrier, by the side of which was a guard-house. Though it was not till 1598 that all the main gates were fitted with drawbridges, the wooden bridges that served before that could doubtless easily be destroyed in cases of emergency. Double-folding doors and portcullises protected the gateways themselves. Once past there, the enemy was far from being in the town, for the road led through extensive advanced works, presenting, as in the case of the Laufer Thor outwork, a regular place d'armes. Further, the road was so engineered as not to lead in a straight line from the outer main gates to the inner ones, but rather so as to pursue a circuitous course. Thus the enemy in passing through from the one to the other were exposed as long as possible to the shots and projectiles of the defenders, who were stationed all round the walls and towers flanking the advanced tambour. This arrangement may be traced very clearly at the Frauen Thor to-day. The position of the round tower, it will be observed, was an excellent one for commanding the road from the outer to the inner gate.

The entrance and exit of the Pegnitz were two weak spots, calling equally with the gates for special measures of defence. They were completely barred by "Schossgatter" as they were termed—strong oak piles covered with iron—set beneath the arches that spanned the river. Strong iron chains were stretched in front of them, forming a boom to prevent the approach of boats. The tower at the exit of the Pegnitz was erected, we know, in 1422. It is mentioned by sixteenth-century chroniclers as the Schlayerturm, and, though it has lost its former height, it serves to-day in conjunction with the adjoining building over the water as a jail.

The most vulnerable points were thus provided for. The rest of the enceinte consisted of the ditch and walls and towers. There were two lines of walls and towers enclosing a space which in peace-time served as a game-park. Celtes in his poem in praise of Nuremberg boasts of the rich turf growing there, upon which grazed splendid herds of deer. The Tiergärtner Thor, however, did not derive its name from this game-park (Tiergärten), but from another earlier one belonging to the Burggrafs.

The interior line of walls was the first to be built. It was made about three feet thick and twenty-two feet high. Originally there were no buttresses to it (as one may gather from the short length of old wall, north of the Spittler Thor, where the inside of the wall is plain), but afterwards buttresses were added along the whole of it, at a distance of eighteen feet or so from centre to centre. About four feet broad, they projected some two feet beyond the actual wall. They are joined by circular arches, the coins of which are walled up. The blinded galleries thus formed are still frequently used as workshops.

INTERIOR OF THE WALLS

The top of the wall is about three yards broad, thanks to a coping stone which projects on each side. Along the outer edge of the coping stone runs a crenelated wall, only a foot and a half thick. Seeing that it was already at the time of construction exposed to artillery, the thinness of this wall is somewhat surprising. Probably the Nurembergers knew that the neighbouring nobility could not afford a heavy and expensive siege-train. A roof, composed, according to the poet Celtes, of tiles partly glazed, was erected over the crenelated wall and thus formed a covered way. The crenelles were furnished with hanging shutters, which had a hole pierced in them and were adapted therefore either to the fire of small pieces or of arquebuses.

At intervals of every 120 or 150 feet the interior wall is broken by quadrilateral towers. Some eighty-three of these, including the gate towers, can still be traced. What the number was originally we do not know. It is the sort of subject on which chroniclers have no manner of conscience. The Hartmann Schedel Chronicle, for instance, gives Nuremberg 365 towers in all. The fact that there are 365 days in the year is of course sufficient proof of this assertion! The towers, which rise two or even three stories above the wall, communicated on both sides with the covered way. They are now used as dwelling-houses. On some of them there can still be seen, projecting near the roof, two little machicoulis turrets, which served as guard-rooms for observing the enemy, and also, by overhanging the base of the tower, enabled the garrison to hurl down on their assailants at the foot of the wall a hurricane of projectiles of every sort. Like the wall the towers are built almost entirely of sandstone, but on the side facing the town they are usually faced with brick. The shapes of the roofs vary from flat to pointed, but the towers themselves are simple and almost austere in form in comparison with those generally found in North Germany, where fantasy runs riot in red brick. The Nuremberg towers were obviously intended in the first place for use rather than for ornament.

Parallel with the interior town wall there ran an exterior lower one, which, together with the former, enclosed a space, to which we have already referred, varying from fifty to twenty feet in breadth. We know very little about the original height and form of this exterior wall. It suffered many changes and can no longer be traced in its original shape. Experts hold diametrically opposite views both as to the use and the height of it. But that is the way of experts. We shall probably not be far wrong in concluding that this wall was originally a mere crenelated crowning[31] of the escarp of the ditch; that catapults were worked from the space enclosed by the two walls; and that the chief object of the outer wall and the enclosure was to prevent the enemy from working at the main, or inner, wall and towers with his rams and moveable turrets. Later, when the use and effectiveness of artillery developed and guns supplanted catapults in vigour as well as in fact, some time at the end of the fifteenth or the beginning of the sixteenth century, we may suppose that this old crenelated wall was removed, and the escarp wall of the ditch was raised and strengthened and provided with embrasures for large cannon, and rounded off on the outside so as to neutralise the effect of shot striking the face of the walls. In this form the exterior wall is well preserved, and can be seen at many places in the course of a walk round the outside of the town. At many points in the circumference, but chiefly where the fortifications are accessible (e.g. near the Frauen Thor) the parapets of this curtain-wall present a somewhat remarkable arrangement. The parapets, pierced with embrasures for cannon, are surmounted by timber hoards or filled in with brick and mortar, like the old English half-timbered houses. In these hoards (wooden galleries roofed in with tiles) arquebusiers and even archers, who were still employed at that period, might be placed. Pieces in battery were covered by these hoards just in the same way as pieces in the "'tween decks" of a man-of-war. The crenelles of the hoards were closed by shutters opening on the inside, in such a way as to present an obstacle to the balls or arrows fired by the assailants placed on the top of the glacis.

The outer, like the inner wall was provided with towers. These were thicker in construction but lower and less numerous than the interior ones. They were placed at intervals of 200 to 250 feet and amounted in all to forty or thereabouts. The chief purpose of them was to flank and command the ditch and thus to prevent the enemy from building a dam across it. With this object they projected some distance into the ditch.

Simultaneously with the alterations of the exterior wall small bastion-like towers were also constructed, chiefly at places where the wall formed an angle, and where the enemy could not therefore advance in line. From these towers a searching fire could be maintained in all directions, sweeping both the ditch and the ground in front. The strong, low, semi-circular tower at the Haller Thor is supposed to be the oldest work of this description.

Lastly, in the second half of the sixteenth century, the large bastions which bring us in touch with modern ideas of fortification were built. We may instance the bastion adjoining the Neue Thor, called the Doktors Zwinger because the doctors had their summer garden there. And in 1613 the Vöhrderthor-Zwinger was added to the old town-wall. It was designed by Meinhard von Schönberg, and built by Jakob Wolf, the younger. But in 1871 this magnificent structure, with the armorial devices which decorated the four corners of it, was enclosed in the Vestner Thor Zwinger.

An account of the fortifications of Nuremberg would be incomplete if no mention were made of the Landwehr—a continuous line of defence which was thrown up at some little distance from the town about the middle of the fifteenth century, in the time of the first Marggravian war. The Landwehr was a ditch with an earthen parapet strengthened by stockades, barricaded at the crossings of the roads with obstacles and moveable barriers, and defended by blockhouses in which guards were always kept. The main object of this fortification was to afford shelter to the country people, and to secure them and their goods and cattle from the raids of the enemy. Only the merest fragment of the "Land-ditch" remains, viz., the Landgraben, running through the Lichtenhof meadow.

It will be gathered from these dry details that the chief note struck by the fortifications of Nuremberg is that of picturesque variety. The defences have been built at different times and form no stereotyped pattern. Walls, towers, and bastions of varying types and shapes, suggesting the ideas of different ages, succeed each other in pleasant confusion. The walls themselves, now high, now low, now with, now without roofing, here crenelated with narrow loopholes and arrow-slits, there fitted with broad embrasures for heavy guns, seem to be typical of the place and to suggest to us the recollection of her chequered career.

At the end of our long perambulations of the walls it will be a grateful relief to sit for a while at one of the Restaurations or restaurants on the walls. There, beneath the shade of acacias in the daytime, or in the evening by the white light of the incandescent gas, you may sit and watch the groups of men, women, and children all drinking from their tall glasses of beer, and you may listen to the whirr and ting-tang of the electric cars, where the challenge of the sentinel or the cry of the night-watchman was once the most frequent sound. Or, if you have grown tired of the Horn- and the Schloss-zwinger, cross the ditch on the west side of the town and make your way to the Rosenau, in the Fürtherstrasse. The Rosenau is a garden of trees and roses not lacking in chairs and tables, in bowers, benches, and a band. There, too, you will see the good burgher with his family drinking beer, eating sausages, and smoking contentedly.

CHAPTER VI
THE COUNCIL AND THE COUNCIL HOUSE— NUREMBERG TORTURES

Da ist in dieser Stadt
Ein weiser, fürsichtiger Rath,
Der so fürsichtiglich regiert
Und alle Ding fein ordinirt.
—HANS SACHS, Lobspruch der Stadt Nürnberg.

WE have seen how in gradual and piecemeal fashion the Council, as representative of Nuremberg, acquired the character of an imperial state on an equality with the reigning princes and territorial lords. The special mark of sovereign power, the higher jurisdiction, was accorded in perpetuity to the Nuremberg Council through an edict of Frederick III., 1459. The Council was composed originally of such burghers as the community saw fit to elect. But gradually it came about that only the moneyed classes, large merchants, large land-owners, and court-officials admitted to the citizenship took part in the election, and that, within this circle again, those who had already held office formed themselves into a specially privileged group. So there resulted in Nuremberg, as everywhere else, the formation of a special town-aristocracy of those families eligible to the Council, which in Nuremberg particularly, where the original suffrage soon had to give place to the Council's right of self-election, developed into the most pronounced exclusiveness. The final result was the separation of the citizens into the governing families and into the remaining classes cut off from any influence upon the town government, and represented in general by the Trades Guilds. This antithesis, which existed in all towns, led everywhere, in the fourteenth and fifteenth centuries, to violent conflicts; in our town, to the riots of 1348, to which we have already referred.

The families eligible to the Council composed the Patriciate, the origin of which can no longer be traced in detail. The Patricians were not, as often in other towns, burghers of long standing, for in the fourteenth century and later, even up to the beginning of the sixteenth century, it happened that foreign families settling here were at once accepted as eligible to the Council. This is a circumstance which does not at all correspond to the usual conception of the burgher exclusiveness in the Middle Ages; but on the contrary it betrays a certain liberality.

The Patricians appear with others of the nobility as witnesses to documents, and are not infrequently given precedence over the territorial nobility. They carried shield, helmet, and seal; their hatchments hung in the churches, they held fiefs from the princes, and were eligible to church dignities. The Patriciate, however, did not by any means occupy itself wholly with military service and knightly exercises. Many of them carried on wholesale businesses and manufacturing trades. This occurred pretty generally throughout the Middle Ages, as also in the sixteenth century, though their descendants denied that they were ever connected with trade.

As the burghers were in general capable of bearing arms, the governing families especially kept themselves in military practice. They led the armed burghers or the mercenaries in the wars of their country, and many of them obtained in the service of the Emperor, or elsewhere, the dignity of knighthood.

As early as the fifteenth century the Patrician families claimed the rights of knighthood and heraldry like territorial nobles. Probably the tourney held in 1446, on the occasion of a Patrician wedding, and represented in life-size stucco-work on the ceiling of the upper corridor in the Town Hall, by Hans Kuhn, 1621, was intended as a manifesto to this effect.

At any rate it is recorded that this tourney vexed the nobles very sorely, "as they opined, it did not become the Nuremberg families to tilt in noble conflict or to indulge in such knightly pastime; it was indeed generally held that this tourney had had no little influence in bringing about the great Margravian War which soon followed." In the year 1481, and again in 1485, in the Heidelberg and Heilbronn tournament regulations, the Town Patriciate's right of tourney was formally contested.

Though we do not know how their prerogative arose, we certainly find that by 1521 the number of actual Patrician families was limited to forty-three, whilst, by the end of the century, only twenty-eight are left eligible for the Council. They formed a close and very exclusive corporation, clinging very tightly to their fabricated privileges. "Anno 1521," runs an old statute, "it was declared and set down by the Elders of the Town of Nuremberg which families have always from time immemorial danced and may still dance in the Town Hall."

We cannot deny that the short-sighted policy so often pursued by Nuremberg to her own undoing was due to the narrow and selfish oligarchy thus formed. But if we blame them for the decay we must also give them full meed of praise for the ripening of the prosperity of Nuremberg. The truth seems to be that the government of oligarchies of this nature, formed, not of all the wealthy families, but of a Patrician order of certain families, is, owing to the varied interests of the remaining society over whom they rule, peculiarly difficult to overthrow. Moreover, it is at first likely to lead on the State to success and prosperity: for at first the prominence of particular families represents the triumph of the fittest, the rise of those best able to govern, to conduct commerce, to encourage industry and art. But when in the course of nature these families begin to decay and cling all the more obstinately to their rights, it is then that the weakness of the position appears and the State is involved in the ruin of its most degenerate members.

It is noticeable that many of the early measures of the Council bore a decidedly socialistic character. We may instance the establishment of public baths, and the storing up of corn against the time of famine, besides the foundation of a great town brewery, which is the origin of the famous Tucher brewery of to-day, and the keeping of public stallions to improve the breed of horses, a measure that resulted in Nuremberg becoming famous for its chargers. On the other hand, as an instance of the jealous tyranny of the Council, we may quote the case of Christoph Scheurl. When he, the "Oracle of the Republic" as he was called, threatened to appeal to the Imperial Chamber against a sentence of the Council they replied by torturing him in the cruellest fashion for three weeks.

The public attitude of the Councillors being of this somewhat grandmotherly kind, it is not surprising that they left the young members of their families very little liberty in placing their affections. Love affairs and marriage for love were in fact not regarded with favour. Girls were betrothed by their parents at eight years of age and married at fourteen, often to old men of sixty or seventy. A couple were very seldom permitted to initiate for themselves an affair of the heart. So when Leonhard Groland, against good manners and tradition, had begun a love affair with Catherine, daughter of Hans Hardörfer, and this was discovered, the precocious lover was punished with two months' imprisonment and banished for five years from the town. When a father did allow his son to choose his own wife he very seldom allowed him to woo her. They tell us how when the young Paul Tucher said that he would like to marry Ursula, daughter of the late Albrecht Scheurl, his father did the wooing for him, and went to Andreas Imhof, her guardian, and these two "with unshaken calm and dignified respectability" arranged the dowry and settlements. The public betrothal took place first in the Rathaus and then in the house of the bride. The wedding, after many formalities, took place not in the church, but before the portal of the church,[32] and only after the marriage service was completed did the bridal pair enter the church to partake of the holy sacrament. After the service the bridal party danced in the morning and then, after dinner at the bride's home (where it was customary for the pair to reside for a year), another dance took place in the evening; in the case of members of the Patriciate, in the Rathaus. These proceedings were regulated by laws by which the Council continually strove to repress the tendency to luxury and extravagance which always accompanies commercial prosperity.

The Rathaus, the heart of the old trading Republic, fronts the chancel end of the Sebald-kirche, a position architecturally unfortunate. The original Councilhouse, which was shared by the Council with the Clothiers Guild, stood in the present Tuchgasse. But in 1332 the Council bought from the Heilsbronn Monastery a house on the site of the present Rathaus, and here they built themselves a new Council-house into which they first moved in 1340. In its oldest form the Rathaus consisted only of a large hall, large enough to hold with comfort and dignity the numerous assembly that might gather there on the occasion of a Reichstag. All that now remains intact of this hall is the outer architecture on the east side. The oldest portions of the Rathaus are to be seen from the interior quadrangle and from the Rathausgasse, the street at the back.

RATHAUS (WINDOW)

In 1514 new rooms were added. They are mostly by Hans Behaim and are very good specimens of late Gothic. In 1520 the Rathaus Hall was renovated and altered and the side walls were painted after Durer's designs, by Georg Pencz and other pupils of the master. The hall was again restored and adorned with new pictures in 1613. Two years later the great chandelier, by Hans Wilhelm Behaim, was placed there. Two copies of it were added in 1874.

The Rathaus took almost its present form in 1616. The architect, Eucharius Karl Holzschuher, adapted, so far as possible, the old Rathaus to the new Italian style of building which now enclosed it. The outbreak of the Thirty Years War, however, prevented the completion of his plan. The north-east portion of the Rathaus has indeed only recently been finished after the designs of Dr A. von Essenwein. The imposing Renaissance façade confronting St. Sebald's is nearly 300 feet long and consists of two stories containing thirty-six windows apiece. Three Doric portals form the entrances, and are ornamented with sculptures of reclining figures—Justice holding the scales and Truth with a mirror, Julius Cæsar and Alexander, Ninus and Cyrus—by Leonhard Kern. The sculptor received the moderate wage of 100 gulden per figure.

Entering the first court by the central portal, we see in front on the right the charming old Gothic gallery, supported by three pillars. In the centre of the court is a bronze fountain by Pankraz Labenwolf (1556); in the second court is the Apollo fountain of Hans Vischer.[33] The principal[34] staircase (r of central entrance) leads to the Great Hall or Council Chamber already referred to (1332). The arched wooden ceiling dates from 1521. The hall is 130 feet long and 40 feet wide and contains the chandeliers and the paintings after Durer's designs mentioned above. The latter, on the north wall, have been much spoiled by the effects of time and of incompetent restoration. The first of them represents the Triumphal Car of Maximilian I. drawn by twelve horses. Victory holds a laurel wreath over the Emperor, who is attended by the various Virtues. Behind the car follows an animated procession of Nuremberg town musicians. The second design is on the well-worn subject of Calumny—Midas with his long ears sitting in judgment on Innocence who is accused by Calumny, Fraud, Envy, and so forth, whilst in the background appear Punishment, Penitence, and Truth. On the right of the judge (our left) who sits between Ignorance and Suspicion, are the words: Nemo unquam sententiam ferat priusquam cuncta ad amussim perpenderit, on the left the same sentiment in German:

Ein Richter soll kein Urtheil geben
Er soll die Sach erforschen eben.

Over the little door is written "Eins manns red ist eine halbe red. Man soll die Teyl verhören bed." (One man's rede is but half the rede. The other side should be heard.)

The frescoes (now scarcely visible) between the windows are by Gabriel Weyer (1619?). As both Bædeker and Murray state that "among them is a representation of the guillotine, which is thus proved to be two centuries older than the French Revolution," it may be worth while to remark that nothing of the sort is proved. The falling-axe, fall-beil, the Italian caraletto here represented, was of course much used at this time, as the engravings of Lucas Cranach, Georg Pencz and others and as our own Halifax Gibbet and Morton's Maiden show. But the guillotine, properly so-called, was a revived and modified form of this. The instrument then took its name from the inventor of these modifications, M. Guillotin, a philanthropic French physician, who designed "to reduce the pain of death to a shiver" by this machine;

"Qui simplement nous tuera
Et que l'on nommera,
Guillotine."

as the royalist song first phrased it.

The bronze railing, by Peter Vischer, which once separated the lower from the upper half of the hall has now disappeared.

The small hall on the second floor is used now as the city court. It has recently been repaired and contains, besides portraits of modern Nuremberg worthies, some pompous allegorical paintings by Paul Juvenell (1579-1643).

In the Rathaus as in the Castle and Museum some very fine specimens of old German stoves are to be seen. The stucco-relief on the ceiling of the corridor on this floor we have already mentioned more than once.[35]

The Municipal Art Gallery (gratuity) on the third floor contains an interesting collection of paintings that deal with the history of Nuremberg. The most remarkable historically is the Banquet held in the Rathaus on the occasion of the Peace of Westphalia (1649), by Joachim von Sandrart (1606-1688). Thirty of the forty-seven figures at the table in this piece are portraits from life.

The power over life and death was given, as we have said, to the Council along with the other rights of the Schuldheiss in 1459 by Frederick III. Till then the Emperor had reserved to himself the power to give to any individual he chose this right, "Ban über das Blut in der Stadt zu richten." It was an evil thing now to fall into the hands of the Council. Prisoners even during their detention before trial were made to suffer more severely than the worst modern convicts. The accused were put into the Loch, the hole which formed a part of the cellar of the old Rathaus, where there are twelve underground cells, each about two yards square, and two yards high.

Entering the Rathaus by the portal nearest to the Schöner Brunnen we turn to the right, ascend a flight of steps and ring the bell for the

Hausmeister,[36] who will guide us with lanterns to those gloomy caverns which like the Piombi of Venice cry shame on the inhumanity of man. We follow our guide down a narrow stone staircase to the dungeons cold and dark as the grave. Over the various entrances were symbolic figures of animals: the two last being ornamented with a red cock and a black cock. No one seems able to say what these strange hieroglyphics denote.

The cells were never cleaned, but were warmed by a brazier in the winter. Two of them are furnished with stocks; in each there is an angular wooden couch; in some, when the sight has got gradually accustomed to the darkness, we become aware of a ghastly cleft in the floor. Flaubert, Poe, Scott, and Victor Hugo never fail to make my blood run cold with their descriptions of tortures, but the pages of "Salammbo," of the "Pit and the Pendulum," of "Old Mortality," or "Les Misérables" have no such terrors for my imagination as the actual sight of these deep and horrid dungeons wherein so many hundreds, innocent and guilty alike, have been incarcerated and suffered, with no Anne of Geierstein to deliver them. Presently we pass on to a room of still more horrible interest—the torture-chamber where the judges (Die Blutrichtern) sat, whilst their wretched victim, far removed from human aid and human sympathy, was "examined" till a confession was wrung from him. This vaulted room in the Loch was called the "Chapel." Over it is written "Folterkammer, 1511" (Torture Chamber). On the wall was inscribed the jingling verse—

"Ad mala patrata hæc sunt atra theatra parata."

Revolting as the idea of torture is to us, it would not be fair to concentrate our indignation on the Nurembergers, as we are tempted to do, when we see these things and still more when, in the Castle, we visit the stupendous collection of torture-instruments, those melancholy monuments of human error. For torture as a system of trial, as the great alternative to the ordeal, has received the sanction of the wisest lawgivers throughout far the greater portion of the world's history. It is, indeed, only quite recently that we have in practice acknowledged Quintilian's objection to torture—that under it one man's constancy makes falsehood easy to him whilst another's weakness makes falsehood necessary. History, too, has shown us the evil effects of this system upon the judge, who became inevitably eager to convince himself of the guilt of the poor wretch whom he had already caused to suffer. How completely the prisoner thus became a quarry to be hunted to the death is shown by the jocular remark of Farinacci, a celebrated authority in criminal law, that the torture of sleeplessness invented by Marsigli was most excellent, for out of a hundred martyrs exposed to it not two could endure it without becoming confessors as well. This form of torture was practised in England even without the continental limit of time. But on the whole, torture in England fell short of the best continental standard. Still, it remains true to say that human ingenuity could not invent suffering more terrible than was constantly and legally employed in every civilised community. Satan himself, one writer exclaims, would be unable to increase its refinements. A visit to the Tower of London will prove that Nuremberg was not a solitary and disgraceful exception to the manners of her day. The robber-barons, who flourished under King Stephen in England used the same methods as their German brethren to extract ransoms from the rich merchants they captured, using knotted ropes twisted round the head, crucet-houses, or chests filled with sharp stones in which the victim was crushed, sachentages, or frames with a sharp iron collar preventing the wearer from sitting, lying, or sleeping. A visit to the Castle of Nuremberg shows us that the rich merchants were ready to use similar arguments to the robber-barons.

When the prisoner had been brought into the torture chamber and the professional gentlemen (the Hangman and the Secretary) had decided how much the patient could bear, operations began. A circular opening on the inside of the room above the entrance marks the place behind which sat the person who took down the prisoner's confession. Innumerable devices and instruments had been invented, as we see in the Castle, by using which separately and in combination the confession was extorted. Burning candles held under the arms were found very effective and the favourite Spanish methods, the Strappado (suspension by the arms behind the back with weights to the feet), pouring water down the throat and applying fire to the soles of the feet were in frequent use. We find many varieties of the "little ease" or rack in the Castle. The severity of the instrument is attested by the signature of our Guy Fawkes before and after being submitted to that ordeal. But even less attractive than this must have been the peine forte et dure. John Gow, it will be remembered, in "The Pirate," stands mute even when his thumbs were squeezed by two men with a whipcord till it broke, and again when it was doubled and trebled so that the operators could pull with their whole strength. But his fortitude gave way and he confessed when he had seen the preparations for pressing him to death with the peine forte et dure, a board loaded with heavy weights. A peculiar atrocity marked the torture system of Scotland. Torture retained its place in that kingdom's laws as long as she preserved the right of self-legislation. Her system could not surpass, but it serves to illustrate the fiendish barbarities of the Nuremberg questions. Readers of Sir Walter Scott will remember his description of the "boot"—an iron frame in which the leg was inserted and broken by iron wedges driven in with a hammer. The penni-winkis, thumb-screws, and caschielawis, iron frames for the leg heated from time to time over a brazier, were also favourite instruments both there and here.

It is not surprising that such persuasion usually succeeded in producing a confession from the prisoners, whether true or not, of their own or of other people's guilt. They were not infrequently compelled to confess to crimes which they had never committed[37] and were hanged for murdering persons who afterwards were found to be alive and well. Real criminals, however, often refused to speak; for habitual and professional malefactors used to torture each other regularly in order to be hardened when brought to justice. But in that case their wives and children often proved less reticent. Confession having been secured the Council appointed a day of judgment for the armen, "poor fellow," as they termed him. If when he came before them he still persisted in his confession he was condemned. But condemnation depended on the confession of the criminal, and the Church had long maintained that confessions obtained under torture were invalid. If, therefore, when brought before the Council he recanted he was tortured again, and as often as he retracted this process was repeated until a confession apart from torture was obtained. The humane intervention of the Church thus resulted in a redoublement of cruelty. Even after condemnation, if the convict told the clergyman, who came to prepare him for death, that he was really not guilty but had confessed only because of the torture, the Council on hearing of it had to begin all over again. This became such a nuisance that they warned the clergy not to talk to the condemned too much about temporal matters! After sentence had been passed by the Council a public trial of an entirely formal character was held, very wearisome to the condemned wretch, who probably knew that it was so empty a form that it was held even if the prisoner had already succumbed to the torture or committed suicide in the cells.

In Nuremberg, as elsewhere, various methods of punishment were employed. Much ingenuity and some humour were displayed in making "the punishment fit the crime." The shrew was tamed, as in England, by the application of the Brank or scold's bridle—an iron framework placed over the head in such a way that a plate covered with spikes, which was attached to it, fitted into the mouth. Thieves, like English authors, had their ears cut off. This operation was performed on the Fleischbrücke. The tongues of blasphemers were torn out, and if the banished returned to the city their eyes were gouged out. The latter treatment was often applied in the East to junior princes not required to be heirs. But there the removal of the eyeball gave way, in later times, to the drawing of a red-hot sword blade across the eyeball. In Italy the use of a heated metal basin (bacinare) was preferred. Whilst, in England, we punished drunkenness, as lately as 1872, with confinement in the stocks, the use of the ordinary Nuremberg punishment—"The Drunkard's Cloak"—a barrel worn after the manner of a cloak—was almost confined to Newcastle. The ancient Moslem punishment for wine-drinkers—the pouring of melted lead down the offender's throat—does not appear to have been in vogue. Other devices shown in the Five-Cornered Tower are the Spanish horse, which suggests the modern American method of "riding on a rail," the finger-cramp for bad musicians, pipes for excessive smokers, faces to be worn by husband-beaters, ducking-stools and the wheel, last used in 1788, and the cradle, last used in 1803.

Even the sentence of death was variously performed. Robbers were hanged; murderers beheaded; worse criminals were torn asunder by horses or broken on the wheel. Sinners against the Church were exposed barefooted and bareheaded and hanged before the church doors; sinners against morality were branded. Jews—if it was a question of hanging them—were always hung from the end of the gallows' beam, so that they and the Christians might swing from a different place. Boiling oil does not seem to have been indulged in, though it was used in France for mere counterfeiters, and in England for poisoners. The Bishop of Rochester's cook for instance was treated in this manner in 1630. Terrible as these atrocities were, they are also terribly recent. The last burning at the stake in Germany took place in Berlin, 1786, and in the same year at Vienna occurred the last case of breaking on the wheel. The victim was tortured with red-hot pincers as he walked to the place of execution. And in England the execution of the rebels after the "45" was carried out in exact accordance with the statute of treason of Edward III., 1351, by which the unhappy victim of justice must be drawn to the gallows and not walk; be cut down alive and his entrails be then torn out and burnt before his face.

Women in Nuremberg, as in France and England, were not exposed on gibbets in chains but were buried alive, till 1515, when at the hangman's request they were drowned instead. In 1580 they took to being decapitated. Women who had murdered their husbands were bound to a cart on the way to execution, bared to the waist and tortured with red-hot tongs. The condemned criminal usually walked from the

HENKERSTEG (HANGMAN'S TOWER)

Rathaus over the Barfüsserbrücke to the Frauenthor, where the gallows stood. On the way priests confessed him; pious people prayed for him and supported him with draughts of wine. It is satisfactory to learn that the feeling of the people was usually in favour of the "poor" thing. Fellow-feeling made them wondrous kind, so that if the hangman bungled his business and failed to kill his subject outright the mob might prove dangerous. But the executioners, who lived in the picturesque Henkersteg, were usually masters of their art.[38] They tell us of one great artist who in 1501 killed two robbers almost at a blow. He placed them back to back, two or three yards apart, and took his stand between them. He beheaded the first one, who was kneeling, then with the same sweep, swinging round in a circle, he whipped off the other's head. Clearly he was not devoid of professional pride, and worthy was he to be compared with the executioner in Anne of Geierstein who boasted that

"Tristrem of the Hospital and his famous assistants André and Trois Eschelles are novices compared with me in the use of the noble and knightly sword," and who claimed "if one of my profession shall do his grim office on nine men of noble birth with the same weapon and with a single blow to each patient, hath he not a right to his freedom from taxes and his nobility by patent?"

The day-book of the Nuremberg executioner, 1573-1617, shows that no less than 361 were executed, and 345 were beaten with rods and had their ears and fingers cut off in that period. Besides these there were doubtless many dungeon executions and much cellar practice as well. There were also the victims of the Secret Tribunal, the Vehme-Gericht.

After leaving the torture-chamber we pass the entrance to a passage, inaccessible now by reason of the masses of fallen stone, which leads beyond the town to a distance of nearly two miles, and emerges (it is said) in the forest near Dutzendteich. It was used to despatch envoys, and as a means of access to, and escape for, the Senate in troublous times.

The passage which we follow was constructed about 1543. It runs beneath the streets towards the Castle, making a circuitous course and passing under the Albrecht Dürer Platz. It varies in height from 3 to 7 feet, and, as it nears the Castle, is hewn out of the living rock. Presently we pass on the right the passage which leads down to the Deep Well (see Chap. V.); and then at last we emerge first into the Thiergärtnerthorthurm and then on to the Castle bastion—the Schlosszwinger. This bastion is now a well-kept garden, and the empty, spreading embrasures for guns are now covered with creepers. Our guide leads us out into the Burgstrasse. A few years ago it was possible to descend again into the passages, traverse the inner side of the town-wall and pass into the Castle dungeon—the secret prison of the Vehme-Gericht. Underground passages led thither both from their own tribunal—a hall now used as a warehouse in the Pannier-Gasse—and from the private residences of the Senators. There, too, was that deep and dismal abyss[39] which was wont to receive the mangled remains of the prisoners, mostly of rank, who had been condemned to "kiss the maiden"—die verfluchte Jungfer. He upon whom doom had been passed was forced, after a night spent in her presence, into the embraces of the famous female figure, which stands to-day with Sphinx-like placidity in the Castle. Gradually by cunningly-contrived machinery the Maiden grasped the unhappy man with iron arms and pressed him crushingly to her bosom. But from her body and from her face sharp spikes sank as gradually into his eyes and flesh, piercing him through and through. At last the arms relaxed from their cruel embrace, but only to precipitate him, a mass of ghastly laceration, into the pit below, where the body was received upon sharply-pointed bars of steel placed vertically at the bottom, and was cut to pieces by wheels armed with knives which soon completed this inhuman work of secret destruction. This subsequent cutting into a thousand pieces may be compared with the Chinese Ling-chee, and the Bodoveresta prescribed by Zoroaster for incompetent physicians. Besides its horrid appeal to the imagination, it was doubtless useful in concealing the identity of a prisoner secretly condemned and secretly executed.

There are various parallels to the Nuremberg Maiden. A similar instrument was invented by Nabis, a Spartan tyrant, who named it the Apega, after his wife. But the famous Morton's Maiden in the Museum of Antiquities in Edinburgh is simply a beheading machine, something after the manner of a guillotine. Tradition says that the Regent, Earl of Morton, introduced it into

Scotland and was the first to suffer by it. This is a story as old as the Bull of Phalaris. But it is not likely that Morton introduced it and he was certainly not the first to suffer by it. Similarly the rack was called Exeter's Daughter because the Duke of Exeter is said to have introduced it into England. So, too, the Scavenger's Daughter in the Tower of London took its name from Sir William Skevington, a lieutenant of the Tower under Henry VIII., who revived the use of an iron hoop, in which the prisoner was bent heels to hams and chest to knees, and was thus crushed together unmercifully. In all these cases, it will be observed, the instrument took its title of Maiden or Daughter from the grim contrast that would strike the popular mind between the soft embraces of a girl and the cruel greeting of the machine. It was the sweetest maiden he ever kissed, said the Marquis and Earl of Argyle when he suffered death by Morton's Maiden. So in the navy the gun to which a sailor was lashed before being flogged was termed the Gunner's Daughter.[40] So, too, in the days of the French Revolution, as Dickens tells us, the figure of the sharp female figure called La Guillotine was the popular theme for jests: it was the best cure for headache, it infallibly prevented the hair from turning grey, it imparted a peculiar delicacy to the complexion, it was the National Razor which shaved close; who kissed La Guillotine looked through the little window and sneezed into the sack. In Nuremberg this grim jest was translated into literal earnest. But it must have been difficult for the sufferer to appreciate the hideous humour of the thing.

Not long ago there was an exhibition of torture instruments in London. The Nuremberg Maiden was represented, and round her neck hung a placard with the legend: "Maiden: Nuremberg." A cockney, the story runs, read out this inscription to his companion: "Syme old gyme," was the comment; "Myde in Germany." And it was.

CHAPTER VII

Albert Durer and the Arts and Crafts of Nuremberg. (Michel Wolgemut, Peter Vischer, Veit Stoss, Adam Krafft, etc.)

"Wie friedsam treuer Sitten
Ertrost in that und Werk
Liegt nicht in Deutschlands Mitten
Mein liebes Nüremberg."
—WAGNER, Die Meistersinger.

"Here, when Art was still Religion, with a simple, reverent hart,
Lived and laboured Albrecht Dürer, the evangelist of Art;
Hence in silence and in sorrow, toiling still with busy hand,
Like an emigrant he wandered, seeking for the Better Land.
Emigravit is the inscription on the tomb-stone where he lies;
Dead he is not—but departed,—for the artist never dies."
—LONGFELLOW.

AT Nuremberg, as elsewhere, in the Middle Ages, every trade formed a close corporation, the rules and ordinances of which were subject to the Council alone. These unions, besides enjoying a monopoly of their particular trade, aimed at producing good work after their kind, and at "living together peacefully and amicably, according to the Christian law of brotherly love." Wages and prices were fixed, the relations of masters and subordinates were regulated by the corporations. Equality as well as fraternity was aimed at. Each master was allowed only a certain number of apprentices and workmen, who might not work at night, on Sundays, or on Feast days. Occasionally, in the case of artists whose work was in very great repute and demand, the Council relaxed this rule. By special privilege Adam Krafft was allowed to increase his establishment of workers. The trade-corporations paid great attention to the quality of the goods produced. They were always anxious that only products which were "in the eyes of all good, irreproachable, and without flaw," should be delivered. To guarantee their quality and soundness goods were carefully inspected before being put on sale: shoes or works of art, bread or beef—all alike came under the eye of inspectors appointed by the respective associations. Punishment for infringement of the rules was severe. Two men were burnt alive at Nuremberg in 1456 for having sold adulterated wine.

The modern publican would doubtless be surprised at such treatment.

The youth who was destined for a certain trade had to be apprenticed to some master of that trade, "who," say the rules of the time, "must maintain his apprentice night and day in his house, give him bread and attention (and in some cases even clothes), and keep him under lock and key." The master, who was responsible for his apprentice's work, had also to teach him his trade, and to see that he was brought up in the fear of God, and that he attended church. When the apprenticeship (Lehrjahre) expired the young worker set out on his travels (Wanderjahre) for one, three, or even five years, visiting foreign countries, and learning all he could of his trade. Then he returned and occupied himself, whilst working for a master, in endeavouring to produce a piece of work—his masterpiece—which should entitle him to be admitted to the rank of master.

ALBERT DURER'S HOUSE

That this system had faults, economically, is undeniable. That it produced good work and engendered in the craftsmen a personal interest and pride in their work, is equally certain. Among the craftsmen of Nuremberg in her golden age were Albert Durer, Peter Vischer, Adam Krafft, Veit Stoss, and a host of others eminent in their line. It was under the conditions we have sketched that they learned and laboured.

· ·

Among the most treasured of Nuremberg's relics is the low-ceilinged, gabled house near the Thiergärtnerthor, in which Albert Durer lived and died, in the street now called after his name. The works of art which he presented to the town, or with which he adorned its churches, have unfortunately, with but few exceptions, been sold to the stranger. It is in Vienna and Munich, in Dresden and Berlin, in Florence, in Prague, or the British Museum, that we find splendid collections of Durer's works. Not at Nuremberg. But here at any rate we can see the house in which he toiled—no genius ever took more pains—and the surroundings which impressed his mind and influenced his inspiration. If, in the past, Nuremberg has been only too anxious to turn his works into cash, to-day she guards Albert Durer's house with a care and reverence little short of religious. She has sold, in the days of her poverty and foolishness, the master's pictures and drawings, which are his own best monument; but she has set up a noble monument to his memory (by Rauch, 1840) in the Durer Platz, and his house is opened to the public (on payment of 50 pfennige) between the hours of 8 A.M. and 1 P.M., and 2 and 6 P.M. on week days. The Albert-Durer-Haus Society has done admirable work in restoring and preserving the house in its original state with the aid of Professor Wanderer's architectural and antiquarian skill. Reproductions of Durer's works are also kept here.

The most superficial acquaintance with Durer's drawings will have prepared us for the sight of his simple, unpretentious house and its contents. In his "Birth of the Virgin" he gives us a picture of the German home of his day, where there were few superfluous knick-knacks, but everything which served for daily use was well and strongly made and of good design. Ceilings, windows, doors and door-handles, chests, locks, candlesticks, banisters, waterpots, the very cooking utensils, all betray the fine taste and skilled labour, the personal interest of the man who made them. So in Durer's house, as it is preserved to-day, we can still see and admire the careful simplicity of domestic furniture, which distinguishes that in the "Birth of the Virgin." The carved coffers, the solid tables, the spacious window-seats, the well-fitting cabinets let into the walls, the carefully wrought metal-work we see there are not luxurious; their merit is quite other than that. In workmanship as in design, how utterly do they put to shame the contents of the ordinary "luxuriously furnished apartments" of the present day! Simplex munditiis is the note struck here.

The artists of those days gave themselves no airs: they were content to regard themselves merely as successful workmen. The same hands that carved the most splendid cathedral stalls were ready to lavish equal care on the most insignificant domestic utensil: whilst the simplest artisan was filled with the ambition to turn out work truly artistic. He aimed at perfection, sharing in his master's toil and triumphs, and hoping, no doubt, to produce some day a masterpiece himself.

And what manner of man was he who lived in this house that nestles beneath the ancient castle? In the first place a singularly loveable man, a man of sweet and gentle spirit, whose life was one of high ideals and noble endeavour.[41] In the second place an artist who, both for his achievements and for his influence on art, stands in the very front rank of artists, and of German artists is facile princeps. At whatever point we may study Durer and his works we are never conscious of disappointment. As painter, as author, as engraver or simple citizen, the more we know of him the more we are morally and intellectually satisfied. Fortunately, through his letters and writings, his journals and autobiographical memoirs we know a good deal about his personal history and education.

Durer's grandfather came of a farmer race in the village of Eytas in Hungary. Durer, it has been plausibly suggested, is a Nuremberg rendering of the Hungarian word Ajtó = door = Eytas. The Open Door, Azure, in his canting coat of arms seems to confirm this. The grandfather turned goldsmith, and his eldest son, Albrecht Durer the elder, came to Nuremberg in 1455 and settled in the Burgstrasse (No. 27). He became one of the leading goldsmiths of the town: married and had eighteen children, of whom only three, boys, grew up. Albrecht, or as we call him Albert Durer, was the eldest of these. He was born May 21, 1471, in his father's house, and Anthoni Koberger, the printer and bookseller, the Stein of those days, stood godfather to him. The maintenance of so large a family involved the father, skilful artist as he was, in unremitting toil.

"My dear father," writes Durer, "passed his life in the midst of great toil, and difficult and arduous labour, having only what he earned by his handiwork to support himself, his wife and his family. His possessions were few and in his life he experienced many tribulations, struggles and reverses of all sorts: but all who knew him had a good word to say of him, for he clung to the conduct of a good and honourable Christian. He was a patient and gentle man, at peace with all men and full of gratitude to God."

The portrait he has left of his father (at Munich) corresponds exactly to the character he has thus described. It is the trustful, strenuous face of a worn but strong old man, who seems to accept without regret, in the glad possession of a conscience free from all reproach, a life deprived of all comfort and worldly pleasure. He took great pains to bring up his children in the way they should go.

"My father took much trouble over our education. He brought us up to the glory of God: his chief desire was to keep his children under severe discipline, so that they might be acceptable to God and to man. Every day he urged us to love God and to show a sincere affection for our neighbours." Of his mother, Albert Durer writes, "It was her constant custom to go much to church. She never failed to reprove me every time that I did wrong. She kept us, my brothers and me, with great care from all sin, and on my coming in or my going out, it was her habit to say 'Christ bless thee.' I cannot praise enough her good works, the kindness and charity she showed to all, nor can I speak enough of the good fame that was hers."

His father, who was delighted with Albert's industry, took him from school as soon as he had learned to read and write and apprenticed him to a goldsmith. "But my taste drew me towards painting rather than towards goldsmithry. I explained this to my father, but he was not satisfied, for he regretted the time I had lost."

**ALBERT DURER AS A BOY.
FROM A DRAWING BY HIMSELF AT THE AGE OF
THIRTEEN**

Benvenuto Cellini has told us how his father, in like fashion, was eager that he should practise the "accursed art" of music. Durer's father, however, soon gave in and in 1486 apprenticed the boy to Michel Wolgemut. That extraordinarily beautiful, and, for a boy of that age, marvellously executed portrait of himself at the age of thirteen (now at Vienna) must have shown the father something of the power that lay undeveloped in his son. So "it was arranged that I should serve him for three years. During that time God gave me great industry so that I learnt many things; but I had to suffer much at the hands of the other apprentices."

Painting was already in vogue at Nuremberg in the fourteenth century, but it was never much encouraged. One of the reasons may perhaps have been that there was little opportunity for fresco painting here, as in Italy; for the Gothic style of architecture offers no large surfaces that seem to demand the relief of colour and drawing. Painting was regarded at first merely as an assistant of architecture, glass-blowing and sculpture, for the purposes of decoration and ornament, and painters therefore always continued to be treated as mere artisans of one craft or another. "Here I am a master," writes Durer from Italy, "at home a Parasite." But, however regarded, the art of painting had attained to the dignity of a separate existence when, in the fourteenth century, it was called in to supply the place of sculpture and to furnish altar-pieces and memorial pictures attached to monuments. These latter, "epitaphs," are highly characteristic of northern art, and no better examples of them are to be found than in the great churches of Nuremberg. Many of them, in their original positions, can be seen in the Churches of St. Lorenz and St. Sebald, executed for the great burgher families—Imhoffs, Tuchers, Holzschuhers, etc.—on the death of one of their number. An early example is that of Paul Stromer (1406) in St. Lorenzkirche.

The oldest Nuremberg picture is said to be an altarpiece in St. Jakobskirche. A great advance on this awkward work is the celebrated Imhoff'sche Altar-piece in the Lorenzkirche (1418-22). Of the same period, but more full of colour and movement, are the pictures of the Deokarus Altar in the same church, of the Altar of the Sacristy in St. Jakobskirche, and notably of the Tuchersche Altar in the Frauenkirche (1440). The figures in this picture are more severe and also more vigorous than the graceful, soft, full figures of the Imhoff'sche Altar-piece.

The names of the painters of these works are unknown. Berthold, who was commissioned by the Council in 1423 to paint the interior of the Rathaus, is the only early painter of note whose name has survived. To him some of the earliest epitaphs are safely to be attributed.

So far no outside influence had affected the work of the Nuremberg painters. They were content to supply their pictures with plain gold backgrounds and to subordinate the composition of them to the requirements of the folding divisions of the altar-pieces, carved in stone or wood. The grouping is therefore often crowded and the drawing and arrangement of the limbs and figures frequently approaches the grotesque. But presently, and probably through the agency of Martin Schongauer, the famous engraver and painter of Colmar, the influence of the Flemish School began to make itself felt. The introduction of landscape backgrounds and a great improvement in drawing and composition are noticeable, and may be traced in the Löffelholz Altar-piece in St. Sebald's (1453). In these respects and in the smooth and brilliant colouring, not quite perfectly harmonised, Michel Wolgemut's (1434-1519) earliest works show the influence of the Flemish School in full vigour. It was in 1473 that he married the widow of Hans Pleydenwurf, a painter of some reputation, and in his house, beneath the old Castle, proceeded to carry on the firm of Wolgemut and Pleydenwurf. From this workshop all the principal paintings of that period would seem to have issued. It is extremely difficult to determine how far the pictures that have hitherto passed under the name of Michel Wolgemut are really his. The master has certainly failed as a rule to stamp his own personality on his works. This is no doubt due in great part to the fact that he left much of each picture to be done by his pupils and assistants. The "firm" took a frankly business view of their handiwork. The amount of personal attention Michel Wolgemut gave to a picture probably varied with the price paid for it. It is unfortunate that Durer in many cases followed the same custom. He found that his careful and elaborate style of painting was simply beggaring him, and he frequently therefore allowed his paintings to be finished by his assistants.

Some common characteristics of the Pleydenwurf-Wolgemut School soon impress themselves on us as we study their works in the German Museum, or the Churches of St. Lorenz, St. Sebald, St. John, and St. Jakob. The drapery is stiffly drawn but the colouring remarkably clear and brilliant. The modelling of the limbs, not founded on Durer's close studies of the nude, still leaves much to be desired. The female type is at first sight graceful, but on closer acquaintance we find it soulless and unsatisfying. The prominent cheekbones, straight noses, mild expression of almond-shaped eyes, thin lips and lifeless mouths produce an impression very different from that caused by the almost painful intensity of Durer's portraits. As the fifteenth century draws to a close an increasing severity of design and hardness of expression becomes noticeable. It is not altogether fanciful, I think, to attribute this in part to the stern independent spirit of the Reformation and in part to the prevalence of engraving. For Wolgemut, with Wilhelm Pleydenwurf, paid much attention to woodcarving,[42] and aided doubtless by their youthful apprentice, Albert Durer, illustrated the Schatzbehalter (1491) and the Hartmann-Schedel Chronicle (1493), published by Koberger. The influence of this style of work is perhaps traceable in the flatness and severe modelling of the hands, feet, and faces, and in the stiff movement of the figures in Wolgemut's pictures.

Wolgemut is seen to best advantage in his single figures of saints, as in his Peringsdörffer masterpiece, from the Augustinerkirche, now in the German Museum, the only painting of importance known to have been produced in his studio during Durer's apprenticeship. But even in his best pieces we see little more than the fine feeling of a skilful workman. We look in vain for inspiration, in vain for imagination, we listen in vain for any echo from that world of Perfect Beauty which Durer and the greatest artists have known in part and striven to express. And yet, somehow, his best works do appeal to us and stir our hearts. What the secret of that appeal may be is a question which will doubtless find various answers. Quot homines tot sententiæ. For me it is that Wolgemut speaks in the naïve, straightforward tones of the Middle Ages, and decks the actors of the Sacred Story in the clothes and colours of his own time and his own surroundings. The atmosphere of his pictures is laden with subtle associations. If there was no note of poetry in Wolgemut, still, round the landscapes in his pictures, there hovers a tone like the echo of some old folk-song that has been sung and yet lingers in the air.

. . . .

Albert Durer always entertained the highest respect for his master, and in 1516 painted the immortal portrait of him in his eighty-second year, now in Munich.

When in 1490 his apprenticeship was completed Durer set out on his Wanderjahre, to learn what he could of men and things, and, more especially, of his own trade. Martin Schongauer was dead, but under that master's brothers Durer studied and helped to support himself by his art at Colmar and at Basle. Various wood-blocks executed by him at the latter place are preserved there. Whether he also visited Venice now or not is a moot point. Here or elsewhere, at any rate, he came under the influence of the Bellini, of Mantegna, and more particularly of Jacopo dei Barbari—the painter and engraver to whom he owed the incentive to study the proportions of the human body—a study which henceforth became the most absorbing interest of his life.

"I was four years absent from Nuremberg," he records, "and then my father recalled me.... After my return Hans Frey came to an understanding with my father. He gave me his daughter Agnes and with her 200 florins, and we were married." Durer, who writes so lovingly of his parents, never mentions his wife with any affection: a fact which to some extent confirms her reputation as a Xantippe. She, too, in her way, it is suggested, practised the art of cross-hatching. Pirkheimer, writing after the artist's death, says that by her avariciousness and quarrelling nature she brought him to the grave before his day. She was probably a woman of a practical and prosaic turn, to whom the dreamy, poetic, imaginative nature of the artist-student, her husband, was intolerably irritating. Yet as we look at his portraits of himself—and no man except Rembrandt has painted himself so often—it is difficult to understand how anyone could have been angry with Albert Durer. Never did the face of man bear a more sweet, benign, and trustful expression. In those portraits we see something of the beauty, of the strength, of the weakness of the man so beloved in his generation. His fondness for fine clothes and his legitimate pride in his personal beauty reveal themselves in the rich vestments he wears and the wealth of silken curls, so carefully waved, so wondrously painted, falling proudly over his free neck. Joachim Camerarius, the first rector of the Melanchthon Gymnasium in Nuremberg, tells a pleasant story of how the aged Giovanni Bellini once asked Durer to present him with one of the brushes with which he drew hairs.

"Durer immediately produced several ordinary brushes such as Bellini himself used, and begged him to take the best, or all if he would. Bellini said 'No, I don't mean these. I mean the ones with which you draw several hairs with one stroke. They must be more spread out and more divided; otherwise in a long sweep such regularity of curvature and distance could not be preserved.' 'I use no other than these,' Albrecht replies, 'and, to prove it, you may watch me.' Then taking up one of the same brushes, he drew some very long, wavy tresses, such as women generally wear, in the most regular order and symmetry. Bellini looked on wondering, and afterwards admitted that no human being could have convinced him by report of the truth of that which he had seen with his own eyes."

"Nature had given him a body," says the same writer, "noble in build and structure, consonant with the beautiful mind it contained. His head was expressive, the eyes flashing, the nose nobly formed, and what the Greeks called τετράγωνον (Roman). His neck was long, and his chest broad; his thighs muscular, and legs powerful."

And most noteworthy of all are his exquisitely beautiful hands and fingers, which strike us equally in the portrait of the boy of thirteen, and in the Munich portrait which forms our frontispiece. No one who studies the latter picture can fail to notice how closely the countenance of Durer approaches the ideal type of Jesus Christ in art. The artist, indeed, was conscious of this himself, for his own representations of Christ bear a resemblance to his own features.

On his marriage Durer did not proceed to live in the house of his parents-in-law as was customary, but, for some reason, took up his abode in his father's house. It was his ambition to excel as a painter, but it is as an engraver that he won his hold on the world—and still retains it. Copperplate engraving had been practised as early as the first quarter of the fifteenth century. It had been developed out of the goldsmith's art, and perfected by the masters E. S. and Martin Schongauer. There was a great demand for engravings. Accordingly, with a view to earning the much needed money for his family, Durer at first devoted himself to this art. We can trace clearly enough the progress of the artist as he endeavoured to produce not merely the simple representation of a subject, but by the aid of landscape backgrounds, a picture, an artistic whole on the copper. For this purpose he turned to account his early studies of Nuremberg scenery and his charming drawings of Nuremberg, the Pegnitz, and the houses to which he was ever devoted. Piracy of his works soon followed on and proved his popularity. Literary piracy, it will be seen, if not yet respectable, is at any rate of some antiquity. Meantime he was busy painting the portraits of members of patrician families, of his father, of himself. For these we must not seek in Nuremberg, but an example of his painting at this period (circa 1500), is to be found in the Pietà, now in the German Museum. In painting, it was Durer's rule to deal only with sacred subjects or portraits. The much damaged and inferior work, "Hercules with the Stymphalian Birds," in the same museum forms an interesting exception to this rule. But in his engravings Durer did not confine himself to any one subject: sacred and secular history, mythology, animals, satire, humour, architecture, land and water scapes, portraits, all formed material for his receptive and strenuous mind. His humour may be studied in his designs for Maximilian's "Book of Hours," and there, too, his mordant satire lashes the faults of vain women and the gaucheries of proud and foolish peasants.

We have already had occasion to refer to the circle in which Durer moved in these days; but special mention should here be made of Willibald Pirkheimer, his great friend and patron, the most generous Mæcenas of sciences and art in Nuremberg. Scholar and statesman, writer, orator, and soldier, his house and splendid library in the Herrenmarkt was the centre of intellectual activity in Germany, and the chief meeting-place of the Humanists. Maximilian I., Conrad Celtes, Eobanus Hesse, Luther and Melanchthon, and especially Ulrich von Hutten and Durer were among his most favoured and frequent guests. He was a constant correspondent

ST. ANTHONY, FROM THE ENGRAVING BY ALBERT DURER. BACKGROUND OF NUREMBERG SCENERY

also of Reuchlin and Erasmus. A martyr to gout, he was naturally choleric, but he had the humour to write a poem in praise of gout. His quick temper and vehement opinions led to his quarrelling in time with every friend except the gentle Durer. Coarse and caustic was his wit: and it is only under his influence that Durer ever shows these qualities. Pirkheimer was, in fact, a great man, a very great man, in his day; but he lives now through his friendship with Durer, and through the portrait, that marvellous engraving so full of character, which Durer published in 1524.

Besides copper-engraving and painting Durer also turned his attention to wood-engraving, and by his admirable work and designs began to give it its place among the pictorial arts. One of his earliest woodcuts is entitled The Men's Bath. It represents a group of nude male figures in one of those open-air public baths in the Pegnitz, which are still used in Nuremberg, and of which an old writer says: "A solicitude particularly attentive to the needs of the working classes and to the health and well-being of artisans, servants and the poor, has established baths in the towns and villages: it is a habit very praiseworthy and profitable to the health to take a bath at least once a fortnight." There were a dozen such public baths at Nuremberg, often visited by Durer no doubt in his pursuit of the study of the nude. He continued to pour forth works drawn from mythology and church history, until in 1498 he produced that "great trumpet-call of the Reformation," the famous series of wood-cut illustrations to the Apocalypse. In this series, so full of artistic skill and imagination, Durer not only reveals to us the aspirations of his own mind, but he also expresses the thoughts and emotions of the age in which he lived. The Apocalypse, in which under the veil of religious symbolism are made to appear the terrible judgments of the Lord and the peace of his saints, was followed by that sweet and tender poem, The Life of Mary, and by the Great and the Little Passion, two sublime tragedies that leave nothing to be desired in truth of expression and vigour of design. Durer put his whole soul into these religious works—the same deeply penitent, simply trusting soul which he reveals to us in his prayers, his diaries, and his books. How real his subjects were to him, how homely his religion, is indicated by the inevitable manner in which he transfers the scenes of Holy Writ to the ordinary surroundings of his daily life in Nuremberg. Deeply imbued with the religious spirit, he tells this pictorial history of the Christian faith as one to whom it was indeed a living reality and a very intimate part of his life.

But before this immortal series was finished various important events occurred in the life of the artist. In 1502 his father died.

"O all you who are my friends," writes Albert, in words that remind us of St. Augustine, "I pray you for the love of God, when you read the account of my good father's death, remember his soul, and say for him a Pater and an Ave. Do so too for your own salvation, that we may all obtain the grace of truly serving God, and that it may be granted to us to lead a holy life and to make a good end. No, it is not possible that he who has lived a good life should leave this world with regret or fear, for God is full of mercy."

In the following year were produced the tender Virgin and Child, and in 1504 the Adam and Eve, in which the fruits of his study of the nude were given to the world in ideal figures of man before the Fall. Next year another break occurred in Durer's career. Whether, as Vasari says, to secure himself against the piracy of his engravings, or merely in search of fresh knowledge, towards which "his lofty mind was ever striving," Durer paid another visit to Venice in 1505. Here he painted for the German colony, as an altar-piece in the Church of St. Bartolommeo, the Madonna del Rosario, now at Prague. This picture contains portraits of Maximilian, Julius II., Durer, Pirkheimer, and several German merchants. So great was the admiration roused by it that the Doge visited the artist and endeavours were made to induce him to live permanently in Venice. But in 1507, in spite of all temptations, he returned to his native town and proceeded to execute many commissions. In 1508 he obtained an injunction from the Council to prevent the fraudulent copying of his prints. In the same year a Nuremberg worthy, Matthäus Landauer, added a chapel to the almshouses (Zwölfbrüderhaus or Landauerkloster) he had founded in 1501. The chapel was dedicated to All Saints, and Durer was invited to paint an altar-piece for it, representing "The Adoration of the Trinity by all Saints." The result, the Allerheiligenbild, is one of the artist's noblest and most famous compositions, but it too has left Nuremberg. For in 1585 the Rat sold it to Emperor Rudolph II., replacing it by a copy for which they retained the original frame.

In 1509 Durer bought the Durer-haus and took his aged mother to live with him there. He also bought his father's house in the Burgstrasse off his brother. This in itself shows that the stories of his poverty have been much exaggerated. On his death he left 6858 gulden—a very good fortune in those days. His connection with Maximilian, to which we have already referred,[43] no doubt brought him something, though he had difficulty in procuring the payment of the pension allowed him by the Emperor. The Council, in 1510, at last gave a sign that they were aware of the presence of a great artist in their city by ordering Durer to paint the portraits of Charlemagne and Sigismund, to be displayed at the festival when the Imperial insignia and sacred relics—many of which were introduced into the pictures—were shown to the people. These portraits, into the former of which Durer introduced the features of Stabius, Maximilian's poet-laureate, are now in the German Museum, much restored and over-daubed with repaintings.

The illness and death of his mother in 1514 caused Albert Durer very great grief. Most touching is his description of that event.

"Just a year after she had fallen ill, my mother died in a Christian manner, after having received full absolution. Before dying she gave me her blessing, and with many pious words invoked upon me the peace of God, recommending me above all to keep myself from all sin. She had much fear of death, but, she said, she had no fear of appearing before the Lord. She suffered when she died, and I observed that she saw before her something which terrified her, for she asked for holy water, although she had not uttered a word for a long time. At last her eyes grew fixed and I saw Death deal her two great blows to the heart. Then she closed her eyes and mouth and died suffering. I betook myself to reciting prayers at her side, and experienced such paroxysms of anguish as I cannot express to you. May God have mercy on my mother! It was always her greatest joy to speak to us of God, and she saw with gladness everything that could increase the glory of the Lord. She was sixty-three years of age when she died, and I had her interred honourably according to my means. May our Lord give me grace to die a holy death even as she died! May God with all the heavenly host, my father, my mother, my relatives and my friends, be present at my end! May God Almighty grant us the life everlasting! Amen. And after my mother was dead her face became more beautiful than it had been during her life."

Sorrow is the source of most great works of art. In his sorrow Durer produced his three most famous, best-wrought engravings, works full of imagination and of thought, works in which, expressed in exquisite draughtsmanship, lies his whole philosophy. Through St. Jerome in his Library, The Knight, Death and the Devil, and Melencolia, Durer has more than elsewhere revealed himself to us and shown us his outlook upon things, his manner of regarding the world, his criticism of life.

On the death of Maximilian Durer travelled to the Court of Charles V. in order to get his pension confirmed. He succeeded in his object, and, after travelling through the Netherlands, where he was accorded a great reception, he returned to Nuremberg in 1521, having refused the pressing invitation of the Council of Antwerp that he should take up his residence in their city. When he returned he received another commission from the Rat—to design decorative paintings for the great hall of the Council-house. But Durer's health was broken and his prolific imagination was flagging. He seems to have taken little interest in this commission. He chose the time-worn subject of the Calumny of Apelles for one design, and used his unfinished sketch of Maximilian's Triumphal Car for the other. The painting was carried out by Georg Pencz and others of his pupils. Durer's last great imaginative effort was the painting of the Four Preachers, two large upright panels with figures of St. Peter and St. John on the one, and St. Mark and St. Paul on the other. These, as his final message to his native town, he presented in 1526 to his gunstigen und gnädigen Herren, the Council of Nuremberg.

Painter, designer, engraver, mathematician, Durer was also an author. The year before he died, he published his "Instructions how to Use the Compass" and "Instructions how to Fortify Towns, Castles, and Villages," and after his death appeared the four books of his life-long work on "The Human Proportions."

His life had been passed in a strenuous endeavour to perfect his art: he died amid a universal chorus of regret, on April 6th, 1528. His grave is in St. John's Churchyard (No. 649). A plain bronze plate on the headstone bears his well-known monogram and the following inscription:—

ME(ister) AL(brecht) DU(rer)

QUICQUID ALBERTI DVRERI MORTALE
FUIT, SVB HOC CONDITUR TUMULO.
EMIGRAVIT, VIII, IDUS APRILE,
M., D. XXVIII.

"I can truthfully say," wrote Durer to the Council, "that in the thirty years I have stayed at home, I have not received from people in this town work worth 500 gulden—truly an absurd and trifling sum—and not a fifth part of that has been profit." After his death his fellow-citizens became more fully alive to the value of his works, and the worthy shopkeepers began those transactions which gradually stripped Nuremberg of almost all the master's drawings and paintings. I borrow the following account from Mr Lionel Cust's excellent monograph on "The Paintings and Drawings of Albert Durer":—

"The greater part of his drawings, which were made for his own use, appear to have passed into the possession of his life-long friend, Pirkheimer, perhaps handed over by Durer's widow to redeem the many financial obligations under which Durer lay to his friend. The sketch-books used by Durer in the Netherlands seem to have passed into the possession of the Pfinzing family, and were dispersed by their next owner. At Pirkheimer's death the whole of his collections, including the paintings and drawings by Durer, became the property of the Imhoff family, the bankers and usurers of Nuremberg. The Imhoffs, as befits a good, steady, money-making firm, seem to have regarded Durer's works as a marketable commodity. At the end of the sixteenth century, when the Emperor Rudolph II. was forming his great collection of works of art and curiosities, the Imhoffs, knowing his intense admiration for the works of Durer, pressed upon him the collection of paintings and drawings which they possessed. The Town Council of Nuremberg seem to have followed suit with the paintings which were immediately under their control, if not actually in their possession. In a short time Rudolph became possessed of the bulk of Durer's paintings and drawings at Prague or Vienna. Several of the paintings remain in the Imperial collection to this day, and a large portion of the drawings now forms the nucleus of what is known as the 'Albertina' collection at Vienna. Another portion of the Imhoff collection found its way through a collector in the Netherlands, perhaps through one of the Austrian governors, into that of Sir Hans Sloane, and is now in the print-room at the British Museum. These two collections, together with the great collection, which official industry and acumen have brought together at Berlin, are the best field for the study of Durer's work as a draughtsman, although in some of the smaller public or private collections some of the most remarkable examples are to be found.

"The good citizens of Nuremberg continued their work of converting Durer's works into hard cash whenever the opportunity occurred. In 1585 the Town Council persuaded or compelled the governors of the Landauer almshouses to sell to the Emperor Rudolph their great painting of All Saints, replacing it by a copy which, by way of carrying out the deception, was inserted in the original frame designed by Durer. The Adam and Eve also appear to have passed into the same Imperial hands. In 1627 the Council sold to the Elector Maximilian of Bavaria the two great panels of the Four Preachers, Durer's last gift to his native town, and replaced them by copies. The long inscriptions from the Bible were cut off from the original panels and added on below the copies. A few years before, in 1613, they had presented the same Elector with the beautiful Baumgärtner altar-piece, which was torn from its place in St. Catherine's Church at Nuremberg. The two Descents from the Cross followed in the same channel: and the Praun collection at Nuremberg yielded up the portrait of Wolgemut and the portrait of Hans Durer. Worst of all, the portrait of their beloved and honoured citizen, the world-famous portrait of Durer by himself, which had become actually the property of the Town Council, was lent by them to a local painter to copy; this ingenious craftsman sawed the panel in half, and glued his copy on to the back, on which were the town seal and other marks of ownership, and sold the original to King Ludwig of Bavaria. The worthy magistrates never discovered the fraud, or pretended not to, and this copy hangs to-day at Nuremberg a monument of dishonour and fraud. Gradually Nuremberg divested itself of every work by Durer which it could, and rejoiced in its copies and its cash. Ludwig I. of Bavaria took pity on its denuded condition, and gave back to it as a gift the Descent from the Cross, known as the Peller altar-piece, and also apparently returned from Schleissheim the Hercules and the Stymphalian Birds. With the overdaubed paintings of Charlemagne and Sigismund, these appear to be the only authenticated paintings by Durer in his native town at the present day. Three hundred years after Durer's death, a statue was erected to him in Nuremberg, and his house is now preserved and shown as a national relic. Yet little more than fifty years after the erection of this statue, in 1884, the citizens allowed the famous 'Holzschuher' portrait, the last great work by Durer which the town possessed, to be sold by the family, to whom it still belonged, to the Munich Gallery. Truly a prophet hath little honour in his own country!"

Of the pupils and assistants of Durer who carried on his tradition we may mention Hans Schäuflein, Albert Altdorfer, Hans Baldung, Georg Pencz, the two Behaims and the two Sebalds, and Hans von Kulmbach. We meet with many examples of their work in the churches and in the German Museum.

. . . .

As we turn our steps from Durer's house and wander through the Durer-platz to St. Sebald's we come upon the oldest restaurant in Nuremberg, where the devout tourist should not fail to drink ein Glas Bier to the memory of Hans Sachs, Pirkheimer, and Durer, who sat here, drank and talked in days gone by. The Bratwurstglöcklein is a little beerhouse clinging to the north wall of St. Moritz Chapel, and owes its name, I suppose, to the custom of ringing a small bell when the sausage was ready. As to the curious position of this little restaurant we may remark that the practice of bargaining in the sacred precincts was very prevalent at one time, and little booths were frequently built on to the churches. It is only quite recently that the booths attached to the Frauenkirche were broken up.

. . . .

North of the Rathaus runs the Theresien Strasse. No. 7 is the house of Adam Krafft, the greatest of Nuremberg sculptors (1430-1507). The house belonged originally to the Pfinzing family, and is of interest in itself for its architectural features. The figure of St. Moritz on the fountain in the courtyard is by Peter Vischer. Here Adam Krafft, the pious and modest stone-mason, worked at his art to the glory of God. We know next to nothing of the man beyond what we can learn from his handiwork. There is fortunately little reason for believing the legend that he died in great poverty. A friend we know he was of Lindenast and Vischer, with whom, so great was his industry and eagerness to improve in art, he used to practise drawing on holidays, even in his old age; and it is recorded that he made his wife call herself Eva because he was Adam. That quaint humour of his is revealed in the pleasing relief over the gateway of the "Waage" or old weighing-house in the Winklerstrasse. If we would see the counterfeit presentment of the man himself, we must pay a visit to St. Lorenzkirche, and there, on the pedestal of his masterpiece the figure of the master appears with the tools and in the costume of his craft, kneeling in company with his assistants and supporting their beautiful creation.

A simple man, of calm, unruffled temper and fervent faith he must have been, thoroughly representative of the best German spirit of his day. No German artist has portrayed the scenes of Christ's passion with greater depth of genuine feeling. Happily many of his principal works are at Nuremberg. Probably the earliest examples of Nuremberg sculpture are the figures of Adam and Eve and the prophets round the portal of St. Lorenzkirche. They date from the fourteenth century. In point of style and execution it is a far cry from these stern and angular figures to the almost supernatural grace and lightness of Krafft's Pix within the cathedral. Well did legend pay him the pretty compliment of saying that he knew the art of founding stone like bronze. Tender and graceful as the artist here shows himself, the strength and vigour of his reliefs are equally remarkable. His treatment of the folds of garments seems to reflect the influence of the Netherland school, and to point to a dangerous striving after the effects of painting. For his subjects Krafft rarely went outside the New Testament, which he interpreted in the terms of Nuremberg life and dress. His figures, like those in the works of his contemporaries at Nuremberg, are in most cases short, not to say dumpy, and reflect, no doubt, the ordinary type of human form around him. But always the homely Nuremberg costumes in which they are clad seem to bring the scenes portrayed nearer to our hearts; and thereby when a Mary draws to her breast the head of her crucified Son, or a Magdalene at the feet of Jesus waters His feet with her tears, we are impressed the more vividly with sympathy for their sorrow.

One of his earliest works, if, as I think, it is indeed by him, is the Last Judgment over the Schauthüre, on the south-east side of St. Sebaldskirche. His earliest works of unquestioned authority are the Seven Stations of the Cross on the Burgschmietsstrasse. These are a series of bas-reliefs on seven pillars, each representing a scene in the passion of our Lord. Starting from the house of the founder they mark the way to St. John's churchyard. Some of them are much defaced by time and some have been carefully copied by Burgschmiet,[44] but here and there we can still recognise the vigorous touch of Adam Krafft, and they still keep green the memory of their pious founder. Martin Ketzel, somewhere about the year 1470, had undertaken a pilgrimage to the Holy Land. Struck by the fact that the distance between Pilate's house and Golgotha was exactly that between his own house and St. John's Churchyard, he returned home with various measurements, determined to erect at certain intermediate stations some pieces of sculpture commemorative of our Saviour's passion. To his dismay when he arrived he discovered that he had lost his precious measurements. There was nothing for it but to return to Jerusalem and take the measurements afresh. For he could trust no one to perform so important a task for him. This time he was more successful, and Adam Krafft was commissioned to provide the reliefs. Starting from Pilate's house, which was represented by Ketzel's own house—Thiergärtnerthorplatz (opposite Durer's house—it is adorned by the statue of an armed knight) the pillars were placed at intervals, marking the spots corresponding to those where Christ was said to have rested on the real Dolorous Way to Mount Calvary. Calvary itself is represented at St. John's. Each pillar bears an inscription:—

1. Hir begegnet Christus seiner wirdigen lieben Muter die vor grossem hertzenleit anmechtig ward. 200 Srytt von Pilatus haws.

2. Hir ward Symon gezwungen Cristo sein krewtz helfen tragen. 295 Sryt von Pilatus haws.

3. Hir sprach Christus Jr Döchter von Jherusalem nit weint über mich, sünder uber euch und ewvre kinder. 380 Srytt von Pilatus haws.

4. Hier hat Christus sein heiligs Angesicht der heiligen Fraw Veronica auf iren Slayr gedruckt vor irem Haws. 500 Sryt von Pilatus Haws.

5. Hier tregt Christus das Creuz und wird von den Juden ser hart geslagen. 780 Srytt von Pilatus Haws.

6. Hier felt Cristus vor grosser unmacht auf die Erden bei 1000 Srytt von Pilatus haws.

Then on a small eminence by the gate of the Cemetery we behold the last sad scenes of Calvary reproduced. It is a noble group which moves us alike by the pathos and dignity of its treatment and by the beauty of the inscription.

7. Hir legt Cristus tot vor seiner gebenedeyten wirdigen Muter die in mit grosem Herzenleyt und bitterlichen smertz claget und beweynt.

In the Holzschuher Chapel near at hand is Krafft's last work (1507) the Burial of Christ. In this piece, which lacks the fervent feeling of his earlier representations of Christ's passion and was probably chiefly executed by his assistants, the figure of Joseph of Arimathea is a portrait of Adam Krafft. Krafft in his prime (1492) had dealt with the same subject in the Sebald-Schreyer-tomb on the outer wall of the Choir of St. Sebaldskirche, facing the Rathaus. The "Burial" in St. John's Church seems cold and hard compared with the pathos and beauty of this masterpiece, so finely composed and exquisitely wrought.

Other works of Adam Krafft's which well repay study are:—

1496. Bearing the Cross, St. Sebaldskirche.

1501. The Last Supper, Mount of Olives and Betrayal, behind the High Altar, St. Sebaldskirche.

1504. The Annunciation, on the house at the corner of Winklerstrasse and Schulgässchen.

1499. The Crowning of Mary (Pergenstorfer Relief) in the Frauenkirche.

1499. Madonna with Child, on the corner-house, Wunderburggässlein.

1501. Crowning of Mary, in the Tetzellchapel of the Ægidien Church.

But most important of all stands in the St. Lorenzkirche the wonderful Pix, Ciborium, Weibrodgehäuse, or Sakramentshäuslein, wherein were deposited the elements of the Eucharist, previous to consecration. This "miracle of German art" (1496-1500) was made on commission for Hans Imhoff, a member of the great family of merchant princes, who died in 1499, a year before it was finished, though long after it was due to be delivered. His heirs, however, recognised the merit of the master who, inspired by friendly rivalry with Vischer's Sebaldusgrab, completed at last so great a work of art. They gave to Krafft 70 gulden more than the 700 gulden he asked, and to his wife a mantle worth 6 gulden.

SAKRAMENTSHÄUSLEIN. (ADAM KRAFFT)

Nuremberg, so rich in legend, tells a story of the origin of the Pix. A servant of Hans Imhoff was accused of having stolen a goblet and, in terror of being tortured, confessed the theft. He suffered death accordingly. But a little while afterwards the goblet was found, full of wine, beneath a bed, where it had been placed, it was surmised, by some guest who had been drinking too freely. As an atonement for his hastiness Hans Imhoff dedicated this offering to the Lord.

Similar, but inferior Weihbrodgehäusen by Adam Krafft are to be seen at Schwabach and at Heilsbronn. That by the Master of Weingarten at Ulm rivals though it can scarcely surpass the St. Lorenzkirche masterpiece.

The life-size kneeling figures of the master, in the middle with cap, apron and mallet, and two assistants, the one with a measure and the other with a chisel, support the balcony which runs round the Ciborium. The pillars of the balustrade are adorned with eight figures of saints, including St. Lorenz (with gridiron) and St. Sebald.

On the pillars of the Ciborium itself (beneath which are small angels and escutcheons), are the statues of Moses, John, Mary, and James the Less.

Above the receptacle rises a spire like a bishop's crosier, representing perhaps the crook of the Good Shepherd. It is ornamented with statuettes of saints, and as the Holy Sacrament was instituted to commemorate the death of the Redeemer the artist has added reliefs representing episodes of the Passion, which with the Resurrection complete for all believers the fruits of the Holy Supper.

- 1. Christ comforting the Women.
- 2. The Holy Supper.
- 3. The Mount of Olives.

Above these again are four patriarchs and eight angels holding signs of the passion, which interpreted as instruments of torture may have given rise to the story of the origin of the Pix. Then—

- 4. Christ before Pilate.
- 5. The Crown of Thorns.
- 6. The Crucifixion. SS. Mary and John and a kneeling figure (the Church?).

On the pillars above stand the four Evangelists(?) and above all the figure of the risen Saviour, the right hand stretched out in benediction, the left holding the banner of victory.

But apart from the details of the carving, it is the grace of the fretted Gothic pinnacle of finest filigree stonework that seizes our attention. Tapering, or rather mounting airily on high it carries the eye up to the spandril of the vaulting of the choir, soaring like the notes of a flute-like voice, and embodying, as it were, the utterance of some deeply spiritual aspiration. The delicate elaboration of this wonderful stonework seems to have overcome all terrestial heaviness. Higher still and higher, it springs from the earth like Shelley's skylark, but it fades not from view. For when, some sixty feet from the ground, the bend of the vaulting checks its further growth, it bows its beautiful head and like a lily on its stalk or snowdrop on its stem terminates in a pendant flower. It is indeed a miracle of rare device. So slender and graceful is it and withal so clear-cut that the triumph of the artist over his material seems almost unearthly, whilst the spring and proportion of the whole and the sharpness of the carving redeem him from the imputation of making an inappropriate use of stone. In this, as in the Schreyertomb, it is usual to trace the influence of Durer on the sculptor. To me it seems more probable that Adam Krafft's style with its excessive minuteness influenced Albert Durer and was in turn influenced by Martin Schongauer.

Wood-carving (as a visit to the Museum will demonstrate) flourished exceedingly at Nuremberg. There were indeed so many carvers there towards the end of the fifteenth century that it is difficult to understand how they all gained a livelihood. The greatest artist among them, if we except the unknown master of the Nuremberg Madonna in the Museum, was certainly Veit Stoss. Born in 1440 he was of abstemious and frugal habits and lived till 1533. In 1477 he gave up his rights of citizenship, went to Poland, and at Cracow made a great reputation by the high altar and choir-stalls he carved for the Church of St. Mary there. Like Durer he was very versatile—a carver in wood and stone, painter, engraver, mechanician, and architect. But unlike most of the great artists of this period, his character was stained by a considerable crime.

On returning to Nuremberg in 1496 he was nick-named the Pole and was presently condemned on a charge of forging a signature to a document which was to substantiate his claim against a Nuremberg merchant, whom he accused of having cheated him out of a sum of money. He was sentenced to be branded on both cheeks—a gentle punishment, seeing that a forger was liable to lose both eyes. The Council also compelled him to swear that he would never leave Nuremberg, but, when he found that no one would work with him, he fled. But later, the Council pardoned him and received him back. They seem to have appreciated his artistic gifts as much as Maximilian. Stoss worked very diligently at Nuremberg and received orders even from Transylvania and Portugal. Whatever his character—and it is fair to add that on the count of forgery he always maintained that he was unjustly accused—his art will always bring him praise. Of his numberless altar-pieces, crucifixes and Madonnas, the very beautiful wood gilt crucifix and the much-admired Angels' Greeting, both in the Lorenzkirche, are the most famous. His earliest work in Nuremberg is a painted carving of the Madonna and Child on the north wall of the Frauenkirche, executed for the old Welser Altar (1504). Veit Stoss, it is pointed out in his later work, exhibits the increasing influence of Albert Durer, but nowhere more unmistakably than in the "Englischer Gruss" (1518)—the Angelic Greeting, which hangs from the roof of the Lorenzkirche, a work of tender piety, in which the delicacy of the figures is very noticeable. Formerly the Greeting hung in the choir suspended by a costly chain. But owing to the torrent of coarse abuse which Osiander, the great preacher and reformer, hurled against it, it was wrapped up in a green sack, on which were set the Tucher arms. Later on, the chain was replaced by a rope. Then the Greeting was moved about from church to church till at last it returned to St. Lawrence's. But it was insecurely hung, and in 1817 it fell from a height of 50 feet and was broken to pieces. It was very skilfully put together again by the brothers Rotermundt. But the huge crown which originally surmounted it was not restored.

Celebrated as this carving is, and beautiful as are many of the individual figures and details in the medallions, the Angelic Greeting as a whole is, I confess, too florid and too heavy for my taste. So that, rather than be dishonest in my enthusiasms, I will only add (without superciliousness) that for those who like this sort of thing, this is the sort of thing they like.

The praying Mary, who holds in her left hand a book, her right hand being laid upon her breast, and an angel with the staff of the Annunciation, stand alone, over life-size, in the centre of a rose-wreath frame. Over the wreath is carved God the Father, sitting between two angels, with crown and sceptre, blessing the figures beneath. Other angels hovering about Mary make heavenly music. Under the wreath, Eve's serpent (with the apple), is being conquered by the Ave with which the Angel of Annunciation greets Mary.

On the wreath itself, seven round medallions in low relief represent the seven joys of Mary:—the Annunciation, Visitation, Birth of Christ, (cf. the Rosenkranz-tafel in the Museum), Adoration of the Wise Men, Resurrection of Christ, Pouring out of the Holy Spirit, and Crowning of Mary.

....

Krafft and Stoss worked in the Gothic style, but Peter Vischer (1455-1529), the bronze founder, except in his early works, of which there are no examples in Nuremberg, shows the influence of the Italian Renaissance. Perhaps this had come to him through Jacopo dei Barbari, whose influence on Durer we have noted. However that may be, Peter Vischer remains a truly original artist. And yet, the son of a coppersmith, he ever continued to regard himself as a simple artisan. With a workman's cap, and a large leather apron round his waist, with hammer and chisel in hand, the signs of his calling, he has portrayed himself to us in his most beautiful work of art— the shrine of St. Sebald. There, in a niche facing the altar, stands, thick-set and full-bearded, the modest, pious labourer, whose reputation had spread beyond the limits of Germany, and whose bronze work, if we may believe the chronicler, once "filled Poland, Bohemia, Hungary, and the palaces of princes throughout the Holy Roman Empire." Seldom did prince or potentate come to Nuremberg without paying a visit to Vischer's workshop. Adam Krafft and Sebastien Lindenast, the coppersmith who made works of art of copper "as if they had been of gold or silver," and who is responsible for the copper figures which adorn the Frauenkirche clock, were his two bosom friends. They seemed, we are told, to have but one heart. All three were equally simple, disinterested, and ever eager to learn. "They were like brothers: every Friday, even in their old age, they met and studied together like apprentices, as the designs which they executed at their meetings prove. Then they separated in friendly wise, but without having eaten or drunk together."

The masterpiece[45] of Peter Vischer is without doubt the shrine of St. Sebald, the highest expression of German art in this kind. Imagination, which is so much lacking in most German art, is found here in plenty, and in a still higher degree the artist displays his sense of form and his careful attention to detail. To find any work of the fifteenth century which can vie with this in richness of fancy and in depth of feeling, as well as in successful handling of bronze, we must go I think to Ghibellino Ghiberti's gates of the Baptistry at Florence. The criticism, however, which must be passed on the Sebaldusgrab is that the parts are very much greater than the whole; but the beauty and finish of the details are so great that once we are within range of their influence we forget and forgive any fault that may have caught our eye in the proportionment of the complete structure.

It was in 1507 that Vischer received the commission to make this superb receptacle for the bones of St. Sebald. For twelve years he with his five sons laboured, though their labour was often interrupted by want of funds. Private subscriptions failed to supply the cost even of the 15,700 pounds— about 7 tons—of metal used. At last when, in 1519, Anton Tucher in moving words had told the citizens in St. Sebald's Church that they ought to subscribe the 800 gulden still wanting "for the glory of God and His Holy Saint," the money was forthcoming, and the monument was completed.

The iron railings which surround it were made by George Heuss, who was also responsible for the clockwork at the Frauenkirche and the mechanism for drawing water at the deep well on the Paniersberg.

Round the base of the shrine runs the following inscription:—"Peter Vischer Bürger in Nürnberg machet dieses Werk, mit seinen Söhnen, ward vollbracht im Jahr, 1519. Ist allein Gott dem allmächtigen zu lob und St. Sebald dem Himmelsfürsten zu ehren, mit Hülf andächtiger Leut von dem Almosen bezahlt."

That is the keynote of this wonderful structure. Through years of difficulty and distress the pious artist had toiled and struggled on with the help of pious persons, paid by their voluntary contributions, to complete a work "to the praise of God Almighty alone and the honour of St. Sebald." No words, one feels, can add to the simple dignity and faith of that inscription. It supplies us with the motive of the work, and it supplies us also with the interpretation of the various groups and statues which form the shrine. To the glory of God,—we are shown how all the world, all nature and her products, all paganism with its heroic deeds and natural virtues, the Old Dispensation with its prophets and the New with its apostles and saints, pay homage to the Infant Christ, who enthroned on the summit holds in his hands the terrestrial globe. To the honour of St. Sebald,—the miniature Gothic chapel of bronze, under the richly fretted canopy some fifteen feet high, contains the oaken coffer encased with silver in which the bones of St. Sebald lie; and below this sarcophagus, which dates from 1397, are admirable bas-reliefs representing scenes and miracles from the life of the Saint.[46]

At the feet of the eight slender pillars which support the canopy are all sorts of strange figures and creatures suggestive of the world of pagan mythology, gods of the forest and of the sea, nymphs of the water and the wood. Between them are some lions couchant, which recall to the memory Wolgemut's Peringsdörffer Altar-piece. At the four corners are candlesticks held by most graceful and seductive winged mermaids. But the most famous and the most beautiful figures are those of the Twelve Apostles, which stand, each about two feet, on high brackets and in niches on the pillars of the canopy. Clad in graceful, flowing robes, their expression and whole attitude expressive both of vigour and of tranquil dignity, these statues are wholly admirable. I know no sculpture or painting which conveys to a higher degree the sense of the intellectual and moral beauty and strength which centred in these first followers of Christ. That characteristic pervades them all, but the unity of suggestion is conveyed through a variety of individualities and of actions. Each apostle stands forth distinct in the vigour of his own inspired personality.

Those at the east end of the monument are St. Peter and St. Andrew; on the north, or right side as we face these, are SS. Simon, Bartholomew, Thomas, and Matthew; on the south, or left, SS. John, James, Philip, and Paul; and on the west SS. Thaddæus and Matthias.

The apostles are surmounted by the forms of the Fathers of the Church, or rather perhaps of the twelve minor prophets. Beneath the apostles, on the substructure in a niche facing west, is a fine statue of St. Sebald, and at the corresponding place on the other end of the monument is the excellent statue of P. Vischer himself, to which we have referred.

Right at the bottom, at the foot of the four corner pillars, are the nude figures of Nimrod with his bow and quiver, of Samson with the slaughtered lion and jawbone of an ass, Perseus with sword and shield and in company of a mouse, and innumerable other little animals; Hercules with a club. Between these heroes, in the centre of either side, are female figures representing the four chief manly Virtues—Strength in a coat of mail with a lion, Temperance with vessel and globe, Truth with mirror and book, and

Justice with sword and balance. In all, besides the apostles and prophets, there are seventy-two figures, in the presentation of which amidst flowers and foliage the exuberant fancy of the artist has run riot. But all are subordinated to the two central ideas which animate the whole, and all are executed with a delicacy and finish little short of marvellous. The whole fabric rests on twelve large snails with four dolphins at the corners.

Peter Vischer died in 1529 and was buried in the Rochus Churchyard. His sons and Pankraz Labenwolf proved worthy successors in his art. Labenwolf was responsible for the Gänsemännchen fountain in the Gänsemarkt, the fountain in the Court of the Rathaus and perhaps for the St. Wenzel in the Landauerbrüderhaus. After Peter Vischer's death his sons received an order to complete for the Great Hall of the Rathaus a very beautiful bronze railing, which their father had begun in 1513 for the family of Fugger in Augsburg, who, however, had withdrawn their commission. This railing, which divided the Great Hall, was a work of very great artistic excellence. But it was taken away in 1806 by the Bavarian Government, and sold for the weight of the metal. It was probably melted down by the purchaser for the sake of the bronze. Anyhow all trace of this beautiful work of art has disappeared.

We have now dealt with the most famous of the Nuremberg craftsmen. It would be wearisome to do more than mention a few of the leading names amongst those who excelled in other branches of art. A host of locksmiths, glasscutters, potters and stovemakers, bookbinders and carvers turned out in the golden age of Nuremberg work which has never received its artist's name, but which continues to delight us. The painted glass, which in spite of much modern restoration is one of Nuremberg's most priceless possessions, is often by unknown hands. But we can name such artists as Schapfer and Helmbach and later Veit, Augustin and Sebald Hirschvogel, Guttenberger, Juvenell, Amnon, Kirnberger and Springlin. Especially is it the case with the early glass in the smaller churches that we must label it Pictor Ignotus. The principal churches contain painted glass windows which surpass even those of Ulm and Cologne. In St. Lorenzkirche there is the Tucher window (1457) by Springlin; whilst the Volkamer window (1493), representing the family and patron saint of the donor and the genealogical tree of Jesus Christ, is justly claimed to be, for richness and depth of colouring and for elaboration of design, one of the noblest windows in the world. It can only be doubtfully attributed to Veit Hirschvogel. To him, however, belongs the credit of the Maximilian window in St. Sebald's (1514), and the Margrave's window (1527), designed by Kulmbach, in the same church. There, too, is a window by Kirnberger and the Bishop of Bamberg's window (1493), which may perhaps be by Katzheimer of Bamberg.

There were at one time fifty masters in the goldsmith trade, whose delicate work, excellent in execution and varied in design, was renowned throughout Europe. The fact that in 1552 nine hundred pounds' weight of silver and silver-gilt ornaments was taken from the churches and sold by order of the Council, will show how rich Nuremberg was in this respect. But we can do here no more than mention the names of Ludwig Krug and Wenzel Jamnitzer and Augustin Hirschvogel, goldsmiths and painters on enamel.

Of armourers and metal-workers there were Hans Grünewalt, who died in 1503, and his son-in-law Wilhelm von Worms, whilst Martin Harscher (1523) and Kaspar Endterlein (1633) were chief among the makers of waterpots and candelabra. Sebald Behaim, the great gunsmith; Hieronymus Gärtner, the architect; Jakob Püllman, the clockmaker and locksmith, also claim mention.

Nuremberg was the home of invention as well as of industry. Christopher Denner invented the clarionet in 1690, and Lobsinger the air-gun in 1550. Cannon were first cast here about the year 1350, and in 1500 Peter Henlein made the first watches, which, from their shape, were called Nuremberg eggs. Specimens may be seen in the Castle and in the Museum. Erasmus Ebner discovered the particular alloy of metals which we call brass, the brass of earlier times being apparently of different combination, and one Rudolph invented a machine for drawing wire in 1360. About the same time the first paper-mill in Germany, if not in Europe, was established at Nuremberg; and here at the latter end of the fourteenth century playing-cards, though not invented, were certainly printed. Last, but not least, the honey cakes, which still introduce the German child to the name of Nürnberg, were famous as our Banbury cakes, and much appreciated by princes in the Middle Ages.

It will be seen that the proverb—

"Nürnberg Tand geht durch alle Land,"

was no empty boast, and we can now understand the force of the rhyme—

"Hätt' ich Venedigs Macht,
Augsburger Pracht,
Nürnberger Witz,[47]
Strassburger Geschütz
Und Ulmer Geld
So wär ich der Reichste in der Welt"

CHAPTER VIII
THE MEISTERSINGERS AND HANS SACHS

"Here Hans Sachs, the cobbler poet, laureate of the gentle craft,
Wisest of the Twelve Wise Masters, in huge folios sang and laughed....
Not thy Councils, not thy Kaisers, win for thee the world's regard;
But thy painter Albrecht Durer and Hans Sachs thy cobbler-bard."
—LONGFELLOW.

"Heil Sachs! Hans Sachs!
Heil Nürnbergs theurem Sachs!"
—WAGNER, Die Meistersinger von Nürnberg.

IT is impossible to be in Nuremberg many hours without becoming conscious of the fact that there once lived and died here a poet, who is still, as Wagner calls him, the "darling of Nuremberg." His name is heard and his portrait seen on every side. In the Spital-Platz stands the monument erected to his memory in 1874 (Johann Krausser). His house in the Hans Sachsgässlein,[48] much restored and rebuilt since he lived there, is marked by a tablet. Who then was this great man? A cobbler—and more than a cobbler, a poet.

Hans Sachs, the son of a master-tailor, was born 5th November 1494, and died January 20, 1576. Apprenticed to a shoemaker he yet always found time, he tells us, to practise the lovely art of poetry. His first teacher was Lienhard Nunnenbeck. But it was during his five years of travel (Wanderjahre), in which he visited the greater part of Germany, that he formed his determination "to devote himself to German poetry all his life long." In 1516 he returned from his travels to Nuremberg, made his "Master piece," and became a "Master Singer." We have already seen how ardently he supported the Lutheran teaching, and we have referred to his poem (1523) "Die Wittenbergische Nachtigall."[49] His object was always both to amuse and to instruct. Even his light poems usually end with a moral. He strove to make the new teaching popular by versifying and translating passages from the Old and New Testaments. He was apt, however, to be too vehement in the expression of his convictions. So violent was he against Roman Catholicism that in 1527 the Council, anxious as ever to preserve peace and quiet, forbade him to write any more books or rhymes on that subject.

Hans Sachs was twice married. His first wife died in 1560, and the following year he married the beautiful widow, Barbara Harscherin, whose beauty and worth he praises in one of his most pleasing poems, "Der Künstliche Frauenlob," written after the manner of the Minnesingers:—

"Wohlauf Herz, Sinn, Muth, und Vernunft
Helft mir auch jetzt und in Zukunft,
Zu loben sie, so fein und zart,
Ihre Sitt', Gestalt und gute Art,
Auf dass mit Lobe ich bekröne
Die tugendreich', erwählte Schöne,
Dass ich ausbreite mit Begierde
Wohl ihres Frauenwesens Zierde.
Vor allen Frauen und Jungfrauen,
Die je ich thät mit Augen schauen
Hin und wieder in manchem Land,
Ward keine mir wie die meine bekannt
An Leibe nicht, nicht an Gemüthe,
Die Gott mir ewiglich behüte...."

We have mentioned both Meistersingers and Minnesingers. It may perhaps not be superfluous to add a word or two on the difference between these. The Minnesingers flourished in the twelfth and thirteenth centuries. They were mostly of noble birth, and, in an age when poetry and chivalry kissed each other, they exclusively cultivated the poetic art, living in kings' palaces, or wandering from court to court, and composing and singing pure and beautiful little love poems, in which the meadows and flowers sparkle, as it were, in the sunlight of their song. Best known of these minstrels is Walter von der Vogelweide. He, during his wanderings, visited and sang in this old town at the Court of Frederick II., himself a Minnesinger. Heinrich von Meissen, surnamed Frauenlob, also visited Nuremberg, but he was the last of the Minnesingers, and was buried at Mainz, 1318. After his time the practice of German poetry devolved almost exclusively on the burgher and artisan class. Close societies were formed: the rules of poetry and singing were taught in their schools. Versecraft became one of the Incorporated Trades. The Sängerzünfte, or Singers' Guilds, flourished chiefly at Augsburg, and on the Rhine at Strasburg, Mainz, and Worms. The Meistersingers, ever anxious, but all unable to clothe themselves with the fallen mantle of ancient glory, speak of the "Twelve old Masters" (including Tannhäuser, Walter von der Vogelweide, Wolfran, etc.), as having lived together and formed the first society of Meistersingers, under Otto I. The truth is that these Twelve Masters were Minnesingers, and did not live together. Longfellow's phrase, "Wisest of the Twelve Wise Masters," cannot, therefore, be correctly applied to Hans Sachs. The Incorporated Poets, we must confess, though they derived many of their rules and metres from the Minnesingers, managed to degrade the old German Minnesinging to a close, artificial, and philistine art. The final pitch of absurdity was reached, when in 1646 was published Harsdörfer's "Nuremberg Funnel, for pouring in the art of German poetry and rhyme, without the aid of the Latin tongue, in six lessons." Succeeding ages have thanked Harsdörfer for that phrase. "Nürnberger Trichter" has passed into a proverb. The first celebrated master-singer of Nuremberg was Hans Folz (1470), whom Hans Sachs called a "durchleutig deutschen Poeten" (noble German poet). It is to be noted that the poems of the Meistersingers were always sung to music, and often had to be written to a particular tune. Hence the stringent rules made for their formation: hence, too, when prizes were given for the fewest mistakes in mere technique, the great attention paid to form and metre, and the gradual elimination of true passion and poetry. Nuremberg had always fostered music. The art of lute-making, as of organ-building, had found a home there. Borkhardt, the famous inventor of musical instruments, built the St. Sebald's organ about this time. Conrad Gerler's instruments, too, were much sought after. In 1460, for instance, we find Charles the Bold, Duke of Burgundy, sending for three lutes for the players at his Court. An extremely good and interesting collection of old musical instruments will be found in the German Museum. In this connection should also be noted there a picture of the Meistersingers' singing school.[50]

The reputation of the Nuremberg school of poetry and singing was greatly enhanced by Hans Sachs. Remarkable for his own personality and literary fertility, he was also famous for reducing all the rules of the Meistersingers to writing, in a code which lasted till 1735. But, in spite of his attention to rules, he, at any rate, showed some poetic and original talent. It is for this reason that Wagner makes him, in "Die Meistersinger," recognise the real poetry in Walter, though the latter's impassioned song does not conform with all the artificial rules of the Guild, mere paper rules which added nothing to the sound or rhythm of the words. For, as all the world knows, Hans Sachs has achieved a second lease of life on men's lips, through the genius of Richard Wagner, dramatist, poet, satirist, and wonderful musician, who, in this opera, laughs at the conceit of the Incorporated Poets in assigning an extravagant antiquity to their Guilds, and at their pedantic sacrifice of matter to form. No more vivid and humorous picture of mediæval German life and of the people of quaint old Nuremberg has ever been drawn. Though "Die Meistersinger von Nürnberg" was not published till 1867, Wagner had already as early as 1851 sketched out the plan of an opera which was to display the triumph of genius and genuine passion over pedantry and conventionalism in art.

The passage[51] from "Eine Mittheilung an meine Freunde" is worth quoting here.

"Immediately after the completion of this work" (Tannhäuser), he writes, "I was permitted to visit some baths in Bohemia to restore my strength. Here, as always, when I have been able to withdraw from the atmosphere of the foot-lights and my duties in the theatre, I soon found myself in a light and joyous humour. For the first time, and with artistic significance, a gaiety peculiar to my character declared itself. Capriciously, and yet not without some premeditation, I had determined a little time previously to write as my next work a comic opera. I call to mind that I had been influenced in arriving at this decision by the well-meant advice of good friends, who wished to see an opera of a 'lighter kind' composed by me, because this, they said, would open the German theatres to my work, and so bring about that success, the invincible want of which had undoubtedly begun to threaten my worldly circumstances with serious embarrassment. As, with the Athenians, a gay satirical piece followed on a tragedy, so suddenly there appeared to me, on that holiday journey, the picture of a comic play, which might suitably be attached as a satirical sequel to my 'Battle of the Bards at Wartburg.' This was 'Die Meistersinger zu Nürnberg,' with Hans Sachs at their head. Hans Sachs I conceived as embodying the last appearance of the artistically productive folk's-spirit, and as such I opposed him to the vulgar narrow-mindedness of the master-singers, whose very droll, rule-of-thumb pedantry I personified in the character of the 'Marker.' This Marker, as is well-known (or as is perhaps not known to our critics), was the overseer appointed by the Singers' Guild to 'mark' with strokes the faults against the rules committed by the performers, especially if they were candidates for admission to the Guild. Whoever received a certain number of strokes had versungen—failed in his singing." (The singer sat in a chair before the assembly: the marker was ensconced behind curtains, and gave his attention chiefly to marking mistakes in singing, in Biblical history, in Lutheran German, in rhymes, music and syllables.) "Now the eldest of the Guild offered the hand of his young daughter to that master who should win the prize at an approaching public singing-competition. The marker, who has already been wooing the maiden, finds a rival in the person of a young knight, who, fired by reading the 'Book of Heroes' and the old Minnesingers, leaves the poor and decaying castle of his ancestors to learn in Nuremberg the art of the master-singers. He announces his candidature for admission to the Guild, being inspired thereto by a sudden passion for the Prize-Maiden, 'whom only a Master of the Guild may win.' He submits himself for examination, and sings an enthusiastic song in praise of women, which, however, provokes such incessant disapprobation on the part of the marker that ere his song is half-sung he has 'failed in his singing.' Sachs, who is pleased with the youth and wishes him well, baffles a desperate attempt to carry off the maiden, and thereby finds an opportunity of deeply annoying the marker. The latter, who, with a view to humbling him, has already been turning rudely on Sachs about a pair of shoes not yet finished, plants himself at night before the maiden's window, in order to make trial of the song with which he hopes to win her by singing it as a serenade. By so doing he hopes to secure her voice in his favour at the adjudication of the prize. Sachs, whose cobbler's shop is opposite the house thus serenaded, begins singing loudly as soon as the marker strikes up, because, as he informs the infuriated lover, this is necessary if he must keep awake to work so late: that the work is pressing nobody knows better than the marker himself, who has dunned him so mercilessly for the shoes! At last he promises the poor wretch to stop singing on condition that whatever faults he may find, in his judgment, in the marker's song, he may be allowed to mark according to his shoemaker's art—namely, with a blow of the hammer upon the shoe stretched on the last. Then the marker sings: Sachs strikes on the last again and again. The marker jumps up indignantly. Sachs asks him nonchalantly whether his song is finished. 'Not nearly,' he cries. Then Sachs laughingly holds up the shoes outside his shop, and declares that they are now quite finished, thanks to the 'marker's strokes.' With the rest of his song, which in desperation he screams out without a pause, the marker fails lamentably before the lady, who appears at the window violently shaking her head. Disconsolate, he asks Sachs next day for a new song for his wooing. Sachs gives him a poem by the young knight, pretending not to know its source: only he warns him to secure an appropriate tune to which it may be sung. The conceited marker thinks he has nothing to fear in that respect, and sings the song before the public assembly of masters and people to a quite inappropriate tune, which so disfigures it that he once more and this time decisively fails altogether. In his mortification he accuses Sachs of having cheated him by providing so base a song. But Sachs declares the song is a very good one, only it must be sung to a suitable tune. It is then agreed that whoever knows the right tune shall be the victor. The young knight does this and wins the bride: but rejects with disdain the admission to the Guild now offered to him. Sachs humorously defends the Master-Singers' Guild, and closes with the rhyme—

"Though should depart
The pride of Holy Rome,
Still thrives at home
Our sacred German art."

The "Marker," thus pourtrayed in The Meistersingers, is Sigs Beckmesser, who is one of those whom Hans Sachs mentions as having taught him. There is nothing remarkable in Hans Sachs being a shoemaker as well as a Meistersinger, for the Guild was chiefly composed of weavers and shoemakers. What is remarkable is that he was something of a poet as well as a Meistersinger.

The Guild had to get special leave from the Council each year to maintain their singing schools. This leave was sometimes refused, on the ground that the Masters sang lascivious songs, and bawled them rather than sang. Their meetings occurred principally in the Church of St. Catherine, after afternoon service on Sundays—usually once a month. Public performances took place thrice a year, at Christmas, Easter and Pentecost. The public were invited to these great assemblies by placards representing a rosegarden and David playing the harp before our Lord on the Cross. This placard also announced the subjects chosen and the forms of songs allowed on the occasion.

As an author, Hans Sachs was astonishingly prolific. Besides his songs, he wrote fables, eighteen books of proverbs, comedies, tragedies and farces (in which he himself acted). Altogether, the number of his works reached the huge total of 6205. Some of his plays—and some were in seven acts—were acted in the Marthakirche and some in the Rathaus. From Sachs' time the drama began to make headway in Germany; but it was not till after his death that it received its first great stimulus, when the English strolling players began to come through Germany, acting Shakespeare's plays among others no doubt, and the more blood-curdling scenes from Ford and Webster. In 1628 the Council provided for such performances by building the Fencing School, "for fencing and comedies" on the Schütt, next to the Wildbad.

Nürnberger Spruchsprecher

Sachs was above all things a popular poet. He reflects both the good and the bad side of the people he represents. At his best we find in him that mixture of religious gravity with fresh and pungent humour which is so characteristic of the German spirit of those days. The narrative poem "Der Schneider mit dem Panier" is a good example of this, and is free from that coarseness which too often disfigures his writings. Nor must we forget to mention the long poem, "Ein Lobspruch der Stadt Nürnberg," a descriptive eulogy of his native town. His narrative style is plain and straightforward, his manner pleasingly naive, though often both prolix and prosaic, his humour original and unaffected, if too frequently rough and Rabelaisian. But we can forgive him much for his robust good sense and shrewd irony. The first line of one of his poems—

"In dem Zwanzigsten Kapitel" (of the Bible)

will show how prosaic he can be: his well-known couplet on himself—

"Hans Sachs war ein Schuh-
Macher und Poet dazu,"

is a fair example of the roughness of his versification.

Hans Sachs is buried in St. John's Churchyard, and what is shown as his grave is numbered 503. But whether that is actually his grave seems to be somewhat uncertain.

On the whole, literature was far behind art in Nuremberg. But we must not pass over the institution of the Spruchsprecher, the poet laureate of the town. He was a speciality of Nuremberg, and had to deal in rhyme with the occasion of all weddings and festivals, when called upon. He rejoiced in a special dress, and was invented, it seems, about the middle of the fifteenth century.

One other Nuremberg poet is worth mentioning—Johann Konrad Grübel, "the Nuremberg Philistine," as Goethe called him in compliment. A comic, dialect poet of the people, he was first-rate of his kind. He died in 1809, and a statue of him by Professor Wanderer adorns a little fountain near the house of Hans Sachs.

CHAPTER IX
THE CHURCHES OF NUREMBERG

Der Kirchen act sind in dem Ort
Darin man predigt Gottes Wort.
—HANS SACHS.

NUREMBERG is rich in churches, those sermons in stones so much more eloquent than any words that ever fell from the lips of the preachers. The Gothic style has been finely called the true architectural expression of Christianity. In her churches Nuremberg possesses some of the finest specimens of the pure German Gothic style. They exhibit, it is true, the common failing of German architecture. Exquisite, though sometimes extravagant, in detail, they fall far below the masterpieces of the French architects in the proportionment of the whole.

St. Sebald, the patron saint of Nuremberg, affords one more proof of the fact that a prophet is not without honour save in his own country. It is, indeed, not even known what his country was. His history and even his name are so unfamiliar to any but Nurembergers that it will be of interest if I add here the record of his life from the account written by an eleventh-century (?) monk.[52]

Born at the beginning of the eighth (?) century, Sebald was the son of a Christian king: but as to whether his father was King of the Danes, Britons or Irish or a petty chief on the Danube biographers differ. Sebald's parents had long been childless, but at last when all hope seemed gone, God heard the prayers of his servants and gave them a son. Sebald was born. The boy grew up waxing in years and virtue, learning the lesson of the love and fear of the Lord, obedience to his parents and charity to all men. At the age of fifteen he was sent to Paris to study theology, in which he quickly eclipsed all the scholars of his own age and many of riper years. He returned to his home full of wisdom and honours and was betrothed to a beautiful and virtuous maiden. But before the marriage was consummated he fled from the things of this world, and, leaving his wife, his father and mother and his inheritance, he chose the chaste and solitary life of a hermit. Within the lonely recesses of a dense wood he passed his days in prayer and fasting and his nights in self-inflicted chastisement. Fifteen years passed and then the hermit made his way to Rome, whence Pope Gregory the Second despatched him in company with SS. Willibald and Wunibald to go forth and preach the gospel, succour the feeble, confirm the good, and correct errors of doctrine. Together the holy men pursued their way, praising the

Lord with cheerful heart, until at length it came to pass that weary with journeying and exhausted by storm and wind, they grew faint with hunger, and his two companions called upon Sebald to provide them with food. Then, having comforted them with doctrine, he departed from them a little way, and when he had poured out his soul in prayer, lo! there came an angel from heaven bringing to them bread that had been baked under the ashes. And when they were now come to the parts about Vincentia (Vicenza) Sebald, moved by the Holy Spirit, would go no further, but abode as a hermit in the wood. His fame spread abroad. From far and near, even from Milan and Pavia, people flocked to hear from his lips the wonderful works of God. But, amongst those who came, came also an unbeliever who scoffed and blasphemed at the prophet and his message. Then Sebald prayed to God that a sign might be given, and immediately in the sight of all, the earth opened and the scoffer sank up to his neck. Then the hermit prayed with a loud voice and interceded for him, so that he was delivered,[53] and he and many of the unbelievers embraced the true faith.

Sebald now left Italy and came to Ratisbon (Regensburg), bringing the gospel into the wilds of Germany. At Ratisbon, after crossing the Danube in a miraculous manner, he stayed for a short time and mended, by the power of prayer, a vessel which his host had borrowed and broken.

At last he came to Nuremberg and settled there in the forest, in the heart of the Franconian people, teaching them the word of God and working miracles. On one occasion, we are told, he sought shelter in the house of a poor but churlish mechanic. It was winter: the snow lay on the ground and the wind howled over the frozen marshes of the Pegnitz. But the signs of charity did not shine brightly in the host. Sebald called upon the man's wife to bring more wood for the fire so that he might warm his body: for he was chilled to the bone. But though he repeated his request the niggard host forbade his wife to obey. At length the Saint cried out to her to bring the cluster of icicles which hung from the roof and to put them on the fire if she could not or would not bring the faggots. The woman, pitying him, obeyed, and in answer to the prayer of Sebald, a flame shot up from the ice and the whole bundle was quickly ablaze. When he saw this miracle the chilly host gave the hermit a warmer welcome (frigidus hospes ad ipsum factus est liberalis). Perhaps, it has been suggested, we may see in this pretty story an allegory of how Sebald quickened the flame of divine love within the icy Franconian natures, which it seemed as impossible to warm with grace as the winter's ice. Sebald's host now, to make amends, sallied forth and bought some fish in the market, contrary to the regulations of the authorities, and, being caught, was blinded. But the holy hermit restored to him the light of his eyes.

Sebald clearly foretold the date of his death: the place of his burial was appointed by a miracle. At length, says the chronicler Lambert Schagnaburgensis, full of good works, he fell on sleep in the town of Nuremberg. The bier of the Saint was drawn by untamed oxen. And they, when they had reached the spot chosen for his resting-place, refused though goaded to the utmost to move any further. Thus was the site of the church afterwards built to the patron saint of Nuremberg determined. Those who ministered to him swung incense over the dead body of the old hermit and lit candles above it. Now there was a woman, a sinner, whom Sebald had turned to the love of the true God. In memory of her sins and in expiation she wore about her arm a hoop of iron. And she came to see the dead hermit. It chanced that one of the candles above his head was crooked, and she stretched forth her arm and set it straight. At that moment the iron band burst. So she knew that the saint, when he entered into the presence of God, had not forgotten the poor woman whom he had converted on earth and that God had heard her prayer, and that her sins, which were many, were forgiven, as the broken ring signified.

Many other miracles were attributed to the ashes and relics of the saint which lie in the beautiful shrine in St. Sebalduskirche.[54] We have spoken at length of this exquisite work of art (p. 208), to which, says Eobanus Hessus in his poem on Nuremberg, no words can do justice and with which not even the greatest artists of past ages could have found fault.

"Musa nec ulla queat tanto satis esse labori
Nec verbis æquare opus immortale futurum;
Quod neque Praxiteles, nec Myron, nec Polycletus,
Nemo Cares, nemo Scopas reprehendere posset."

The east end of St. Sebalduskirche faces the Rathaus: but the western is the oldest portion of it. Here the St. Peter's or Löffelholz Chapel, as it was called later, after the Nuremberg family of that name, with its crypt and choir (Engelschörlein), and the lower part of the two towers[55] date from the beginning of the thirteenth century. They belong, in their original state, to the Romanesque style of architecture; whilst the nave affords a beautiful example of the transition to Gothic forms and the magnificent east choir is in the purest German Gothic. We may conjecture that the church was originally a basilica with a Romanesque east choir, flanked by two small adjoining aisles, corresponding to the west choir which is still preserved, and with a nave in the shape of a cross. Then, about 1309, they began to build broader and higher aisles in place of the low and narrow ones, and, in so doing, half concealed the old round-arched windows. But the most important alteration must have been when they pulled down the old east choir and began to build (1361) the Gothic choir, which together with the rest of the church has been recently and carefully restored. Twenty-two pillars 80 feet high support the vaulting. The two simple, slender towers at the west end, some 260 feet high, were apparently completed towards the end of the fifteenth century. According to tradition, the southernmost of these is built on piles—a tradition that reminds us of the swamps and marshes that once stood here, in the days when the narrow circumference of the first town wall did not cross if indeed it reached the river (see Ch. V.). In the base of each tower is a Romanesque doorway: over the southern one, in the tympanum, a high relief in stone represents the Trial of St. Helena. On the north side of the north tower is a low relief of the Crucifixion, a memorial to Burkhard Semler, 1463. Beneath the towers is the crypt in which was once the tomb of Konrad von Neumarkt, the founder of the Convent of St. Catherine. This, the oldest Nuremberg tomb, is now in the German Museum. The colossal bronze crucifix outside the west end, against the middle window of the St. Peter Chapel, was presented by the Starck family in 1482. It is attributed to H. Vischer, father of Peter Vischer, and has some merits as a work of art, though the figure is that of a Hercules rather than of a Christ. It was repaired in 1625, on which occasion the Nurembergers incurred the nickname of Herrgottschwärzer, or Blackeners of God. For, the story runs, the Cross was made of silver, and the Council ordered it to be coloured black in order to protect it from the roving bands of soldiers who passed through the town in the Thirty Years War.

BRAUTTHÜRE, ST. SEBALDUSKIRCHE

On the north side of the church the beautiful Brautthüre (1380?) or Bride's Door (see p. 154) is especially worthy of attention. Very richly and daintily carved, the outer and inner arches form a porch which was meant to protect the bridal pair from the inclemency of the weather when they stood here for the first part of the marriage service. On either side of the pointed arch are the figures of the Madonna and Child and of St. Sebald with his pilgrim's staff and a model of the Sebalduskirche in his hands. The ten intercolumniated statues on the inside walls of the porch represent the five wise and the five foolish virgins (at present being restored). Within the entrance appear Adam and Eve with a half-length Christ above them, and the snake and apple-tree of Eden.

On the buttresses of the east choir are some sculptures in half-relief, representing the Passion, and at the east end, facing the Rathaus, is the Schreyer Monument (Schreyer's Begräbnuss), a high relief by Adam Krafft (1492). Nobly conceived and nobly executed, these representations of the Passion and Burial of Christ are among the most noteworthy of the master's works. Especially beautiful in grouping and in feeling is the Grablegung—the Laying in the Grave. Sebald Schreyer, who died in 1520, was a keen patron of art and, as churchwarden of St. Sebald's, devoted to the interests of his church. In recognition of his services, and as he was the last of his family, the rule which had lately come into force that all citizens except the clergy must be buried in St. John's Churchyard, was set aside in his case, and he was buried in the east choir of the church to which he had devoted his life and fortune. For the Begräbnuss of Adam Krafft and Vischer's Sebaldusgrab owed their existence chiefly to Schreyer's care and encouragement.

The animals on the capitals of the door of the south aisle are full of characteristic humour. One may trace here some of that mockery of the monks in which the mediæval masons not infrequently indulged, and of which there is a famous example at Strasburg. St. Peter with his key and a crowned Saint with a sword are on either side of the door itself. A partly gilded Last Judgment occupies the space above the arch. It will be found interesting to compare the numerous figures of it with those on the main entrance of the Lorenzkirche, to which they are strikingly akin.

Above the door called the Schautthüre (show-door) on the S.E. side of the church, near the guard-house, is a Last Judgment (1485), probably by Adam Krafft (see p. 200). It is a fine and interesting work. At the top, beneath four hovering angels and between twelve Apostles, Christ sits on a rainbow to judge the world. The earth is his footstool. Mary and John Baptist (the figures remind us of those in the Rosenkranztafel in the Museum) intercede for the poor souls who are rising from their graves. On one side they are conducted (with crowns of glory on their heads) by an Angel to the gates of Paradise, over which waves the triumphant banner of Christ. On the other side the Devil, who is also similar to the Devil in the Rosenkranz, with the head of a cock, drags his prey into the jaws of hell. The figures are all strong and full of animation. In the midst of the group of those rising from the dead, between the kneeling figure of the founder, Hartmann Schedel, and his arms, is a Latin inscription which gives us to understand that Hartmann Schedel, to whose memory this relief was erected, died Dec. 4, 1485.

For admittance to the church we must knock at the Anschreibethüre, the portal on the N.W. side.[56]

This Anschreibethüre—so called because it was customary to enter the names of the dead on a register kept here for that purpose—was renewed in 1345. It is adorned on either side with the figures of Gabriel and Mary (Annunciation), and above with a relief of the Death, Burial (the unbelieving Jews falling prostrate before the coffin) and Crowning of Mary. Note the figures of female saints on the capitals.

On entering, our first impression is one of disappointment. A vile whitewash disfigures the walls, whilst the fact that the church has not been designed by one hand as a complete whole deprives us of that satisfied sense of perfect proportion for which we are forever hoping but so often in vain. But as we grow more familiar with the details of this church the feeling of disappointment vanishes and we are left grateful if not completely satisfied.

On our right is the St. Peter's or Löffelholz Chapel, and we notice that this, which forms the western end of the church, has been altered from a Romanesque into a polygonal apse. The pointed cells of the vaulting make up five-eighths of an octopartite compartment. Thus the old double-apse arrangement of Romanesque buildings is retained at St. Sebald's; but the west end is in the transitional, the east in the pure German Gothic style. By introducing this pointed vaulting into the older Romanesque shell of the St. Peter's Chapel, the Engelschor above it, or Angels' Choir as it is called, has been concealed from view. But we can easily see where it springs from the apex of the great arch which forms the entrance to the Chapel.

The lofty central nave is, as we have already said, a good example of the transition to Gothic architecture in German churches, when the horizontal lines of the Romanesque style were giving place to the upright and upward tendency of the Gothic. The sexpartite vaulting, the broad but pointed arches, the substitution of rolls for the flat and square-edged vaulting ribs, the clustering of the shafts and the flanking by shafts of pointed windows are all eloquent of this tendency. The pillars, too, begin to be prolonged in extent and diminished in thickness, and the line is no longer interrupted by the rectangular effect of square capitals. The varied patterns (flowers, pearl strings, etc.) of the capitals here should be noted.

The walls beneath the clerestory are relieved by a triforium, which had no place in the conceptions of the original Romanesque architects. There is here no gallery set apart for the young men, as there frequently is in the triforium of an early German church. This triforium consists only of a row of low, pointed openings supported by short pillars, variously ornamented.

The east choir (1361-1377) is a building of the same period as the Frauenkirche. Compared with the rest of the church its dimensions are a good deal exaggerated. Nor is it placed symmetrically as regards the axis of the older part; for it inclines considerably to the north. Regarded in itself, however, it must be admitted to be a splendid building, the lofty and airy effect of which is greatly enhanced by the single row of tall windows. The light streams in through beautiful stained glass. The windows, however, are really too tall in proportion to their breadth (50 feet by 8). The mullions, too, nearly 40 feet in height, are more interesting as triumphs of masonic skill than admirable as features of architectural design.

Contenting ourselves with these general observations as to the building itself, we will here add a list of the principal objects of art which will catch the attention of the visitor to the church.

In the Löffelholz Chapel stands conspicuous the highly decorated bronze font wherein the Emperor Wenzel was baptized (1361, see p. 42). At the base are statuettes of the four Evangelists. It is said to be the oldest existing product of the Nuremberg foundries.

The altar-piece in memory of Kunigunde Wilhelm Löffelholz (1453) is by an unknown painter. Scenes from the life of St. Catherine are depicted on a plain gold background. It is the earliest Nuremberg work to show any trace of the Netherland influence: but, unfortunately, it has been painted over at least once. There are three other pictures in this chapel, of an earlier date, by unknown artists.

The two-winged Haller Altar-piece (N. near the Anschreibethüre) may very likely be an early work of the Master of the High Altar-piece in the Frauenkirche. The background is of gold: the subject is Christ on the Cross between Mary and John; on the wings, the Mount of Olives and SS. Catherine and Barbara.

In this picture the cramping of the figures and the crude drawing of the hands and feet are noticeable, but in the modelling of the heads there is much that is very noble and very beautiful.

On the pillar next to (S.) the Haller Altar is a relief, "Carrying the Cross," by Adam Krafft, 1496.

Later and more vigorous works by the same master are the Last Supper, Mount of Olives and Betrayal (1501), reliefs 5 feet high by 5 feet broad on the E. wall of the Choir. The Betrayal is distinctly the best composed and most telling of the three. The Last Supper, the arrangement of which is somewhat crowded and confused, has the interest of exhibiting in the Apostles portraits of some members of the Council. The Apostle with the goblet is said to be Paul Volkamer (the founder) and he with the small cap Adam Krafft himself, or, it may be, Veit Stoss, to whom the sculptures, on the strength of the monogram V.S. on them, are now usually attributed.

We need not stay long over the Tucher Altar with its ever-burning lamp, founded by the first baron Tucher, 1326, and its seventeenth-century altar-piece, or the painting by Joh. Franz Ermel (1663) of the Resurrection, over the Muffels Altar next the Schauthüre, or the new pulpit (1859) by Heideloff and Rotermundt. The choir-stalls and the Pix (N.), with its old sculptures, dating from the second half of the fourteenth century, are worth examining, as also are the numerous reliefs on the pillars of the choir. The Crowning of Mary on the first choir pillar on the north side is attributed to V. Stoss. On a column to the right of the pulpit hangs a copy of Durer's Interment of Christ, with the armorial bearings of the Holzschuhers, and opposite, beneath a copy of Rubens' Day of Judgment, is another painting by Durer, little worthy of him, in which figure the Imhoff family, Willibald Pirkheimer and the artist himself (on the right).

The Carrying of the Cross (Tucherische Kreuztragung), on the column next to the Sebaldusgrab, can only doubtfully be attributed to Wolgemut (1485).

The Madonna and Child on the next column was cast by Peter Vischer's son.

The great Crucifix, with SS. Mary and John, of the High Altar was executed by Veit Stoss in 1526, when he was now in his eightieth year. The head of the Christ is a masterpiece of expression. The lower part of the High Altar is modern, and was carved by Rotermundt after the designs of C. Heideloff (1821).

In the choir also (N. wall), we find a good example of the work of Hans von Kulmbach, who passed from the school of Jacopo dei Barbari (Jakob Walch) to that of Durer. The Tucherische Tafel (1513) shows the influence of the latter in a very marked manner: Durer may, in fact, have supplied the designs for it. In the centre of the triptych is Mary enthroned, crowned by two angels. The holy Child on her knee is trying to seize an apple from the Mother's left hand: but both Mother and Child are looking out of the picture. The five Bellinesque angels, who, clad in brightly coloured garments, and playing various musical instruments, stand at Mary's feet, are altogether charming. On either side of the throne are SS. Catherine and

Barbara, whilst on the right wing are SS. Peter and Lawrence, presenting the founder, Provost Lorenz Tucher, to Mary, and on the left are St. John Baptist and St. Jerome. A mountain scene forms the background of the picture, which for all that it owes much to Durer owes much also to the individuality of Kulmbach.

Near this is a commemorative escutcheon of the Tucher family, by Holbein, and below it a small wood carving, said to be by Albert Durer.

The Adam and Eve in Paradise over the Schauthüre is by Joh. Creuzfelder (1603), and was placed there by members of the Behaim family.

One of the chief features of interest in the Sebalduskirche is the stained glass. The Tucher and Schürstab windows, according to Rettberg, contain some late fourteenth-century glass, but would seem to have been much restored. The Fürer window was first set up in 1325 (Christ before Pilate). In the Bishop of Bamberg window (Wolf Katzheimer, 1493?) are the portraits of Kaiser Heinrich, Kunigunde, Otto, Peter, Paul and Georg, and in the corners four Bishops, and over all four Gothic canopies.

The Maximilian window is by Veit Hirschvogel (1514). The Emperors Maximilian and Charles V. stand on a ground of white tracery, with their consorts, patron saints, and arms.

The Margrave's Window is by the same artist, after the designs of Hans von Kulmbach. It was only completed after Hirschvogel's death (1527), and has quite recently been restored. The single figures of the Margrave Friedrich von Ansbach and Baireuth, and of his wife and eight sons, are on a white ground. SS. Mary and John the Evangelist above, and the Margrave's arms on the sides. In the foreground, an inscription and an architectural substructure in the shape of a temple, according to the fashion of stained glass at this period.

Finer, better designed and considerably larger than St. Sebald's is the Church of St. Lawrence. It is one of the best examples of pure German Gothic. Outside and inside, in form and in detail, it exhibits both the beauties and the defects of the German style when pointed architecture was developed according to the taste and feelings of the Germans, uninfluenced by French inspiration.

With regard to detail, amid so much that is admirable, now and again the besetting sin of German art makes itself felt—that lack of self-restraint, that prodigality and extravagance, one may almost call it, of ornament, by which the effect of gorgeous richness is obtained indeed, but at the sacrifice of distinctness. Even in the beautiful windows this is the case. The multiplicity and intersection of the lines tend to blur the "dry light" of the dry beauty of a perfect design.

With regard to form, viewed from the exterior, two features strike the eye and remain in the memory. On the one hand, the enormously high and grossly ugly roof of the choir which overwhelms the building produces the ludicrous effect of a camel's hump. It is unrelieved by pinnacles or even by the flying buttresses which seem to lift the soaring Gothic naves of France into a world beyond our ken. Once again, as in St. Sebald's, the notes of symmetry and proportion are lacking. Some flying buttresses do indeed figure in the nave where the side-aisles are not, as in the choir, of the same height as the central nave. These buttresses, however, are decidedly clumsy. On the other hand, the richly decorated western front, with its towers, rose window, open parapet and light gallery connecting the towers, is a pure and pleasing specimen of German art.

According to tradition the St. Lorenzkirche stands on the site of an older, Romanesque chapel which bore the name of "zum heiligen Grab" (Holy Sepulchre) and was erected for the spiritual needs of the inhabitants when houses first began to be built on this side of the Pegnitz.

ST. LORENZKIRCHE, FROM THE RIVER

As it now stands the church dates almost entirely from the latter part of the middle ages. Begun in 1278 it was not completed till 1477. Of the two towers (250 feet in height) that to the north was built in 1283, the other about 1400. The square portion of each and the elevation of the gable between them are crowned by a light and beautiful open parapet. The north tower, with its roof of gilded metal, was burned down some thirty years ago, but has been carefully rebuilt. The towers terminate in octagonal storeys and spires. At the top of the square portions are wide openings, divided by many mullions, suggesting the gridiron on which St. Lawrence was broiled. Why the church was dedicated to this Spanish saint I have not been able to discover. The stately portal (25 feet wide and 42 feet high), and the rose window (33 feet in diameter), recently much restored, belong to the fourteenth century. During the fifteenth century the church was repeatedly enlarged, and, in 1439, the foundation-stone of the lofty choir was laid. The plans were designed by Konrad Roritzer, who came here from Rothenburg.

At the laying of the foundation-stone a miracle occurred. The pulley which was to raise the stone broke. The workmen then broke the stone, so heavy was it and impossible to raise. And when they had done so, they found inside a hewn cross. Probably, says the sceptical German historian, this was all arranged in order to stir the enthusiasm and to promote the generosity of the people on behalf of the new church.

The figures of Adam and Eve and of the prophets, etc. on the Hauptthor, the Grand Portal, are the earliest specimens we have of Nuremberg sculpture. They date from the fourteenth century. The reliefs of the scenes from the Life of Christ and the Last Judgment are later, like the reliefs on St. Sebald's and the Bride's Door.

HAUPTTHOR (ST. LORENZKIRCHE)

A central pillar divides the Hauptthor into two halves, and bears a Madonna and Child. The arches above the two doors, which are separated by this pillar, contain high reliefs of the Birth of the Saviour and Adoration of the Magi (left), and The Slaughter of the Innocents and Flight into Egypt, and the Presentation in the Temple (right). In the spandrels of these arches are four prophets.

In the upper half of the great arch are represented the Crucifixion, and on the right side Christ before Pilate and Christ bearing the Cross; on the left the Burial and Resurrection of Christ. These scenes correspond to those depicted on the sides of the entrance hall.

The remaining space in the tympanum of the arch deals with the Last Judgment. Two angels blowing the last trump, and two others (restored) holding the instruments of the passion, surround the Judge, whose feet are set upon the Sun and Moon, and He judges the just and the unjust. At His side SS. Mary and John kneel and intercede. The inner curve of the arch contains the twelve Apostles and the outer the twelve Prophets. Below are the above-mentioned life-size statues of Adam and Eve, next to whom two other figures stand, the Scripture in their hands, expounding, one may fancy, to the parents of mankind the story of the Redemption, which the reliefs of the gateway have thus told in stone.

Similar in workmanship to the figures of this portal is the statue of Christ, with flowing beard and folded hands, which is near the door on the south-west side. This in its turn will remind us of a statue of Christ, with hands pointing to the wound in His side, in the St. Jakobskirche. The Brautthüre or Bridal Door on the north side of the church was built in 1520, but it shows little trace of the Renaissance spirit. (Recently restored.)

Of the fine though crumbling old piece of sculpture—Gethsemane—near this door, I can find no history at all.

High up on the roof of the choir outside rises a pole with a hat upon it. Two choir-boys (the story runs) who were playing marbles in the church fell to quarrelling, and one of them who held the two marbles in his hand, maintained his rights with the exclamation, "Devil take me!" Thereupon the Devil immediately appeared and wrung the boy's neck. At the corner of the St. Lawrence schoolhouse, on the pedestal of St. Lawrence, you may see carved in the stone the head as it was twisted on the trunk. The hat on the pole on the choir is that of the unfortunate chorister.

ST. LORENZKIRCHE (N.)

Entering the church by the north-west door, near the Tugendbrunnen (see Ch. X.), we notice that the nave is twice as high and broad as the aisles which are thus subordinated to it. But, as in St. Sebald's, the three aisles of the choir are of equal height. Here there are two stories of windows, instead of a single row of tall ones. Two visits should be paid to St. Lawrence's in order to see the full effects of this church—one in the morning when the sun is shining through the windows of the polygonal east end, and one in the afternoon when the light streams through the glorious rose window in the west.

Plain, slender pillars carry the vaulting of the choir with its flat spidery network. A gallery which runs round the whole choir is reached by a staircase next the sacristy (s). The sacristy should be looked into both for the sake of its own beauty and for the sake of the choral books, illuminated by Jakob Elssner(?) (d. 1546), and a baptismal basin by Endterlein (d. 1633).[57]

The east end of the choir contains splendid windows (see p. 213). The subject of the first, on the north side, behind the altar of St. John, is the wanderings of the children of Israel; of the second the Passion, of the third the Transfiguration, of the fourth the donor, Emperor Frederic III. and his consort, of the fifth, Saints and Fathers of the Church.

But far the finest and most famous of the windows is the sixth, the Volkamer window. It is a "Jesse" window, displaying the genealogical tree of Christ, and, below, the founder and his family. The seventh, or

Schlüssfelder window, represents the holy mill and the four Evangelists with the four Apostles, after Durer, beneath. All these belong to the last half of the fifteenth century; but the eighth is a modern one (1881), commemorating the re-establishment of the German Empire. The Tucher window next the sacristy was painted by Springlin, 1451, and contains beautiful red glass in the early Renaissance style.

Another noticeable window is that on the south side, exhibiting the arms of the Schmidmayer family. The designs are attributed to Durer.

Near this stands one of the old carved chairs, in which the Masters of the Guilds once sat in turn to receive alms.

Of the chief treasures of the St. Lorenzkirche we have already dealt sufficiently with two—the Pix or Ciborium, the Weihbrodgehäuse or Sacramentshaüslein or whatever name we choose to give to Adam Krafft's masterpiece[58]—

"A piece of sculpture rare,
Like a foamy sheet of fountains rising thro' the painted air,"

and the Angels' Greeting, and the still finer wood-gilt crucifix of the High Altar, by Veit Stoss.[59] The six angels in bronze bearing the candles are by Burgschmiet (b. 1796). Anton Tucher dedicated the Angels' Greeting and also the great bronze chandelier, which may contain the handiwork of both Veit Stoss and Peter Vischer. The handsome modern pulpit is by Rotermundt and Heideloff (1839). There is also in the choir some beautiful tapestry (1375?) with figures of the twelve apostles who stand in a scroll-work of wise sayings for our instruction, such as Pis. maister. deiner. zung. dez. ist. dir. not. oder. si. werdint. dir. den. ewigen. dot., and so forth.

The Church of St. Lawrence is rich in examples of the memorial tablets or epitaphs on which the skill of the early painters was chiefly exercised. The altar-pieces and epitaphs founded in memory of some member or another of the great burgher families form a complete gallery of early Nuremberg art and provide moreover a perfect feast for the enthusiastic herald.

We have already spoken of the general tendencies of the Nuremberg artists in the seventh chapter of this little book. Perhaps, therefore, the most interesting way to treat of the pictures in St. Lawrence's will be to mention them in chronological order.

1. Epitaph of Paul Stromer, 1406—next the Rochus Altar, on west wall of the Sacristy. The Redeemer throned on the clouds, surrounded by angels bearing the instruments of the Passion. SS. Mary and John kneel in intercession before Him, and underneath is the family of the founder.

The drawing throughout is strong but severe, and there is considerable harshness in the contours.

2. Epitaph of Frau Kunigunde Kunz Rymensnyderin, 1409. Body of Christ supported by SS. Mary and John. Figures of the founders on either side of the napkin.

3. Wolfgang's Altar (1416?). Resurrection of Christ. SS. Conrad and Wolfgang on the inside of the wings (No. 17, north wall).

4. The celebrated Imhoff Altar-piece in the Imhoff Gallery (north transept). This picture, dedicated by Kunz Imhoff, was painted 1418-22, and is counted the finest achievement of mediæval painting in Nuremberg. In the centre Christ is crowning Mary; on the wings two apostles, at whose feet kneel the founder and his three first wives.

The burial of Christ, with SS. Mary and John, which formed originally the reverse of this altar-piece, is now in the German Museum (No. 87).

A deep love of nature, which reveals itself in the vigorous, homely conception of the forms, is here combined with that spiritual reverence of treatment which inspired the first works of Christian art. In the earnest faces of SS. Peter and Paul we see not merely a reproduction of the traditional types, but faces full of character and originality. They have been carefully thought out as well as carefully carried out. There is individuality again in the sympathetic, the winsome beauty of the countenance of Mary; whilst the countenance of Christ seems to tell us both of the thoughtful earnestness and the gentle dignity of the Saviour.

Notwithstanding their slimness, the figures in the picture are somewhat crowded. The shoulders and necks are powerful, and the hands evince remarkable carefulness in execution. The folds of the drapery, in spite of the simplicity and clearness of them, are by no means monotonous in design. The harmony of colours (green, red, and blue, on a gold background) is strong and happily attuned.

The artist is unknown, but, whoever he was, he had looked upon Nature with loving eyes and worshipped her; and this love of Nature, purified by his deep religious feeling, he had brought to the service of his living faith. Frequently we shall observe in the old Nuremberg artists that this mixture of naivete and reverence in the conception of religious subjects produces too commonplace a representation of them. But here the result is not commonplace, only just towards Nature. The picture, says Dr Janitschek,[60] is like the most beautiful bloom of a period just drawing to a close and already bearing in itself flowers of a more dazzling development.

The Imhoff picture (see below, No. 9) shows similar handling and similar freedom from Flemish influence in the full, soft beauty of the forms. And yet the mastery of Nature displayed in the portraits of the founders reveals to us an artist who was following the same paths as those of the Flemish painters.

5. Epitaph of Agnes Hans Glockengiesserin, 1433. The death of Mary as she knelt in prayer, and portrait of founder. A picture full of tender feeling (No. 11, south side).

6. Theokars Altar (Deocarus Altar, No. 19, north side) 1437, founded by Andreas Volkamer. Christ between six apostles, and below, St. Deocarus between the other six apostles, carved in wood. Below a life-sized painting of the saint.

The wings of the picture, which represent the Transfiguration, the Miraculous Draught of Fishes, the Last Supper, and the Resurrection, and four scenes from the life of St. Deocarus (kneeling before a chapel, healing a blind man, confessing Charlemagne, and on his death-bed), should be compared with the Haller altar-piece of St. Sebald's and the High altar-piece of the Frauenkirche. Though very nearly contemporary with the latter works, this painting is representative of the old school. It exhibits, indeed, great dramatic spirit, though the movements are often awkward, and the

ST. LORENZKIRCHE (INTERIOR)

colouring lacks the strength and brilliancy of the Frauenkirche picture.

7 and 8. A saint in armour, and a suffering Christ with gold background and the Saints Henry, Kunigunde, and Lawrence (with the gridiron), are also probably of the same date.

9. Margaret and Anton Imhoff memorial (1446) (numbered 16, on the north wall of the church). Madonna and Child and four angels, and the founder's family—the father with eight sons, and the mother with four daughters.

The further development of the Nuremberg school of painting, as I have sketched it above (pp. 181-4), may be observed in the following memorial pictures in this church:—

H. Gärtner epitaph, 1462, Madonna and Child, SS. Bartholomew and Barbara (south, near doorway).

Erhard Schon epitaph, 1464, St. Wolfgang and other saints.

Friedrich Schon epitaph, 1464, Birth of Christ, Aaron, Moses, etc.

Hans Lechner epitaph, 1466, Death of Mary (south).

Hans Meyer epitaph, 1473, St. Gregory (No. 13, north side).

Berthold Kraft epitaph, 1475, St. Dionisius (opposite Rochus Altar, south).

Hans Schmidmayer epitaph, 1476, Adoration of the Magi (over stairs leading to Schmidmayer oratory, south).

Leonhard Spengler epitaph, 1488, Christ between SS. Philip and James (No. 15, north side).

Stör Family epitaph, 1479, Christ treading Blood, and Four Evangelists, etc. (north-west).

The Rochus Altar, triptych with scenes from the life of St. Rochus, dedicated by six Imhoff brothers, 1499 (No. 7, west of Sacristy),

and the Krellsche Altar, 1483, which may perhaps be by Wolgemut. It is beneath the Frederick window in the choir, and contains a Madonna and Child and various saints, apostles, etc. The background of this picture represents the town of Nuremberg as it was before the last extension of the walls. (Chap. V.)

By Wolgemut and his school there are several characteristic pictures, of which I may mention here the Burial of Christ (No. 2), the Ascension (No. 3), and the Praying Priests (No. 4). The right wing of the St. Catherine altar-piece (No. 8) is by Wolgemut, and the two pictures of St. Vitus, with his parents and denouncing the idol, are signed by R. F., a painter whose touch is visible in part of the Peringsdörffer masterpiece (see p. 287). The Adoration of the Magi (No. 20) is a fine picture: the Angels bringing the child Jesus to the Virgin (No. 1) bears Durer's monogram.Lastly, the wings of the Nikolaus (No. 6) and of the Annen—or Marien—Altar are by Hans von Kulmbach, 1520(?) (next to the Passion window in the choir).

FRAUENKIRCHE
(Marienkirche, Marienhall)

The Frauenkirche, which occupies the east end of the Haupt Markt, was built, as we have seen (p. 37), under somewhat discreditable circumstances on the site of the old Jewish Synagogue (1355-1361).The brothers Georg and Friedrich Ruprecht are mentioned as the architects, and the sculptor, Sebald Schonhofer, is responsible for the rich ornamentation of the vestibule. This vestibule (restored with the rest of the church some twenty years ago) is unique of its kind. It is conjectured that this part of the church was intended to serve as a kind of treasure-house for the Imperial Crown jewels and relics, which in the year 1361 were certainly shown, as an object of veneration, from the gallery above the main entrance of the church.

**WEST DOOR,
FRAUENKIRCHE**

The plan of the west gate is borrowed in the main from the St. Lorenz portal. There the life and work of Christ, here the life and work of Mary are set forth. Many of the figures strongly recall those of the St. Lorenz statues.

At the corners of the vestibule are statues of Karl IV. and his consort, and SS. Lorenz and Sebald.

Above the rich and massive portal with its fine iron railings is the Chapel of St. Michael, whereon is to be seen an extraordinary old clock known to young and old in Nuremberg by the name of "Männleinlaufen." The chronicles relate that Karl IV., in memory of the "Golden Bull" (p. 39), which was drawn up in Nuremberg in 1356, and recorded what honours and reverences the electors of the Empire were to pay to the Emperor, caused an ingenious clockwork to be mounted over the portal of the church. The mechanism was so contrived that the seven electors passed at noon before the Emperor, who sat upon a throne and received their reverent homage as they passed. The clock was renewed in 1509 by Georg Heuss (even since then it has twice been restored), and the figures were cast by the coppersmith, Sebastian Lindenast. Still, at the stroke of noon, much as in the old mediæval days, the heralds blow their trumpets, the Emperor raises his sceptre, and out from their gloomy chamber the electors file forth and bow low in reverence to the dead representative of an empire which has ceased to exist. And they revive in our hearts something of the child-like pleasure which the Middle Ages took in these elaborate toys.[61]

But a sturdy English Protestant who lived in Nuremberg some forty years ago, took another view of the matter.

"It is generally said to represent the Pope," he writes, "who, seated in a comfortable sort of arm-chair, was formerly accustomed at a certain hour to raise his sceptre and summon the representative figures of the twelve apostles, who accordingly used to make their appearance and do obeisance. That time, however, seems to be gone by. The latter after a while became tired of the ceremony, refused their mechanical homage, and St. Peter himself, it is said, setting the irreverent example, they began to reject the uniformity required in their evolutions." The clock was at that time out of repair.

The subject of clocks leads me to mention what is perhaps not generally known, that as Nuremberg was the inventor of the watch (Nuremberg Eggs, shown in the Museum and the Castle), so also she invented a system of time peculiar to herself. To-day we have the Central Europe system (our 12-hour system), and the Italian or 24-hour system. But at the close of the Middle Ages the Nurembergers, the great clockmakers, had a third plan of dividing the day, called the Nuremberg great hour (Grosse Uhr), for which Regiomontanus drew out elaborate tables. Briefly the plan was this. At the equinox the night was assumed to begin directly after sunset, and day began twelve hours after sunset. This arbitrary "dawn" (Garaus) was sounded by the clock. To this day it is announced by ringing of bells from the principal churches. With the progress of the year, as the days after the equinox lengthened or decreased, time was added to or subtracted from the night or day. For instance, on the shortest day there would be 16 hours night and 8 hours day, and on the longest day 16 hours day and 8 hours night. Again, when the sun set at 6, the "Great Clock would strike 8 at 2 A.M., because 8 hours had passed since sunset. Seasons of the year were, in common parlance, denoted in accordance with this system. "At the time of year when the day strikes 13" would fix a date. The system, it will be seen, was almost as involved as the sentences of a modern German historian. But with all its drawbacks it lasted on, along with the Central Europe system, till 1806. Owing to the great elaboration of machinery required, the hours were usually struck by bell-ringers. But the clock of the Frauenkirche, owing to the additional mechanism needed for its toy-work, probably had to be fitted with the "little hour" from the first.

Besides some old painted glass in the nave (coats of arms of Nuremberg patricians) and some carvings by Veit Stoss, the only works of art in the Frauenkirche that need detain us are the Pergenstorfer tomb (1499), at the end of the north wall of the nave, by Adam Krafft, and close to it the side altar-piece[62] (1440), which was originally the Tuchersche High Altar in the Church of the Carthusian Monastery. We have already had occasion to note more than once how the early Nuremberg painters, before Wolgemut, were struggling to achieve the simple portrayal of Nature and to combine it with the expression of their deep religious emotion. The picture before us is a very good example of this simple and yet sympathetic realism. Let us add that this quality, or combination of qualities, is not borrowed. For the Nuremberg School of Painting remains distinct and peculiar, with very little trace of foreign influence, long after the school of Van Eyck had made itself felt in the regions of the Lower and the Upper Rhine.

In the centre of the picture are the Crucifixion (SS. Mary and John by the Cross, and at the feet of Mary a skull), the Annunciation and Resurrection; on the wings the Birth of Christ and Apostles.

There is a rare conjunction of dignity and life and truth to Nature in these pieces—an individuality too. The Mary is portrayed in the same spiritual mood as that of the Imhoff Altar-piece, but generally the figures are more full of vigour and the countenances more full of expression than in that picture. In depicting the body of Christ, which is carefully proportioned and in which the muscle-play is planned with evident care, the artist, we can see, has wrestled with Nature, and not failed altogether in his attempt to gain the mastery over her. The figures of the Apostles are sturdy, thick-set, and in their faces is an expression of concentrated power. The drapery falls in broad, well-arranged masses. The colouring is deep and clear, and the rich harmony of strong red, blue and yellow (gold background) is happily supplemented by a luscious green.

St. Ægidienkirche

The Church of St. Ægidius, or St. Giles[63] (Ægidienplatz) was founded originally by Conrad III., it is said, for some Scotch benedictine monks. But, with the exception of the side chapels, which still remain and are in the highest degree interesting, it was burnt down in 1696, and rebuilt 1711-18 in the debased, and to Nuremberg utterly inappropriate, style of that period. The High Altar-piece is a Pietà by Vandyck (nineteenth-century angels above). Behind this are two bronze reliefs, one, the beautiful "Entombment," is by Peter Vischer the younger, the other by his brother Hans. The eighteenth-century paintings on the ceiling are by J. D. Preisler.

But apart from the Vandyck, the Ægidien Church is well worth a visit for the sake of the Eucharius, the Tetzel and the Wolfgang's Chapels. The first of these is much the oldest (1140), and is in the late romanesque or transitional style. The Roman vaulting, such as we have seen in the chapels at the Castle, is combined with a mixture of round and pointed arches. The pillars are slender, with broad capitals. The capitals of the centre pillars distinctly suggest Byzantine influence. The two altars here are by Veit Stoss.

The St. Wolfgang's Chapel dates from the end of the fourteenth century. There are here two pictures (1462 and 1463) and a piece of sculpture (1446), Grablegung Christi, by Hans Decker, which cannot by any stretch of the imagination be called a spirited work. The chapel is disfigured by a hideous gallery which has been run round it, but the roof is, as they say, sehr interessant.

The Tetzel Chapel (1345) contains a Coronation of Mary, by Adam Krafft, unfortunately much damaged. In the centre Mary is being crowned by two angels. On either side of her are noble figures of God the Father and Christ. Beneath Mary is a group of angels, and beneath God and Christ stand many suppliants. An older and very interesting stone-relief is to be seen on the south-west wall. Some old glass and over seventy coats of arms of the Tetzel family are also placed in this chapel.

There are many other churches in Nuremberg, and several of them have a distinctive charm of their own. But I must content myself with a bare sketch of the chief treasures they possess. Only let me add that any lover of Nuremberg who has time to spare will be rewarded by the discovery of many characteristic details in the minor churches. The richest in works of art is the

St. Jakobskirche.

Chief among these is a Pietà, by the unknown master of the Madonna in the Museum (see p. 278), and the old glass of the windows. The high altarpiece has the distinction of being the earliest specimen of Nuremberg painting. There are, besides, various early reliefs and carvings by Veit Stoss.

The church itself, which was restored in 1824, belongs in its present form to the beginning of the fifteenth century. It was, however, in existence in the twelfth century, for the Emperor Otto presented it and all its property in 1209 to the "Hospital der heiligen Maria der Deutschherrren zu Jerusalem," an order which had long had a firm foothold in Nuremberg, and came, there is evidence to show, continually into conflict with the Council. After the Jakobskirche was handed over to the Protestants in 1634 by Gustavus Adolphus, the Deutschherren held their Roman Catholic services in the Elizabethkapelle, which was completed in its present shape, as the

Elizabethkirche

with its mighty Italian dome in 1885.

The Marthakirche (1365),

right of the Königstrasse as you come from the Frauen Thor, contains little of interest. Like the chapel "Zum Heiligen Kreuz," north-west of the town on the road to St. John's Churchyard, it was founded as the chapel of a pilgrims' hospital, wherein "all poor strange persons, whencesoever they come, are to be harboured for one or two days and provided with food and drink free of charge." Almost facing it is the

Klarakirche (1430).

Here there are some good windows and an altar by Veit Stoss (?), also an Œlberg, an early Mount of Olives by Adam Krafft. Opposite St. Sebald's, on the north side, lies the

St. Moritzkapelle.

Built originally on the present Hauptmarkt, it was removed in 1313 to a site upon what was then St. Sebald's Churchyard. It was restored by Heideloff in 1829 and used, till 1882, as a gallery for some of the pictures now in the German Museum. In the Spital Platz is

The Hospital and Spital Kirche (Heiliggeist Kirche),

founded by Konrad Gross, which we have already mentioned (p. 30). In the courtyard of the hospital may be seen the chapel founded by Georg Ketzel after the great epidemic in 1437. It is built in imitation of the chapel of the Holy Sepulchre at Jerusalem. East of the Spital Kirche stands the handsome

MOORISH SYNAGOGUE

by Wolf.

Since Nuremberg was from early days both pious and comparatively secure, she was naturally one of the first places in Germany where the mendicant friars settled and founded monasteries. The earliest of these was the Augustiner Kloster (beginning of the thirteenth century). The Franciscan Monastery, or Barfüsser Kloster, was built somewhere about 1210, where now the house of the Museum Club and the buildings of the Industrial Museum stand. The Dominican Monastery, built a little later, is now used as the Public Library and Record Office (No. 4 Burgstrasse, Mon. Wed. Fri., 9-12 A.M.). Thanks chiefly to the efforts of Hieronymus Paumgärtner and Erasmus Ebner the Council formed a fine collection from the treasures—mainly manuscript—of the libraries of the various monasteries. This was placed together with the library, which the Council had itself been founding for over a hundred years, first of all in the Monastery of St. Giles, and then in 1538 in its present home. Among the MSS. are a fragment of Durer's work on the "Proportions of the Human Figure," some poems of Hans Sachs, and autograph letters of Gustavus Adolphus, Melanchthon, Luther, Lazarus Spengler, Regiomontanus, etc., besides an amusing one from Ulrich von Hutten, the Knight and Reformer, who herein congratulates an abbot on having renounced celibacy and taken unto himself a wife.

But the most valuable MS. is the almost unique Hebrew Machsor (1331) written on vellum. Its 1100 pages comprise a full collection of Jewish prayers, hymns, and ceremonies up to the thirteenth century.

Amongst other drawings, portraits, prints, and curiosities in the library are a black silk cap worn by Luther and a drinking cup given by him to his friend Dr Justus Jonas. The portraits of the two friends adorn the cup, together with the following inscription:—

Dat vitrum vitreo Jonæ vitrum ipse Lutherus
Ut vitro fragili similem se noscat uterque.

Then, beautifully written and illuminated, there is a breviary (1350?) of an English Queen with the inscription:—

La Liver du Roy de France Charles
Done a Madame la Roigne D'engleterre.

Among the early printed books is a copy of the "Rationale Durandi" (1459, Mainz), of "Boccaccio" (1472, Mantoni), and of the "Florentine Homer" (1488).

Matthäus Landauer's Almshouse—Landauer'sche Zwölfbrüderhaus (east end of Ægidien Platz) has frequently been mentioned. The almshouse has now been turned into a school of technical design, but the chapel (1502) will repay a visit. The roof, supported by two spiral columns, has the cone-shaped pendants of the contemporary English style, very exceptional in Germany. It was for this church that Durer painted his All Saints' picture, now at Vienna.

There were many foundations, in the old days, for the relief of the sick and needy. Amongst others were two houses for waifs and strays, founded no one knows by whom. They were transferred later to the Barfüsser Kloster. In connection with this institution a charming annual procession takes place. One charitable lady, Elizabetha Krauss, left in 1639 a sum of money to provide the children with a good dinner on St. John's Day. In grateful memory the children always go on that occasion to the St. Rochus Churchyard. On their way they must pass the corner house near the Karlsbrücke. On that house is the statue of a youth, busily engaged in pounding with pestle and mortar. People say this figure represents the apprentice of an apothecary who once lived there. And because the apprentice ran away from his work to gaze at the procession of children, who clad in red and white, and, roses themselves, crowned with garlands of roses were wending their way hand in hand to the tomb of their benefactress, his master grew so angry that he killed the lad.

It is in the churchyard of

St. Rochus

that Peter Vischer (90) lies buried (Rothenburger Strasse). In the church itself are some paintings after Durer, some altar-pieces by Veit Stoss (?), and some glass by Veit Hirschvogel. But the chief burial-place of Nuremberg from the sixteenth century, and one of the most peculiar and impressive spots of the town, is the Churchyard of St. John. For this has been the burial-place of the Nuremberg patricians from generation unto generation, ever since in 1517 the Council decreed that everybody, with the exception of the clergy, must be buried in St. John's Churchyard, and no longer in the churches within the town. Such a wise measure of compulsory extramural interment must have been almost without parallel at that time.

The route to this churchyard the reader already knows, for it lies along Burgschmietstrasse, along that road to Calvary marked by Ketzel's pious Stations of the Cross (see p. 200).

A low walk and pillared gateway, over whose broken pediment the willow bends mournfully, mark this place of tombs. The churchyard is sprinkled with trees: to the south, the shadows of a thicker fringe of branches deepen the natural solemnity of the place. It is here that the mighty dead of the White City are sleeping the sleep that knows no waking; but, as we seek the graves of Durer, Sachs, or Pirkheimer, we pass along the rows of flat tombstones quietly, with hushed voices and reverent steps, as if dreading to disturb even the silence of their inviolable repose.[64] On every side of us are emblems of the past glory and pride of Nuremberg. There are no headstones to the tombs, but every slab, in high relief of imperishable bronze fashioned by the skill of the most distinguished artists,[65] bears the coats-of-arms and devices of the civic noble who moulders beneath. What pomp of funeral processions must have ascended the steep from the city, year by year, through that gateway, to convey another, and yet another, wealthy burgher from the busy scenes of commerce and office, to the silent abodes of the dead! Poets and artists, too, as well as patricians, lie here; and the indistinguishable dust of the famous and infamous, of rich and poor, known and unknown, old and young mingles in this still churchyard of St. John.

"Golden lads and girls all must,
As chimney-sweepers, come to dust."

We feel the pathos, the pity of it, as we stand here and read the message of the tombstones; but even more clearly does St. John's Churchyard suggest that other mood:—

"Hark! how the sacred calm that breathes around
Bids ev'ry fierce tumultuous passion cease;
In still small accents whispering from the ground
A grateful earnest of eternal peace."

CHAPTER X

THE HOUSES, WELLS, AND BRIDGES

EVERY other house in Nuremberg, whether in the narrow and crooked side streets, or in the busy thoroughfares, is, as it were, a leaf from some mediæval chronicle. Here, in the Hirschelgasse or the Ægidien Platz, we read the story of some rich merchant prince, returning from Venice or from Palestine, eager to spend some of the fruits of his emprise in the decoration of his house, according to the style of the country which had fascinated him in his travels. There, in the Tetzel-or the Schild-Gasse, we read in the overhanging upper stories the desire of the architect in this crowded mediæval city to utilise every foot of available space, and the device is revealed to us which he adopted when the Council forbade the projection of the ground floor into the street. And those statues of Saints and Madonnas, which still stand in their niches at the corners of so many houses, those reliefs by Adam Krafft or other artists, which adorn the mansions of the great with the story of Christ and His followers, are they not eloquent, in the very lack of variety displayed in the choice of subjects, of the simple child-like faith of the Middle Ages, ever ready to hear once more the story of the Redeemer's suffering for the sake of man who had sinned?

From the varying height, breadth, and styles of the houses the streets of Nuremberg gain the mediæval charm of irregularity. There is the usual happy

HOUSE ON THE PEGNITZ

avoidance of the straight lines which render modern towns so unattractive. The general character of the red-tiled houses here is lofty, with high-peaked gables and frequently with oriel windows. The ornamentation is lavish and smacks of the Renaissance. Especially is this noticeable in the courts within. For even where the front of a house may seem narrow and almost insignificant, on entering it you frequently find a large quadrangle, with open winding staircases and broad, projecting balconies, highly ornamented, which carry back to the street behind.

I mention here a few of the more notable houses, to some of which reference has already been made.

Albrecht Dürer Haus, corner of Albrecht Dürer Strasse.

Albrecht Dürer Birthplace, 20 Winklerstrasse.

Anton Koberger Haus, Ægidien Platz. Opposite the statue of Melanchthon.

Martin Behaim Haus, next door to the above. Here the famous globe of the navigator is kept.

Peller (now Fuchs) Haus, Ægidien Platz. Recently restored.

Willibald Pirkheimer, 35 Ægidien Platz.

Hans Sachs Haus, Hans Sachs Gasse.

Hieronymus Paumgärtner Haus, 23 Theresien Strasse. The relief, St. George and the dragon, is probably an early work by Adam Krafft.

Krafft (formerly Pfinzing) Haus, 7 Theresien Strasse.

Fembo Haus, Burgstrasse. (Opposite the Library.)

Scheurl Haus, Burgstrasse. This house contains the room in which Maximilian I. stayed, carefully preserved.

Topler, now Petersen Haus, Panierplatz.

Tucher Haus, 9 Hirschelgasse.

Rupprecht Haus, next to the above.

Volkamer Haus, 19 Hauptmarkt.

Grundherr (Zum goldenen Schild) Haus, Schildgasse. Where the Golden Bull was drawn up.

Nassauer Haus, corner of Karolinenstrasse.

Peter Vischer Haus, Peter Vischer Strasse.

Palm Haus, 29 Winklerstrasse. This is the house of the bookseller Palm, who was shot by Bonaparte for publishing a pamphlet against him.

Imhoff Haus, Tucherstrasse.

Ketzel Haus (Pilatushaus), Thiergärtnerthorplatz.

Glossner Haus, Adlerstrasse.

Grundherr Haus, 1585 (now the Bairischer Hof Karlsstrasse).

. . . .

"Manch edles Brünnlein strömt darin
Aus goldnen Röhren schnell dahin."

So wrote Hans Sachs in his poem in praise of his native town. And indeed the wells and fountains here are as characteristic though not of course so beautiful as the well-heads of Venice. Far the most important of them is the so-called Beautiful Fountain (Der Schöne Brunnen) in the corner of the Haupt Markt, near the Rathaus. It is in the shape of an octagonal Gothic spire. The construction of it is usually spoken of as contemporaneous with that of the Frauenkirche and the design is likewise attributed to Sebald Schonhofer. But recent researches have shown that it was not built till the years 1385-1396, and that one Heinrich der Palier, or der Parlierer, as he is commonly named in the City Accounts, had the building of it. No doubt he was very much under the influence of Schonhofer, and very likely he may have been his pupil. So much may be gathered from the similarity of the ornamentation on the Frauenkirche and the Beautiful Fountain. In old days, as we have seen, the well was richly painted and gilded. But this is no longer the case. It was carefully restored in great part in 1824 and again at this moment further restoration is in contemplation.

The iron railing which surrounds the fountain was made by Paul Köhn (1586). Curious funnels on levers are used for drawing the water, and they remind one irresistibly of that reductio ad absurdum of the Meistersingers' Guilds, Harsdörfer's "Nuremberg funnel" for pouring in poetry (p. 218).

FLEISCHBRÜCKE

The Beautiful Fountain is a niched and tabernacled monument of stone, over 60 feet high, tapering at intervals to a pinnacle. The niches in the pillars of the lower compartment contain statues of the seven Electors and of nine heroes, the Christian Charlemagne, Godfrey of Bouillon and Cloris, the Jewish Judas Maccabæus, Joshua and David, and the Pagan Julius Cæsar, Alexander the Great and Hector. Above, in the second division, are Moses and the seven Prophets.

The water of this well has the reputation of being remarkably good. Formerly, even more than at present, the Beautiful Fountain was the very centre of Nuremberg life. At the well, as in the days of Abraham, lovers met and the gossips talked, waiting their turn to fill their long, copper pitchers. To-day, too, the Beautiful Fountain is a household word, and parents explain to their too inquisitive children, when they ask how their new baby brother arrived—"Es ist ein Geschenk von dem Schönen Brunnen!"

Of the other fountains we may enumerate the "Gänsemännchen" in the Obstmarkt and the dainty well in the Town Hall courtyard by Pankraz Labenwolf (1553). The son-in-law of Labenwolf, Benedict Wurzelbauer designed the Tugend Brunnen, or Virtue Fountain, which stands at the north-west corner of the St. Lorenzkirche. This was in 1589 when German art was already becoming decadent and mannered. Then in 1687, to celebrate the victory over the Turks at Siklos the "Wasserspeier" was erected in the Maxplatz. It was copied by Bromig from Bernini's original at Rome. Lastly in the Plärrer, opposite the Spittler Thor, is the "Kunstbrunnen"—which commemorates the opening of the first railway in Germany, between Nuremberg and Fürth.

The bridges, of which over a dozen span the Pegnitz in its course through the town, must once have added greatly to the picturesqueness of the place. But the Pegnitz is liable to sudden and violent spates which have continually swept away the old bridges. The modern ones cannot boast of any great inherent beauty. The Fleischbrücke, indeed, was built by Peter Carl it is said on the model of the Rialto. But it requires a kindly imagination or a bad memory to admit any comparison between the two.

Over a gateway near this bridge will be found the figure of a large bull, with the inscription—

[66] "Omnia habent ortus suaque incrementa, sed, ecce!
Quem cernis numquam bos fuit hic vitulus."

Town mottoes of this kind were common enough in the old days. A quaint example is that which was inscribed over an entrance of the city of Arras in Belgium. Originally it ran—Les François prendront Arras, lorsque ce chat prendra le rat. When the French had taken the town in 1640 they erased the letter p in prendront and thus cunningly caused the inscription to read in their favour.

CHAPTER XI
GERMAN MUSEUM

(Entrance in the Vordere Karthäusergasse. Open 10-1 A.M. and 2-4.30 P.M. summer, 2-4 P.M. winter. Fee, 1 mark. Free Sundays, and in winter also on Wednesdays. Sticks, etc., must be left in the entrance hall (10 pfennige). Full catalogue (German) 50 pfennige. Certain sections of the Museum, including the collections of prints, seals, medals, tapestry, records and the Library, are reserved for the use of students and artists. The visitor who wishes to study any of these magnificent collections must apply to the director of the particular department.)

THE Museum, which owes its inception to the generosity of Freiherr Hans von Aufsess, and its development to the imperial and municipal co-operation of united Germany, has found a home in the old Carthusian Monastery and Church.

It was in 1380 that Marquard Mendel, a scion of a rich and distinguished Nuremberg patrician family, founded a monastery for the most severe of the ecclesiastical orders on a spot outside the then town-wall. The foundation stone of the Carthusian Church, was laid in the presence of King Wenzel in the following year.

The pious founder took the vows of the order he had thus encouraged, and he lived in a cell of the monastery. The services in the church were so popular that to accommodate the crowds of people who thronged there Konrad Mendel, brother of Marquard, founded an additional chapel—the Mendel Chapel, in 1387. It is now used as a fire-station. Opposite this chapel Konrad also founded an almshouse for twelve destitute citizens. It is still marked by the statue of one of the former inmates.

The prior and most of the monks adopted the Evangelical creed in 1525 and the rich monastery became the property of the town. Both the church and the monastery were for a long while used for very profane purposes until at last in 1856 they were utilised as a storehouse for the Museum. Then in 1873 the old Augustinian Monastery was removed and re-erected as an additional part of the Museum.

So vast and varied is the collection of interesting objects here and so careful and elaborate is the German catalogue that it is at once impossible and unnecessary for me to give an exhaustive account.

The following notes are intended to serve rather as an index than as a complete guide to the treasures of the Museum; but they make more particular mention of things that may prove interesting to those who care for the "Story of Nuremberg."

The various sections of the Museum though called after their original architectural purpose—Saal, Halle, Kreuzgang, Kirche, Lichthofgang, etc., are usually numbered consecutively as if they were all rooms of the same type.

The entrance hall leads into the cloisters of the old monastery (walls decorated with Nuremberg heraldry). The first portion of the cloister contains an historical collection of monuments (mostly casts) arranged chronologically.

ROOM 1 (on left).

Ceiling ornamented with the arms of the towns which under the old Empire belonged to princes and bishops. Weapons and implements of the stone age.

ROOM 2.

Bronze weapons and implements. Coins.

ROOMS 3-7.

Roman antiquities found in Germany and German antiquities from fourth to tenth centuries. The exquisite German gold and metal-work of the Charlemagne period seems to foreshadow the work of the great Nuremberg goldsmiths.

ROOM 8.

Latest acquisitions of the Museum.

ROOMS 10-13.

A very fine collection of characteristic stoves and tiles. The latter, used for covering the walls and floors, took the place of mosaics and are ornamented with leaf-work, stars, rosettes, coats-of-arms or grotesques. The tiles of the stoves, which should be compared with those in the Castle and the Rathaus, were made, in the fifteenth century, to represent chiefly mythological subjects, whilst the seventeenth-century ones betray, as we should expect, Italian influence. A green stove with concave plates (Room 12) and an eighteenth-century rococo specimen (Room 13), from the house of the Löffelholz family are remarkable.

ROOMS 14, 15.

contain some beautiful examples of the locksmith's art; locks, keys, hinges, knockers, and knocker plates, exquisite in workmanship and in design. We have here a real lesson in ironwork, a perfect education in hinges.

ROOM 16.

is the Wilhelms-halle, so-called after Emperor Wilhelm I. It contains a window given by him in 1860, when he was still only King of Prussia. Passing by this and the Hohenzollern-halle opposite and going down the Ludwigsgang, built by the aid of Ludwig of Bavaria (1870) we come to the Reichs-hof, a court (left) in which stands a gigantic cast of the Roland in the market-place of Bremen. Rooms 18-25 are called the Victoria and Friedrich Wilhelm buildings. (More tombs and casts.) On the right of the corridor (Room 26) there now begins a very interesting collection of stained glass which is arranged chronologically. (Twelfth to sixteenth-century glass here.)

ROOMS 27, 28.

The old Refectory of the monks serves now as the home for a collection of German and Italian pottery, majolica and faience, porcelain, glass and stoneware. (German faience, first half of sixteenth century. Augustin Hirschvogel and Nuremberg work, Room 27, cabinets 9 and 16.) Pewter work, end of sixteenth century, by Kaspar Endterlein (Room 28, cabinets 4, 5). English Wedgewood (cabinet 6).

ROOM 29 (Cloister).

Bronze epitaphs from Nuremberg tombstones (cf. St. John's Churchyard).

ROOM 32 (Kirche)

is the old monastic church. It is filled with mediæval church utensils (ninth to fifteenth century), amongst which we may mention the silver casket in which the Imperial insignia used (p. 51) to be hung in the Spital-kirche, and with 150 original examples of plastic work, carvings and sculptures (thirteenth to sixteenth century). The majority of these have no great artistic merit though they have great interest for the student of German art. They represent the period when painting was not yet regarded as a separate art but as the accessory, the handmaiden of sculpture. In the beginning images of Madonnas and Saints were carved and painted; then, first of all on the wings of altar-pieces, and afterwards throughout, the painter took the place of the carver or sculptor. The process is clearly demonstrated in this collection.

I can only call attention to the following:—Cabinet 6, six apostles in a sitting posture, excellent examples of Nuremberg plastic work (burnt clay) at the end of the fourteenth century.

Over the north-west door St. Anna, Madonna and Child, by Michel Wolgemut (1510?). The Nuremberg landscape background is noteworthy. The picture has the appearance of having been recently retouched. Various works of the Nuremberg School and the Pacher School of carving (late fifteenth century), are ranged along the south and north walls. The large fresco Visit of Emperor Otho III. to the tomb of Charlemagne, is by W. von Kaulbach, and was bequeathed by that painter to the Museum. But the gem of the whole collection is the

NUREMBERG MADONNA.

It stands at the back of an early sixteenth-century altar-piece of the Swabian School, facing the tombstone (1592) of Georg Ludwig von Seinsheim. No second glance is required to assure us that we have here not only the chef d'œuvre of

NUREMBERG MADONNA

Nuremberg carving, but also one of the works of art of all time. And yet the name of the master is unknown, and the very date of the work is a matter of dispute. Clearly the beautiful female figure of this sorrowing Mary, this praying Madonna, as she is called (trauende, betende Maria), once formed one of a group, and stood facing St. John at the foot of the

Cross, gazing upwards in that bitter grief which is beyond the expression and abandonment of tears. Who can that artist have been who could select that pose of the head, that poise of the limbs, who could carve those robes, which in purity and flow have never been surpassed in German art, and who could express in the suppliant hands such poignant emotion? Man weiss nicht! And whose touch was so delicate, that with his chisel he could stamp on the upturned face those mingled feelings of sorrow so supreme, yearning so intense, love so human, hope so divine? For all this we can read there still, even through the grey-green coat of paint which certainly had no place in the original intentions of the artist. Man weiss nicht! But this much one may hazard—that it was some German artist, touched by the spirit of the Italian Renaissance till he rose to heights of artistic performance elsewhere never attained by him, and scarcely ever approached by his fellows.[67]

At the end of the choir is the High Altar-piece from Hersbruck, with figures of Mary and the four Fathers of the Church, from the workshop of Wolgemut, who painted the wings once attached to it. This is a good example of Nuremberg work of the kind, with its good and bad points, towards the end of the fifteenth century. On the reverse of this altar-piece is a sadly-faded church banner, richly painted. Figures of Christ, SS. Peter, and Sebald, in a rich Renaissance border, attributed to Albert Durer.

ROOM 33 (Kapelle)

is the old Sacristy on the north side of the church. There are several interesting carvings here, chief of which is the ROSARY (Rosenkranztafel), Judgment-scene, and crowning of Mary, attributed to Veit Stoss. Amongst other important works attributed to, or actually by him, is the frame of Durer's great Allerheiligen picture (see p. 193).

There is also here the original wood model of Labenwolf's familiar "Gooseman" fountain, and a picture of a meeting of the Meistersingers (with Hans Sachs). Winding steps lead up from this chapel to the Volkamer Chapel above.

ROOM 34

is the chapel on the south side of the church. Church utensils, etc., and in the choir arch an iron painted chandelier, dedicated by the son of Martin Behaim, the navigator, in memory of his father.

ROOM 35.

Mediæval furniture, household articles, beds, and doors with splendid ironwork and hinges. Turn (left) down corridor 26 till you come to (right)

ROOM 36.

The coloured portal is a remarkable piece of late romanesque work, and was once the doorway of the Refectory of the monastery at Heilsbronn. More stoves and furniture.

ROOMS 37-45.

Carved woodwork. Room 45, cabinets and tapestry. Goldsmiths' works. Magnificent bedstead of ebony and alabaster (Nuremberg). Turn (left) down corridors 46-48. Historical collection of tombs and stained glass continued.

ROOMS 49-51, and 52 (above).

Guns and weapons from eleventh century. Chased armour.

ROOM 53 (above).

Costumes. Heraldic ceiling.

Hence down the open spiral staircase, past the bear-pit, to

ROOM 54.

Cannons, fourteenth to nineteenth century.

ROOM 55.

Torture instruments and guillotine (end of eighteenth century).

From this point a small staircase in the corner of the cloisters (Room 55) leads to Room 56, containing some interesting examples of early bookbindings. Passing through this room, and turning to the left, we arrive at

ROOMS 57-58,

where we have before our eyes the development of manuscripts, engraving and printing from the beginning of the eighth century. The first room contains many documents and charters, manuscripts, autographs, and illuminations. Besides these there are many sketches, architectural drawings and designs, chiefly heraldic, for works of art. Here, too, is a noticeable collection of wood-engravings, including many fine leaves by Durer (Apocalypse, Passions, Life of Mary), Lucas Cranach, Hans Burgkmair, Grien, Schäuffelein, etc., and of copper-engravings[68] by Durer, Lucas van Leyden, Aldegrever, Altdorfer, Augustin Hirschvogel, etc.

In the next room we enter the region of printed books, and find a well-arranged and delightful collection. In case i., among other examples of the early "Block books" (books printed wholly from carved blocks of wood, from which undoubtedly the idea of moveable type arose), we note the Ars

Moriendi and the Kalendar of Ludwig von Basel (1460?). Of Block books at Nuremberg, we may note that Hans Sporer produced here an edition of the Endkrist (1472), of the Ars Moriendi, 1473, and of the Biblia Pauperum (1475).

The first two books to be printed from moveable type were two Latin Bibles (circ. 1453). Of these, one is known as the thirty-six line, or Bamberg Bible. It was printed by Gutenberg, and is represented in the Museum by two leaves only (case i.). The other is known as the Forty-two line, or Mazarine Bible. It was printed by Gutenberg, in partnership with Fust and Schöffer, and is represented here by one leaf (case ii.). One leaf, too, is all there is here to tell of the 1457 Psalter, with the wonderful capital letters printed by Fust and Schöffer. The extraordinary beauty and perfection of printing in its infancy can never fail to arrest attention. The explanation is obvious. It was not till the scribes, with whom printers had at first to compete in the multiplication of books, had ceased to exist that printers could afford to be careless in their work and indifferent in their choice of types.

Then there are the three books ascribed to Gutenberg's press about the year 1460—

(1) The Tractatus racionis et conscientiæ of Matthæus de Cracovia;

(2) The Summa de articulis fidei of Thomas Aquinas; and

(3) The Catholicon.

The Catholicon type appears again in the Latin-German dictionary known as the Vocabularius ex quo, the second edition of which, published by Nikolaus Bechtermünze at Eltvil, is here represented.

Copies of the first fourteen German Bibles (1466, etc.), with the exception of the second and seventh, will be found in the various cases (iv., v., vii., ix., etc.), and the original editions of Luther's Bible (1523-4) and other writings of his in case xxii. The first German Bible to be printed in Nuremberg (actually the fourth German Bible) was published by Frisner and Sensenschmid, 1473(?), case vii. Illustrations, it will be observed, are introduced into the large initial letters. It was Johann Sensenschmid ("the type-cutter") who, with the aid of Heinrich Keffer of Mainz, a pupil of Gutenberg, first introduced the art of printing into the town (Franciscus de Retza, Comestorium vitiorum, 1470, case vii.). Then in 1471 Johann Müller, or Regiomontanus, as he called himself, came with the object of establishing a private printing press, in order to issue his own works here. He printed his German and Latin Calendar from blocks, and various mathematical works from moveable types. But Anton Koberger[69] (1473-1513) was the greatest printer of Nuremberg. To the zeal with which he produced woodcut illustrations for his great works, the Schatzbehalter and the Hartmann Schedels Weltchronik (cases xiii., xiv.), the growth of the Nuremberg school of engraving is due. Another famous Nuremberg printer closely connected in business with Koberger[70] was Friedrich Creussner, who printed the first German edition of "Marcho Polo, das puch von mangerley wunder der landt vnd lewt" in 1477 (case xii.). In case xix. we find a unique copy of Hans Schmuttermeyer von Nürnberg, Fialenbüchlein, and also the Nürnberger Heiligtumsbüchlein, published by Hans Mair, 1493. The Quatuor libri amorum of Conrad Celtes, poet and humanist, was published at Nuremberg, 1502, with woodcuts after Durer (case xxi.). Durer's writings on the Proportions of the Human Frame, on Perspective, Measurements and Fortification figure in case xxiii., in which also the large coloured woodcuts of the "Abbildung der dreiundzwanzig vom schwäbischen Bunde im Jahre 1523 verbrannten fränkischen Raubschlösser," published at Nuremberg by Hans Wandereisen, are conspicuous. To Nuremberg also was vouchsafed the honour of publishing Melchior Pfinzing's Theuerdank (1517),[71] although it would appear to have been printed by Hans Schönsperger at Augsburg from the handsome type (scarcely improved by the tremendous flourishes) specially cut by Jost Dienecker of Antwerp. It was adorned with over a hundred illustrations— hunting scenes and knightly conflicts—by Hans Schäuffelein, Burgkmair and others. A copy of the second, 1519, edition may be seen in case xxii.

After the death of Koberger, illustrated books in Nuremberg came chiefly from the presses of Jobst Gutknecht and Peypus. Other printers here were:—

- Conrad Zeninger, 1480-1482.
- Fratres Vitæ Communis, 1479-1491.
- Georg Stuchs, 1484-1515.
- Johann Petrejus, 1526-1550.
- Alexander Kaufmann (Greek types).
- Konrad Bauer, 1601. Polyglot Bible.
- Leonhard Heussler, 1596. Joachim Lochner's Chronicle.
- Endter, 1668. Fugger's Österreichischer Ehrenspiegel (case xxviii.).

In this case also is Grimmelshausen's Simplicissimus (Nuremberg, 1685). In the next case (xxix.) is a copy of the pamphlet "Deutschland in seiner tiefen Erniederung," 1806, which occasioned the execution of the publisher Palm (see p. 269), "who fell a victim to the tyranny of Napoleon."

Near this case are two old printing presses, and in case xxx. are the bust, some manuscripts, and the collected works of Hans Sachs the cobbler-poet.

ROOM 59.

Ship models, etc.

ROOM 60 (gallery of the Church).

Old weights and scales.

ROOM 61.

Scientific instruments, dials, early watches and watch-cocks. Durer's Reissfeder. Regiomontanus' astronomical instruments.

ROOMS 62-66.

Old drugs and drug-stores, etc. The old apothecary's shop, decorated with crocodiles and so forth, suggests the familiar scene in Romeo and Juliet.

ROOMS 67-68.

Technical models, globes, maps, etc.

ROOM 70.

Banners of old Nuremberg guilds, signs of inns, trade-marks, etc.

ROOM 70A.

Early Nuremberg toys, dolls' houses, etc. We now come to the

PICTURE GALLERY,

which, if not of great size or of first-rate importance, is eminently interesting to those who care to study the development of Nuremberg art. The pictures are unfortunately numbered and arranged in a somewhat eccentric fashion.

In the small room on the right, as we enter Room 71, are some early pictures which would seem to be the forerunners of the system of epitaphs which obtained so largely in the later Middle Ages. Besides these there are two Byzantine pictures.

The first two sections of Room 71 are taken up with some examples of the Rhenish and old Netherland School up to the end of the sixteenth century.

To Meister Wilhelm of Cologne is attributed the charming Madonna with the pea-blossom (No. 7). Of the same school are Nos. 9, 10, and 17.

Stephan Lockner, Nos. 11, 12, 13, 14, 15.

Rogier van der Weyden (copy), No. 20.

Hugo van der Goes. Cardinal Bourbon. No. 19.

The "Master of the Life of Mary." Nos. 24, 25, 26.

Jan Scorel. Two portraits. Nos. 50, 51.

The "Master of the Death of Mary." Nos. 63, 64, 65.

Bartholomew Bruyns. No. 72.

With the third section of this room begins the collection of Franconian and Nuremberg paintings. As I have already on more than one occasion sketched the characteristics of this school, it would be superfluous to add anything here. But perhaps one may be allowed to express the conviction that no one who studies these pictures will fail to be impressed by the comparative merits of Wolgemut, or go away without ranking the master of Durer higher in his estimation than he was wont to do before he came.

The scenes from the Passion (No. 87), 1400, may be taken to represent the beginnings of the Franconian School of painting. No. 96 is the reverse of that Imhoff altar-piece in the Lorenzkirche with which we have already dealt at some length (p. 249). No. 95—from the Frauenkirche—is an important picture of the same date (1430-40).

The workshop of Pleydenwurff and Wolgemut is very well represented here. The admirable portrait of Kanonikus Schönborn (101), whose figure appears again in the Crucifixion (100) painted for him by the master, and SS. Thomas Aquinas and Dominicus (102, 103) are good examples of Hans Pleydenwurff at his best. Of the numerous pictures by Michel Wolgemut it will suffice to mention in particular the two portraits of old men so full of individuality (Hans Perckmeister and another, 119, 119A), and the Hallersche Epitaph (115), besides his masterpiece, the

Peringsdörffer Altar-piece

(107-110, Room 73; 113 and 114, Room 71, SS. Cosmos Damian, Magdalena, and Lucia). We have seen how Wolgemut usually allowed his assistants to help him in his pictures. The Peringsdörffer masterpiece (1488) was no exception; but in this at any rate the master's own share was very considerable.

The outer sides of the altar contain four pairs of Saints, male and female, standing on Gothic brackets—SS. Catherine and Barbara, Rosalia and Margaret, George and Sebald, John the Baptist and Nicholas. Here we have the most animated of Wolgemut's female figures, the most vigorous and life-like of his men. The notable faces,—finer even than that of the St. Sebald who stands like some great architect holding the model of his

Church, or of the St. Nicholas, with his refined and critical countenance, are those of SS. John and George. The former turns upon us his keen and spiritual gaze, so that his great brown eyes seem to pierce the veil that bounds our earthly vision and to penetrate into the hidden depths of futurity; whilst the latter stands rigid, his every feature—powerful nose, firmly closed mouth, thin but not sunken cheeks—eloquent of a bold and earnest resolution.

Incidents from the life of St. Vitus (Veit) and other saints form the subjects of the inner sides of the picture. Here again there is an inequality both of style and of excellence. The simple countenance of Mary, who holds on her knee a very animated Child, represents a type halfway between that of Rogier and that of Schongauer. The St. Luke, the character of whose head is well worked out, is attractive through his expression of earnestness. But there is far more dramatic power and "soul" in the scene from the legend of St. Bernard, according to which Christ came down from the Cross to his ardent worshipper. There the countenance of St. Bernard is made to exhibit a depth of feeling rarely to be found in Wolgemut; as if the artist's imagination had indeed been lit by something of the glow of the Saint's adoration.

The St. Christopher, who is walking through the stream with the Christ-child on his shoulder, is rough to the point of ugliness, whilst in the landscape, which is beautifully executed, there is a most intimate charm.

In the martyrdom of St. Sebastian, the Saint wears that almost inane expression which often does duty, however unintentionally, for the look of deep suffering in Wolgemut's work. The guard, however, are pleasingly and vividly portrayed. Evidently they are akin to the rabble which is found in the scenes of the Passion in Schongauer's works.

But it is when we come to the scenes from the legend of St. Vitus that we seem to trace only the faintest signs of Wolgemut's style. The composition here bears only a distant resemblance to his, and in the execution the assistant employed must surely have been he who painted the scene of St. Vitus denouncing the idols in the Lorenzkirche (see p. 254), and whose initials are R. F.

The pictures by Albrecht Durer in the Museum we have already mentioned (pp. 188, 193-9).

(1) Hercules and the Stymphalian Birds,   205 Room 72

(2) Kaiser Maximilian,   209 Room 72

(3) Pietà—Mourning over Christ's Body, 206 Room 73

(4) Charlemagne, 207 Room 73

(5) Kaiser Sigismund, 208 Room 73

Besides these originals there are several copies of the master's works, including the excellent copies of the Four Apostles (283, 284) by Johann Georg Fischer. The original inscriptions are retained. The Allerheiligen or Trinity picture, No. 210, is a bad copy in a worse frame.

Among other works by contemporaries or followers of Durer are:—

Bartholomew Zeitblom of Ulm,	145	Room 73
	178	Room 73
Bernhard Strigel,	179, 181	Room 71
	185, 186	Room 72
Martin Schwarz of Rothenburg,	130, 133	Room 71
Hans Holbein the Elder,	164, 167	Room 71
	162, 163	Room 72
Hans Friess of Freiburg,		Room 71, 72
Hans Leonhard Schäuffelein,	221, 223, 225 226, etc.	Room 73
Hans von Kulmbach,	212	Room 71
	213, 214, 216	Room 73
Albrecht Altdorfer,	245, 248	Room 71, 72

Mathias Grünewald,	253	Room 71
Hans Baldung Grien,	194-196	Room 72
Lucas Cranach,	259 262	Room 72
Martin Schaffner,	191, 192	Room 72
Hans Burgkmair,	171	Room 72
	168-170	Room 73
Georg Pencz,	272, 273	Room 74

In the following rooms the decline of German art is historically well represented. But in room 78, which is devoted mainly to painters of the Dutch School of the seventeenth century, mention should be made of the interior by Peter de Hooch (330) and an early portrait of Rembrandt by himself (325) and his powerful St. Paul (326). Johann Kupetzky is also well represented (371-378).

ROOMS 81, 82.

Models of cannons and weapons.

ROOM 83.

A collection of musical instruments: some very rare and costly, but mostly of recent date. There are few from mediæval times. Engravings and miniatures will tell us most about these. But the history of the development of the lute and violin, the clarionet and the piano, can here be traced. Of the early Nuremberg makers, whose instruments are preserved, the chief are—

- Conrad Gerler and Melchior Neuziedler (lutes and violins).
- Hans Meuschen (wind instruments).
- Sigmund Schnitzer (whistles).
- Pachelbel (organs).

The Bavarian Industrial Museum (Königstrasse) contains a collection of patterns and samples, ancient and modern, and a good technical library.

CHAPTER XII
THE ARMS OF NUREMBERG

"Da sass ein Vogel wunderschön,
Wie ein Adler war er anzusehn
Kohlschwarz, der hatt' allda gehecket.
Seine linke Seit' war ihm bedecket
Mit lichten Rosen, roth und weiss,
Fein abgetheilt mit allem Fleiss." ...
HANS SACHS.

NUREMBERG is a happy hunting ground for the herald. The hatchments in the churches and the houses, and the arms in the stained glass windows are very noteworthy.

The arms of the city may be seen carved over the north and south main entrances to the Rathaus. You will also find them roughly painted on a little money-box in Albert Durer's house. Durer, as was natural in an engraver, was fond of heraldic drawing. His engravings of the "Armorial Bearings of the Durer Family," and of "The Coat of Arms, with a Cock," and of the "Arms of Nuremberg," are good examples of his work in this genre, whilst his last piece of pure etching was "The Great Cannon," with the arms of Nuremberg upon it. I take the following account of the seals and arms of Nuremberg from Dr Reicke and Mummenhoff.

It was one of the privileges of the Council to have a seal of its own. Both Mayor and Council had their own seals. The Mayor's seal, known to have existed from A.D. 1225 onwards, was of red wax bearing the Imperial Eagle originally looking to

SEALS OF NUREMBURG

the sinister but afterwards to the dexter, with the legend Sigillum Sculteti de Nuremberg (seal of the Mayor of Nuremberg) which subsequently became Sigillum Judicii de Nurenberch (seal of the Court of Nuremberg). The Council's seal (which first appears on documents of 1243) bore an eagle closely feathered up to the neck, with a human head surrounded by flowing locks and wearing a crown. This town-seal usually bears the legend Sigillum Universitatis civium de Nurenberch (i.e. seal of the community of the citizens of Nuremberg) or even civitatis Norimbergue (of the city of Nuremberg). Somewhat later than the middle of the fourteenth century it had a black letter **N** for counter-seal, and bore the following legend in abbreviated writing, Sigillum secretum Nurembergense, i.e. Nuremberg secret or privy seal. A little later it bore for its counter-seal the proper arms of the city, of which we must shortly speak. Towards the end of the fourteenth century (in 1386) a smaller privy seal appears, similar in form, and bearing the legend Secretum civium de Nuremberch. This was always used as a privy seal for letters of importance. Before this seal came into use the city seal was used for all purposes, and even appended (for greater security) to private documents such as contracts of sale, entailing deeds, testaments and jointures. At a later date this seal was chiefly appended to testaments.

The seals, both of the Mayor and of the Council, though not arms, were used as such; however, their real character was well understood. Even in 1477 the Council decreed that the window which the city proposed to place in the choir of St. Lawrence's Church should be adorned "with the arms of the Council and the privy and common arms of the city." Here a distinction is expressly made between the seal and the arms.

However, the proper arms of the town were—Bendy of six Gules and Argent impaling Or an Imperial eagle dimidiated, sable. The dexter side of the shield is often incorrectly represented as Gules, three bendlets argent. It is also wrong to describe it (as many writers have done), as Barry of six, gules and argent.

Meisterlin applies to the dexter side the term Field of Swabia, which we only mention here because it is still occasionally employed. He gives the same name to the district in which Nuremberg lies (apparently by confusion with the "Gau" of Sualafeld). Nuremberg has accordingly nothing to do with Swabia, as was probably inferred centuries ago. The origin of the arms is obscure. It is however worth mentioning that the Burggraves of Nuremberg bore this "Field of Swabia" as a bordure on their arms. These arms, as we said before, have been used since the second half of the fourteenth century as the counter-seal of the city seal above mentioned, as also on stamped parchment and stamped paper (only introduced towards the end of the seventeenth century), on coins struck at Nuremberg, on public buildings, etc.

The human head on the eagle of the privy seal, afterwards called the "Eagle-Maiden," is explained by Mummenhoff as the face of an emperor with long flowing locks and the Imperial crown on his head. It retains this character throughout the Middle Ages both on the seal, and also when the seal was used as a coat-of-arms. Mummenhoff instances in particular the fine eagle on the town side of the upper story of the Thiergärtner-Gate-Tower. With Albert Durer, however, begins the quite unhistorical transfiguration of this eagle. The emperor's face was no longer understood and was mistaken for a female face; and thus in course of time a series of unjustifiable embellishments produced a coat-of-arms bearing a maiden, described by even a modern historian as an "Eagle-Maiden." In quite recent times a mural crown has been set upon her head. We will pass over the jesting explanations formerly given for this seeming Eagle-Maiden, which would be untenable, were they even serious. We need only mention that when the arms are set out in colours the eagle is Or and the field Azure (and very often Vert). These three coats-of-arms (counting the seals as coats) arranged in different ways were employed on public monuments, buildings and coins, and afterwards on all publications, commissions, ordinances, etc., issued by the Council. Usually the simple eagle is at the top, the so-called Eagle-Maiden below on the right, and the Bends impaling the dimidiated eagle on the left. Frequently, especially on the coins, only the eagle-maiden and the dimidiated eagle appear. Sometimes also we find the

Imperial eagle without the shield surmounting the two lower coats, and, as it were, protecting them with its wings.

The double-headed crowned eagle also frequently occurs, for example on the old Fünferhaus (now the Post-Office) with the date 1521. Here it appears alone, whereas on the Tugendbrunnen it is associated with the eagle-maiden and the impaled dimidiated eagle. It was also employed on the eastern part of the city wall, both on the bastion near the Wöhrderthürlein (pulled down in 1871) and on the line of wall. A really handsome example of this double-headed eagle is to be seen on the entrance to the new Rathaus building from the Fünferplatz. This eagle dates from the seventeenth century and was formerly placed on the arsenal, and consequently bears the inscription:—

"Einst Wächter von Nürnbergs Waffen und Wehr
Jetzt Hüter von Nürnbergs Wohlstand und Ehr."

"Once guard over Nuremberg's weapons and steel
Now keeper of Nuremberg's honour and weal."

According to Lochner it appears to have been left to the taste of the artist whether in such combinations this the real Imperial eagle, or the one-headed, uncrowned eagle of the Mayor should be used.

CHAPTER XIII
ITINERARY, PLACES OF RESORT, HOTELS

THE following scheme may perhaps prove of use to those who have but a day or two to spend in Nuremberg and wish to glance at the chief places of interest:—

(1) Walk round the walls and visit the Castle (Ch. V.).

(2) Going from the Frauenthor down the Königstrasse see St. Lorenzkirche (Ch. IX.), the Nassauer Haus (p. 22), and Tugendbrunnen (p. 273). Then crossing the Pegnitz by the Fleisch—or the Museumsbrücke, arrive at the Haupt Markt and the Beautiful Fountain (p. 270). Visit the Frauenkirche (Ch. IX.) (r.), the Rathaus (Ch. VI.) and St. Sebalds, (Ch. IX.) and look at the Parsonage Window (p. 42), St. Moritzkirche (Ch. IX.) and the Bratwürstglöcklein (p. 198).

(3) Albert Durer's House and Monument (Ch. VII.). St. Ægidienkirche (Ch. IX.) and the Pellerhaus (p. 90). St. John's Churchyard and the Adam Krafft Stations (Ch. IX. and VII.).

(4) German Museum (Ch. XI.), Library (Ch. IX.).

WALKS OR DRIVES FROM THE TOWN.

(1) To the Alte Veste. (Wallenstein's Camp, see Ch. IV.).

(2) Castle of Lichtenhof. (Once the residence of Gustavus Adolphus.)

(3) Dutzendteich.

(4) Schmausenbuch.

HOTELS.

There are several first-class hotels in Nuremberg. The Württemberger Hof has the advantage of being very close to the station and just outside the old walls of the town. The management is excellent and I have met with every comfort and courtesy there. Of the hotels within the walls the Strauss ranks for comfort and cuisine among the best hotels in Europe, whilst of the others the Bairischer Hof, the Goldner Adler and the Wittelsbacher are recommended.

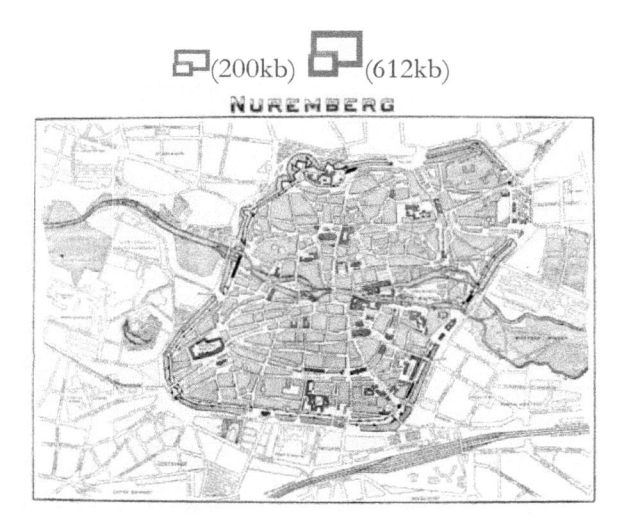

🗺(200kb) 🗺(612kb)

NUREMBERG

Milton Keynes UK
Ingram Content Group UK Ltd.
UKHW030906151124
451262UK00006B/968